PRAISE FOR
DISRUPT
YOUR **CAREER**

"As someone who has made career changes across three continents, four languages and multiple functions and industry sectors, I am convinced that it is crucial to harvest the enormous value created by transitions. Those of us fortunate enough to have gone through the pain and excitement of such uncharted shifts gain in many ways, and organizations would do well to be more open to hiring such people. Claire and Antoine's storytelling capability is impressive, and their frameworks for planning simple and fun to use. This book is of universal value."

—CHARLES AWAD, Senior VP & Chief Marketing Officer,
Oettinger Davidoff

"Too often, career trajectories are reduced to a linear path of experiences, missing out on the purpose, unique strengths and individual circumstances of the talent. But in today's environment, there is no 'one size fits all' anymore. That's why I find Tirard and Harbour-Lyell's approach towards career management so relevant and useful: it provides a holistic process of exploring, experimenting, engaging and expanding to make better decisions and ultimately find career success."

—STEVEN BAERT, Chief Human Resources Officer of Novartis

"*Disrupt Your Career* combines insights drawn from the stories of successful career changers with rigorous research and practical ideas that can be put to immediate use. The book beautifully demonstrates that career reinvention is not only possible, but should be embraced in today's VUCA world."

—KEVIN CASHMAN, Senior Partner, CEO & Executive Development,
Korn Ferry and bestselling author of *Leadership from the Inside Out* and
The Pause Principle

"Every day, as an executive search professional, I meet leaders looking for guidance and creative ways to confront the challenge of career transition. Claire and Antoine have created a truly enjoyable book, which tells compelling and inspiring stories covering all the major, twenty first century transitions, for which people are typically so poorly prepared. They offer sound, systematic frameworks for individuals to plan and execute their own career changes. They also offer models and recommendations for organizations to handle career management strategically and effectively. *Disrupt Your Career* is destined to become the reference for all leaders the world over."

— FABRICE DESMARESCAUX, Managing Partner Southeast Asia,
Eric Salmon & Partners

"Career disruption will happen to everyone – and most of us are ill prepared. This captivating book shows how to understand career transitions and gives fascinating and practical ideas about how best to navigate. A must read for anyone embarking on a life change."

— LYNDA GRATTON, Professor of Management Practice
at London Business School

"Massive change in the working environment is upon us. Our parents were content with 40 years in the same company, a gold watch, and a retirement on the golf course. That is no longer an option. So, you need to be armed with the right tools to survive and thrive in the choppy waters of career management. Whether you are an individual, pondering a big change, or forced into transition by yet another downsizing, or you are leading an organization and hoping to stem the early attrition of your people, there is something in this book for you. The stories are compelling, and the frameworks for action simple and solid."

— PER HEGGENES, CEO, The IKEA Foundation

"In a world where change is the only constant, this book is a must-read for young and seasoned executives alike to take advantage of planned and unplanned changes, and build a successful career."

— ALVIN HEW, Managing Director at The Abraaj Group,
Board Director of Maxis

"More and more people are seeking career change guidance today. Tirard and Harbour-Lyell bring a fresh approach – based on the stories of a diverse and colorful range of career changers – that will inspire many to explore similar moves. Equally, the book provides excellent thinking for organizations, where there is still an enormous need for improved approaches to career management."

— **HERMINIA IBARRA**, Charles Handy Professor of Organizational Behavior at London Business School

"How often have you wondered if those that leave your organization are doing so for the right reasons? What would you give to know more, and lose less? *Disrupt Your Career* holds one of the keys to this increasing challenge for leaders, and outlines a series of insights and processes that can lead to better career comfort for individuals and enhanced, more effective career management for organizations. Tirard and Harbour-Lyell tell the stories that illustrate the career transitions with simplicity and empathy, and make it obvious that we can all learn from them."

— **ÅSA LANDÉN ERICSSON**, CEO of Cygate, board member of Grant Thornton Sweden, Formpipe and Rhenman & Partners

"For a leader in any substantial organization, one major preoccupation beyond attracting the very best people is also keeping them stimulated, challenged and fulfilled. This book provides invaluable insight, research and strategies for improvement in both talent strategy and career management. The stories are inspiring and authentic, indicating new paths to follow, and innovative approaches to managing career paths for both companies and individuals."

— **JEAN-CLAUDE LE GRAND**, Senior VP Talent Development and Chief Diversity Officer at L'Oréal

"*Disrupt Your Career* offers a treasure trove of insight, experience, frameworks and thought-provoking questions for anyone who is contemplating a career transition. Claire and Antoine provide excellent synthesis I wish I had had at my disposal when I made my own transitions. Practical yet conceptually rich, informative yet action-oriented, nurturing yet challenging – an excellent read!"

— **RENIER LEMMENS**, CEO of Viadeo, former Partner at McKinsey, former CEO of Paypal EMEA and investor

"Contemporary careers are nearly limitless for those who have the ability to cross boundaries. And it is in those crossings—in transitions often uncharted and unexpected, to be imagined as much as managed—that careers are made or broken. Tirard and Harbour-Lyell, who have accompanied many professionals through those crossings, distil their wisdom into a compass that will give you confidence to explore new career opportunities and help you navigate the transition towards them."

> —GIANPIERO PETRIGLIERI, Associate Professor of Organisational
> Behaviour at INSEAD

"Successful businesses and economies alike are dependent upon people not only doing their jobs, but also developing and improving through their work. We could all benefit from daring and experimenting more in our careers, and *Disrupt Your Career* shows how, through captivating examples and convincing frameworks for action."

> —KRISTIN SKOGEN LUND, Director General, Confederation
> of Norwegian Enterprise, board member, Ericsson, "Norway's
> Most Powerful Woman", mother of four

"How do you ensure the very best career future for yourself? I've spent 25 years working with individuals who understand the importance of managing their careers, for themselves and for the schools and companies in which they operate. *Disrupt Your Career* makes a significant contribution towards solving this challenge, by illustrating various uncharted transitions with compelling and insightful stories. Their frameworks are strikingly simple, and the book provides invaluable options and strategies for organizations and individuals alike."

> —MATT SYMONDS, Management Columnist for Forbes, BBC,
> The Economist and co-founder of Fortuna Admissions

"An essential, soul-saving guide for anyone navigating a non-traditional career path, including most women. And for the companies smart enough to attract them – and creative enough to benefit from their adaptive skills."

> —AVIVAH WITTENBERG-COX, CEO of 20-first and author
> of *Seven Steps to Leading a Gender-Balanced Business*

to your career

Antoine

to you later

This book is a work of non-fiction. Unless otherwise noted, the authors and the publisher make no explicit guarantee as to the accuracy of the information contained in this book and in some cases, names of people and places have been altered to protect their privacy.

ISBN: 978-1-387-16715-9

Because of the dynamic nature of the Internet, any web addresses or links contained in this book may have changed since publication, and may no longer be valid. The views expressed in this work are solely those of the authors and do not necessarily reflect views of the publisher, and the publisher hereby disclaims any responsibility for them.

Lulu Publishing Services rev. date: 10/12/2017

DISRUPT
YOUR CAREER

How to Navigate Uncharted Career
Transitions and Thrive

Antoine Tirard
Claire Harbour-Lyell

Contents

Introduction

Our careers are no longer linear or plannable, as they once were. Our grandparents and great grandparents would probably turn in their graves if they could compare the complexity of our careers with their forty years of work, gold watch, and golf course career path.

Both of us have managed careers across borders, industry sectors and functions in big and small organizations, both public, private and our own. Averaged out, we have shifted jobs or companies at least seven times. When our teenagers, who still occasionally believe we have something valuable to say on the subject, ask for advice, we know that we cannot credibly give any that begins with "if you go to a great university and work hard, you will be safe and secure for life". If we cannot give that advice to our own offspring, what career advice can we offer? We wrote this book in an attempt to answer that question.

Why Should You Read This Book?

Work and career transitions impact life satisfaction. Most people will spend between a quarter and a third of their life at work. Knowing that there is a correlation between satisfying work and mental and physical health, as well as a similar link between underemployment and poor health, means that the stakes are high for all of us. If transitions in and out of work impact our mental health, then careful, appropriate career transition management becomes crucial not only to enhancing our work satisfaction but also to assuring our well-being.

Professionals and executives frequently make unfortunate, ill-considered career moves. We have both been guilty of this in the past, and have learned a great deal along the way. These career move mistakes include not doing enough research, leaving for better money, or leaving through desperation rather than moving towards fulfillment. Yet job seekers' mistakes aren't random. All of us feel certain psychological, social, and time pressures that can lead to errors of judgment. We believe these mistakes can be avoided – or at least better managed – and want to offer practical advice to help make more profitable career decisions.

Developing resilience and career adaptability has become critical. Over the coming decade, many traditional jobs will disappear while new ones will appear. Career and life transitions will become the norm, as expressed by Lynda Gratton and Andrew Scott in their book "The 100 Year-Life".[1] Careers consist of multiple career steps, or "gigs". Even after many years at the same company, an individual should have the resources to make a career transition where necessary or desirable.

We have experience in career coaching and want to help people. We have both experienced career transitions ourselves, and have together coached numerous professionals about their careers. Our point of view is well-informed, and thanks to our clients and readers, we have amassed a wealth of advice and ideas to share with you. Claire has advised hundreds of young professionals on their early career transitions. She has made professional moves across four continents, seventeen countries and eight languages. Antoine has lived and worked in four countries, while making an impact on thousands of professionals, both as an HR and talent director with Fortune 500 companies, and more recently as a coach and consultant to similar organizations.

Why Talk About Transitions?

One definition of transition that we have found useful is by William Bridges: "Transition is the inner psychological process people go through to come to terms with the new situation, as they let go of the ways things used to be and reorient themselves to the way that things are now."[2]

The difficulty with transitions is that most people are not well prepared for them. Even if they are, they are not used to – or even expecting – the frequency of transitions in their career. Transitions are seen more as an exception, and are mostly viewed as negative events. Yet, instead of perceiving transitions as stressors or trauma, as has been the convention, we want to look at them as potential positive experiences.

We also recognize that the research on transitions, while multidisciplinary by nature, has not been comprehensively addressed. In "Transitions, work histories and the myth of careers" Nigel Nicholson and Michael West make a plea to fill a gap in research: "These (transitions) require but have yet to receive the kind of analysis that social anthropology might bring to bear on the subject. The time is ripe for this within the emerging study of organizational cultures and their social contexts. The study of transitions and how they link to make up 'careers' can be seen as a way of exploring the evolution of social boundaries."[3]

What Do We Mean by Uncharted Transition?

The traditional definition of career uses the metaphor of a "journey". While attractive, we find it is limiting. Journeys have a beginning and an end, with an objective connecting them; this feels somewhat comforting. The danger of this metaphor is that it encourages us to assume that the journey happens at the behest of the traveler alone, rather than being a function of the whole terrain or environment.

Yet, in the increasing economic chaos of the 21st century, the idea of a simple, predictable linear career is dead. All professionals can expect to encounter the unexpected as they progress – or regress – from one year to the next in their professional development. We use the adjective "uncharted" because a professional, like a traveler who cannot yet see an unexplored place on a map, may experience the same discomfort, or indeed excitement, when moving into a role or occupation that is unknown to him or her. The form this unexpected or unusual part takes can vary, but there is one common feature to all of this: nobody is properly prepared for it. Examples of such career transitions, as you will discover in the following chapters, include leaving a corporation to join a non-profit, moving from athletics to business, and returning to work at a former employer.

These uncharted critical crossroads have never before been brought together in this way. We intend to change this by telling the story of some fifty leaders from all over the world, from a broad range of cultures, sectors and backgrounds, showing how they managed, and oftentimes mastered these transitions. We describe the circumstances or motivations that provoke the change, the challenges it creates, how these individuals overcame the transition, and what they did to successfully navigate and grow from it. Gaining an understanding about these special transitions should allow us to understand and better manage careers in the broader sense, even if some shifts are less pronounced than those we discuss here.

How We Approached It

We examined nine different types of uncharted transitions, looking for a diversity of job changes, some of which are already recognized, and some which are more unusual. And we made sure to select transitions across various stages of life and career. These include complete changes of occupation, changes of sector and geography, as well as returns of several kinds. We also made sure to cover both voluntary and involuntary changes, whether these were caused by direct or indirect influences.

The characteristics of these transitions include radical changes, such as leaving the military or moving to the other side of the world; more "mundane" but nevertheless unprepared-for changes, such as the shift from consultant to CEO; slow and fast moves; desired or imposed moves; and sundry other dimensions.

We hope the career transitions covered here are interesting for their variety, intensity, diversity and adversity. They are all developmental, and we remain convinced of their value in the life of each of our subjects, and their relevance to yours.

Our stories take the "field" approach, derived from many hours and days of interviews, which we completed by reference to research and interviews with companies. We have questioned, consulted, scratched our heads, and reflected. The picture is clear in its complexity.

Careers are neither well understood nor optimally managed, and uncharted transitions are a fast-growing phenomenon. They are a source of development, both professional and personal, yet not well studied or supported, either by literature or organizations. Given this relative vacuum, we felt compelled to find a practical approach to look into these transitions and share our learning with you.

In the book, you will find nine story chapters, in which we examine each particular transition one by one, with several characters and examples. We wrote the chapters in a chronological order. We start with transitions typical in early careers, and move on to shifts more likely at the career zenith and beyond. Each of these chapters includes four or five stories of individuals who represent the transition in question. While we have kept the profiles as varied as possible, we have tended to use highly successful individuals, often from our own social and professional circles. We make no apology for this, as they represent the best of the best, and thus exist as examples by which to be inspired. If you notice that many of them come from "a well-known European business school", do not be too surprised.

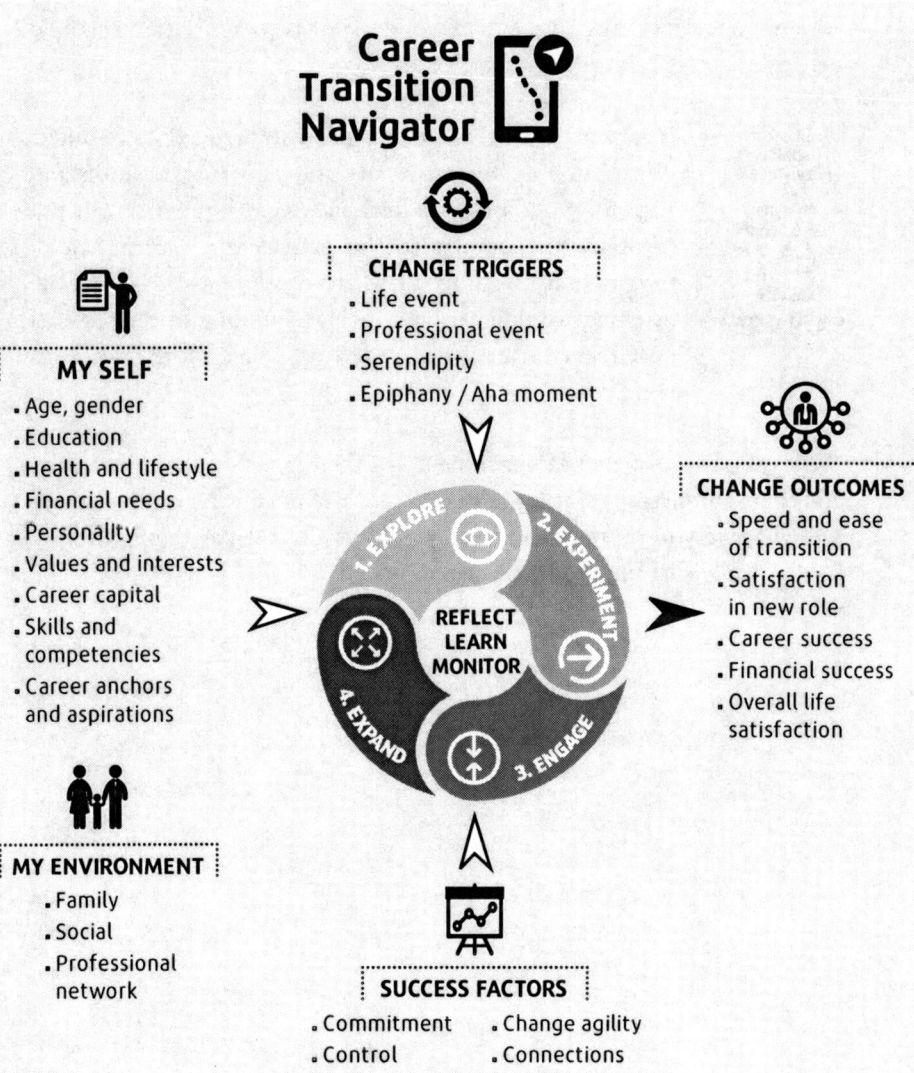

Career Transition Navigator

CHANGE TRIGGERS
- Life event
- Professional event
- Serendipity
- Epiphany / Aha moment

MY SELF
- Age, gender
- Education
- Health and lifestyle
- Financial needs
- Personality
- Values and interests
- Career capital
- Skills and competencies
- Career anchors and aspirations

CHANGE OUTCOMES
- Speed and ease of transition
- Satisfaction in new role
- Career success
- Financial success
- Overall life satisfaction

1. EXPLORE
2. EXPERIMENT
3. ENGAGE
4. EXPAND

REFLECT LEARN MONITOR

MY ENVIRONMENT
- Family
- Social
- Professional network

SUCCESS FACTORS
- Commitment
- Control
- Curiosity
- Change agility
- Connections
- Confidence

Following the stories, both in the story chapters and in the second part of the book, we will give you a series of resources to better manage your career and the careers of your company's people. This will include our Career Transition Navigator (see chart above), a framework to use whenever you are in transition, charted or uncharted. Each time you see one of the stages of the Navigator in action – Explore, Experiment, Engage or Expand – we will signal it, so that you can grasp the multiple ways in which it can be used, and how easy it is to apply (see example below).

Career Transition Navigator

EXPLORE

Realizing at this point that the void needed to be filled, Ton signed up for university, studying Organization and Labor Psychology. He also started volunteering with a crisis hotline, similar to the Samaritans, learning non-judgmental listening. Both the study and the empathic listening would later be critical in building his success as a coach, but for now, he needed work in a more traditional company.

We would like thank all of our subjects for their patience, their generosity and their kindness in assisting us in our task. Before starting on the stories, we will give you more context about the new career paradigm which is so drastically shaping the landscape around us.

Chapter 1

Towards a New Career Paradigm

Ignore this chapter at your peril: if you do not become familiar with the current and rapidly oncoming changes in careers, you risk becoming quickly outmoded and quite possibly replaced by Artificial Intelligence.

The world of work has undergone more changes in the last two decades than ever before. From the beginning of time right up until the industrial revolution, nearly all work was about survival. Whether you were a knight, a peasant farmer or a servant at the local inn, there was little choice of who you worked for, and not much room for advancing from your initial level. Until the late 1700s, there was hardly any notion of "career"; rather, there was a sense that there were those who labored, and those who possessed fortunes and did not need to work at all. Progress along and between social axes did not widely exist, and ambitions were easily stifled.

With the advent of industry in the early 19th century came the rise and rapid development of the corporation. And over the century that followed, careers were made and social ceilings smashed in companies like Standard Oil, Ford, IBM, British Steel and Mitsubishi. During this period, the prize granted to those who were allowed to enter the hallowed halls of such corporations was a "job for life". It seems absurd to have to define this notion today, but some Millennials may have never heard of or observed this notion in action.

During the post-war period of the second half of the 20th century, most parents shared the assumption with their teenagers, that "if you work hard, go to a good school and get a great degree, you will find a stable job and want for nothing." And that was more or less true until the 21st century. Since 2000, this purported truism has been in a state of such intense overhaul that it is sometimes difficult even to catch a glimpse of it at all.

With rapid changes in the landscape, as with every other cataclysmic shift, we need to find new ways to manage our careers. All of us – there are no exceptions. Even in countries with heavy public administrations, such as France or China, the stability and advantages of protected jobs are slowly being eroded. Every single working person on this planet is going to need to have more tools in his or her box with which to tackle this revolution.

Key Forces Behind the Revolution

Many factors are contributing to these shifts, and they make their impact in a variety of ways. We can observe five types of change: lifestyle, economic, corporate, socio-geographic and technological. We will look at these in the course of the book, but there is one that stands above the rest.

Technology brings us the change with arguably the most impact. The internet, the cloud and 24/7 connectivity allow us to go about our business without being there "in person". This kind of facilitation is crucial, as it means that we no longer need to be based where our company is, nor where our clients are, so long as all parties are equipped and willing to use the technologies that are available to make things work. However, technology changes so quickly that it also creates painful necessities – the need to keep up with the advancements, and the challenge that poses, particularly to those of us over the age of sixteen. We need not only to update our skills and knowledge, but also to keep track of entire new job areas that are emerging, such as that of data analytics.

Technology offers a wide range of opportunities to progress. Yet the progress can be slow or painful, especially for the "in-between" generations, who are tech savvy, but did not grow up with it. Without any doubt, the evolution, or revolution, is changing the face of the workplace; this is something we need to understand and manage, whether we use it to leverage change for ourselves or not.

Technology also lies at the heart of changes in lifestyle and life attitudes that are currently such important features in the work landscape. Better medicine and greater access to information allow us to live longer and take better care of ourselves, thus lengthening our lives and our careers. At the same time, we are aspiring not only to longer lives, but also to better living conditions. So we find ourselves in a perpetual tradeoff between time, happiness and money. The result is that proponents of the "four-hour workweek" and lifestyle designers are playing an ever-greater part in our lives. The debate of "live to work or work to live" is simultaneously becoming increasingly complex and less focused on linear work events.

Shifts in the economy lead to shifts in the corporate environment. As our economies become more unpredictable, so jobs will become increasingly unstable. We observe a growing number of temporary contracts and freelance arrangements for tasks that would previously have been covered by a salaried employee with a long-term contract. While this gives us greater freedom as advocates of our own career progression, it also leads to financial and social poverty when things go awry. The social net that used to protect us may well not be as present as it once was, even in paternalistic economies.

We also see companies restructuring with increasing frequency, not necessarily with positive results. It has become fashionable to instigate a restructuring whenever there is trouble. Unfortunately, it does not seem to be so trendy to ensure that the restructuring is being done with proper care. As a result, many previously successful professionals find themselves out in the wilds of the job market, wondering what their next move might be. This too needs understanding and management.

Beyond the restructuring that tends to come in bad times, we see an increasing trend towards flattening hierarchies. Where once, we could enter a company as a graduate trainee, and expect to move inexorably upwards provided we worked hard and built the right relationships, we now face a maze of transverse and networked relationships in which "up" is not commonly a possibility. This requires not only management, but also a deep understanding of the new stakes. In addition to this kind of change, we have those imposed by mergers and acquisitions. The pain of cultural change, whether by fusion or fission, is something that many more companies and individuals experience now than a decade ago.

And finally, there are the challenges and opportunities offered by the global nature of business today. On the one hand, companies are able to grow more easily than in the past, regardless of their readiness for new markets and cultures. This puts things squarely on the employee's side, and there is an increase in the power wielded while determining work arrangements. Those who wish to can push for conditions that are more conducive to growth and development, rather than pure financial gain. Not only are companies mobile, but so are the individuals who work in them. Migration has increased 41 percent since 2000, according to the UN, and that figure does not even take into account the moves that people make inside a country. This means increased uncertainty about opportunities, but it also expands the diversity of the opportunities available. At the same time, we see a shift from industrial manufacturing and mass-consumerism to knowledge and co-creation between consumers and suppliers. The complexity is growing, and we need to manage this at the level of our individual careers.

The pace of change is not abating. The expression "you snooze, you lose" has never seemed more apt. It becomes a necessity to understand and manage one's career in the face of so much chaos, but it is important to recall that amidst the chaos, there is opportunity if we are well-prepared.

Job Changes Are Happening More Frequently and More Radically

Whether it is a cause or an effect, we see a trend for increasingly frequent job changes. While both authors can remember times when it was frowned upon to have a CV with more than one company every five years, it is now common for "successful" executives to be changing as often as every two years. Professor Herminia Ibarra, of INSEAD, in her book "Working Identity", presents her theory of changing careers and career identities, something that was unthinkable only 50 years ago. The heart of her theory is that changing careers means changing ourselves by acting, testing, discovering and adapting: "rather than having one true self, we are many selves throughout our lives".[4] She outlines, in an INSEAD paper of 2004, that "a compelling scholarly argument has been made that career change is on the rise in our society: careers are boundaryless, unfold outside traditional organizational boundaries, business firms continue to downsize, restructure and lay off, and values have changed such that people increasingly change work settings in search of greater autonomy, life balance and meaning in work."[5]

We see evidence for Ibarra's observation everywhere. According to a 2013 study by Right Management, 83 percent of Americans intend actively to seek a new position within the new year.[6] A 2015 LinkedIn study reveals that over the past four years, active job seekers have increased by 36 percent and the global percentage of professionals actively looking has gone from 22 percent in 2011 to 30 percent in 2015. Over the same four-year period, the number of professionals warmly open to change, despite not actively seeking one, has risen by 16 percent.[7] These are not empty figures based on small samples. They are the result of a global survey involving 7 million LinkedIn members and over ten thousand active survey participants.

Job changes are happening not only more frequently, but also more radically. The LinkedIn study also uncovers that as many as one in three job changers were changing their career entirely. This greater individual control of one's career is a significant shift, regardless of economic conditions, and it is incumbent on us all to learn to identify and fit our transferable skills and experiences. According to Boris Groysberg, professor at Harvard Business School, in his article "Five Ways to Bungle a Job Change", "the corporate ladder is being disassembled like a Jenga tower, and even the CEO position is no longer a terminus."[8] This is probably just as well, since the average tenure for a CEO in the 1950s was ten years, in the '60s five years, and today, less than three years.[9] Top level executives will need to stay alert and active, as there is little time to lose in preparing for the next shift.

Will this acceleration of job-shifting change or slow down? It seems unlikely – indeed, it may even accelerate. Later retirement ages are becoming the norm, as governments realize that they will not be able to keep their pension schemes solvent if they do not promote this change. We are also helped by increasingly good and healthy lifestyles that arguably make "sixty the new forty", when it comes to perception, and reality, if we are still working. To aid this change, there are many new types of jobs and skills emerging which may not be the exclusive domain of the young Millennials. There is nothing to prevent a young sixty-five-year-old from learning how to use data analysis to predict future trends. Those who are curious and avid learners may well create that heady combination of nascent technology and a novel approach with the wisdom that can only come from experience.

Thanks to all this change, our lives are becoming multi-staged. An increasing frequency of transitions will become the norm, whether we like it or not. And there is every reason to imagine that further stages not yet even imagined, will be added to the cycle of transitions we already recognize.

A Whole New Career Paradigm Has Emerged

In reality, the shift is not only about the speed and nature of transitions, but also concerns the fact that the entire career paradigm is evolving. For instance, a study carried out at MIT Sloan School of Management observed that a growing number of students had begun to identify lifestyle as their primary career anchor. This number is as high as 50 percent of the students born from the late '80s onwards, according to the study's author, Edgar Schein.[10] The whole notion of career success has changed. Young high-potentials of today are not aiming only for the top company position. We can think of a "Career Lattice", as opposed to a "Career Ladder" , as we move from role to role, function to function, company to company, seeking ever greater interest and satisfaction rather than money or status.

The following table summarizes the many evolutions in career management, contrasting the old and new paradigms.

Career Management Paradigms: Old and New

Dimension	Traditional career	New career
Orientation	Linear, static, rigid	Multidirectional, dynamic, fluid
Boundaries	One or two organizations One or two industries	Multiple organizations Different sectors, occupations
Employment relationship	Job security for loyalty Full-time employment contract Job security for degree	Employability for performance Part-time, flexi-time Freelancing, projects, gigs Degree less obviously useful
Compensation	Salaries and benefits	Contracts and fees
Degree of mobility	Lower	Higher
Work environment	Bureaucratic Office	Shared vision and mission Virtual space and remote working
People focus	Attention to bosses and managers Employees, coworkers	Attention to clients and customers Vendors, entrepreneurs, team members
Core values	Advancement Entitlement Job security	Growth, Marketability Personal freedom and control Lifestyle
Key attitudes	Organizational commitment Loyalty to company	Professional commitment Loyalty to self Work-life balance
Identity	Employer-dependent Job, position, occupation	Employer-independent Life circumstances and contribution to work, family, community
Skills and learning	Firm-specific Finite, broad or job-related	Transferable Lifelong learning
Main career management responsibility	Organization HR departments and line manager	Individual Professional network, mentors, friends...
Success measured by	Career ladder, promotion Pay Status	Psychological success, personal fulfillment Meaningful work, valued skills

An entirely different nature of career – and career path – has emerged. As described by Yehuda Baruch from the University of Southampton, careers have become multidirectional, dynamic and fluid – in contrast with the traditional view of careers, which is linear, static and rigid.[12] The linear career model can be depicted as a mountain-climbing expedition, where reaching the summit is the aspiration and people climb as far and as fast as they can. With the multi-directional career model, the full scale of landscapes is taken into account. You can choose. You can climb the mountain, you can opt for another mountain, take a few hills instead or wander along the plains. You navigate your own career, creating a new path when and where you feel it is right, and you select whichever direction you wish to and feel capable of pursuing in the quest for personal development.

For each individual, the new career management paradigm recognizes that career development is a lifelong process of skill building through a continuum of learning, development and mastery. This process enables each of us to be in charge of our own careers, having enough focus and direction for stability and enough flexibility and adaptability to allow for change along the way.

At the same time, the balance of power shifts dramatically when this attitude prevails. It becomes a challenge to manage individuals who are so strongly focused on their own fulfillment, as opposed to feeling a loyalty and devotion to the corporation, as was previously expected. As managers, we must adjust both our approach and our process to acknowledge the shift, and as individuals, we may embrace the possibilities afforded by this different view on career.

Every element of the new career paradigm outlined in the previous table is on view in the stories you are about to read. As we have both personally made the shift from the old paradigm to the new, and not without some pain, we are well placed to know that it behooves us all to understand the transitions that are not only possible but likely, as a result of the changing environment which we inhabit.

Chapter 2

Far from Home

Starting Your Career Overseas

As we write, there is increasing fear of "others" and "difference", whether that is played out through a post-Brexit UK, or the presidency of Donald Trump in the U.S. Here, we take a more optimistic look at what happens to people who start their careers far from home. Firstly, what makes them take the step away from home comforts? And secondly, how differently does their career evolve over time? Does the wanderlust endure? And what kind of permanent changes come about? We took a look at four successful professionals, each at a different stage of his or her career, and tried to observe patterns and trends, to learn how international assignments can be used more intelligently in every business.

Lily

Lily's move to the UK just before finishing high school in China was not her own choice, though her family situation no doubt predisposed her to this kind of development. Her father had been an expatriate manager of a Chinese multinational since she was a young girl, so she had frequently visited him in France and the UK with her mother. However, it was her parents who dictated that she leave to complete her secondary education in Oxford, saying that they wanted to spare her the terrors of the notorious Chinese university entrance exams.

Lily's move went smoothly, and she describes the two years she spent living with a host family as the happiest in her life. Her excitement allowed her not to be homesick, and she began to explore the cultural differences she faced, never having spoken the English language before arriving in the UK. On moving on to the prestigious London School of Economics, Lily had not particularly contemplated staying in the UK beyond her education years. But she chose to find her own job based on her own abilities, rather than use her parents' network, as she always had previously.

Having set the ambitious goal of obtaining a place on the graduate program at a Big Four audit firm, Lily recently obtained a position at KPMG. Only on entering the firm did she realize that she did not have any real British friends. She did not lack friends in general, but all of them had been Asian until then. She was shocked, but decided to use this as a catalyst for change. The process she underwent to integrate with a diverse British population of colleagues included "learning about beer and rugby, reading 'To Kill a Mockingbird' and finding more out about British music". She observes that "when there is little in common, it is up to me to do the learning and bridge the gap". As for watching football: "that is another language to learn".

The challenge of what comes next is complex for Lily, as she intends to stay in the UK at least long enough to obtain a full residency permit and complete her audit training. However, she knows there will be expectations of her, as an only child, once her parents start to age. She likes her life in the UK, and it now feels like home – she has a flat and a mortgage, and she feels happily rooted there. She realizes she has a broader horizon than her stay-at-home peers, many of whom are still struggling to find a rewarding job and a place of their own, and she seems grateful for her relative freedom.

When asked if her values changed, Lily explains she has developed a more long-term point of view and an openness to others that were absent from her life previously, adding "this gives much more meaning to my existence". Her advice for Chinese students is to get out and socialize with as many different people as possible — to get uncomfortable, and to extend their comfort zone. Lily seems to have done this admirably, adapting beautifully, and whatever the demands of her parents or society in the future, one cannot help thinking that she will manage that too.

Romain

Frenchman Romain has already adapted to more than five cultures and languages in just under thirty years of life. He grew up in a fortunate environment in which his family perceived travel and exploration as important and regularly travelled to a variety of countries. He was educated bilingually in the international section of the lycée near his home in Toulouse, and his vacation jobs included managing a resort in Greece for a local travel company. So it was hardly a surprise that he chose to take a semester during his business studies in Paris to experience campus life in China.

After this early taste of the Orient, he aimed to forge a career in Asia, at whatever cost. However, he did not really have much of a plan for how to make this happen. He had already gone to Singapore to start exploring opportunities when a family link helped him to make contact with the founder of a successful French conference management company. As a result of this introduction, he was hired initially as a project manager for a new event that was due to take place in Hong Kong, but with a view towards him spearheading an Asian business for the company.

Romain has now lived and worked in Singapore for almost three years, built a successful business and is even discussing a financial stake in the company. His pioneering attitude has paid off. He is now waiting to see whether he can get some "skin in the game", in which case he will stay around. If that does not work out, then he will seek out other challenges in alternative faraway places. There is also the possibility of opening his own company, and he is already actively working on ideas.

The work and success that Romain has achieved have made him an attractive prospect for a number of headhunters, though he is clear on the subject: if he wants to stay in the conference business, he will stay where he is. However, he knows that if he wants to move on, it will be to another international opportunity. He also knows that he is perceived as being more valuable than his friends from university in France, who have been more modest in their travels and careers.

When Romain is quizzed on where "home" is, he is firm in responding that Toulouse is his "chez lui". He loves his life in Singapore, but the day we interviewed him, he was in Toulouse to buy an apartment. He says that when he lands in Singapore, he knows he is there to "go to the office". He even goes further, explaining that it feels like going back to boarding school. Not an unhappy boarding school, he is quick to add, but nevertheless a feeling of being "away from home". He enjoys his life as an expatriate, but does not seem to be in danger of becoming a local Singaporean at this point.

Another important element in the argument for Romain's sense of happy non-belonging is that he does not have a serious girlfriend. He is free to jump in a plane at the drop of a hat, and not to feel any tension in his travels or work engagements. He recognizes that this might well change if and when he finds someone with whom to settle down. He would welcome that if it happened, but also seems happy to pursue his freedom and mobility as long as they last.

On further discussion, we discover that some of his siblings live in other countries, and it is thus tempting to believe that the "nurture" part of international living is stronger than ever. Based on the authors' own experience, the travel "gene" seems often to be passed down from one generation to another – but not in all cases, as we discover next.

Gabriel

The story of Gabriel, who is now an IT engineer at Capgemini in France, is one of strong contrast to Romain's. They are of a similar age, but Gabriel has decided to return to France from his sojourn overseas.

Gabriel's family had an interest in the classics, which led them towards holidays in Greece and Italy, but not much further. However, his father pushed him to take Chinese lessons when he started engineering school. Gabriel obeyed, somewhat unenthusiastically. Nevertheless, this opened his eyes to other opportunities.

When a friend of a friend mentioned an internship experience in a Peugeot Citroën joint venture in China, he sent his CV, realizing that the language study would not necessarily help him practically, but its inclusion in his resume just might convince the potential employer. At this point, he had no specific agenda, but was attracted by the idea of doing "something different".

Despite trying to plan for his arrival in Wuhan, Gabriel was hopelessly unprepared. He had neither a place to live nor the language skills required. He found it deeply depressing not to be able to communicate in a language he had believed he could manage. Luckily, with help from his manager, he was able to find accommodation and to begin to improve his language skills, largely through work and social contact with colleagues.

At first, the work environment was not as shiny as he had expected; he found himself in a dark, unheated basement with little support. However, colleagues were helpful, and he began to settle in and manage. He admits that he went to China somewhat scared. As he settled in, he realized his fears were unfounded and that he could have an amazingly rich life there. He opened up, made good friends, and became used to "the Chinese way".

As his internship came to a close, Gabriel returned to France to complete his studies. He soon realized that he had China "on his mind" and focused all his energies on getting another job there. Using his contacts, he obtained another contract and returned to Wuhan, this time working on the French side of the joint venture, where he should have felt much more comfortable. However, homesickness reared its head, and it seemed that Gabriel was not as suited to expatriation as he had thought. His motivation dropped, his learning curve flattened, and he aimed to return to France as soon as he could.

It was after an initial trip home over the first Christmas break that Gabriel began to remove his rose-tinted glasses. He started to notice the pollution. He got used to it but never progressed beyond this to actually "liking" it. He had signed up for eighteen months, and was offered an extension, but he decided to return home at the earliest opportunity.

Contrary to what might be expected, as Gabriel searched for new challenges back home in France, he did not perceive that his foreign experience was valued. He had believed it would be simple to make the transition back to French soil after Chinese work experience with a big brand like Peugeot, but he was proven wrong. He was changing industries, and recruiters could not see the value. In the end, Gabriel took a "bridging" job — a compromise, but one that allowed him to subsequently find a great position at Capgemini.

While Gabriel is happy to have returned to his homeland, he does not exclude the possibility of a return to foreign places. Next time it could be somewhere other than China, and he has kept the desire to learn and develop that is so heavily linked with expatriation. He misses the buzz of developing economies and challenging cultural circumstances, so it may not be long before he takes on the next job away from home.

Richard

Our final character, Richard, is a 55-year-old C-suite executive with oil equipment company TechnipFMC. He is without a doubt a poster-boy expat; he has not looked back ever since his first move away from his New Zealand home upon graduation.

Richard grew up in small-town New Zealand, with nothing particularly predisposing him to an international career. His family expectations were that he achieve a good education and seek out a sound career path. But Richard knew early on that he wanted to explore the wider world. It was perhaps this desire to "get out" that drew him towards French in his high school years. He turned out to be gifted with the language, which was to become critical to his later success. Being a good all-rounder made it difficult to choose a particular subject to study at university, but Richard picked Engineering in the hope that it would take him "out to where the action is". During his penultimate year, he was lucky enough to do an internship in Borneo with oil services company Schlumberger, and he was, as he says, "hooked".

He received an offer to return to a long-term position with the company upon graduation, but then recession hit and he was left in hiatus for a year. During that time, however, he received an invitation to start work in Singapore, and spent the next few years on and off oil rigs, mostly in Indonesia. This life of travel, engaging work and constant adaptation really motivated Richard, and he was happy until he was assigned to Australia, where he felt as if he had been sent back home. The feeling of stagnation was strong enough to start him looking for alternatives, and he accepted a role with a startup company in New Zealand. Unexpectedly, this led to him being appointed General Manager of the company within less than a year, and his life became a whirlwind of crazy energy and chaos in which he learnt a lot; but there was still a piece of the puzzle missing.

Richard started trying to analyze what he wanted. The list included a more predictable, stable life, but overseas and with more responsibility. Failure to be taken seriously for corporate general management roles incited him to find a business school, and he went to INSEAD in France, where he could accomplish the learning required in only 10 months, speak the language he had studied all those thousands of miles away, and learn from others. He was after theory and structure, as he had learnt about management mostly by the seat of his pants.

Career Transition Navigator

EXPLORE

Having excelled in the MBA program, it was Richard's wish to stay in France, or at the very least, Europe. He eventually got the opportunity to take on a role in more general management, with U.S. oil equipment company FMC Technologies in their operation in the French countryside, not far from the campus of INSEAD. He acted as a bridge between the U.S. and French cultures, rapidly becoming the global expert on managing intercultural teams and managers, which set him apart from his peers.

For the past twenty years, Richard's career has continued to develop within FMC with postings in Germany, then back to France, where Richard and his American wife feel that they are at home. They keep allegiance to their own countries, cultures and languages, but their third country means that they keep balance. Many of the past ten years have been spent in the Houston headquarters of FMC, but Richard and family keep their ties to their adopted home.

When asked to what he ascribes his success, Richard is quick to talk about a willingness to go anywhere and do anything, to get far beyond his comfort zone. He uses the word "adventure" a lot, and cites adaptability as a key competency for international careers. His advice to those contemplating a path similar to his is to take risks young: "if it does not work out, you have the time and space to recover".

There is also much talk of the need for solid leaders, with experience frequently adapting to new and uncomfortable situations. He sees a lack of such skills in those he interviews for roles in his team, and feels this to be a real threat to the future of business. Young people need more experience leading others, and this is exactly the kind of experience that they can get by doing the sort of work Richard did while still in his study and early corporate years.

What's Going On? The Search for Adventure and Learning

Starting your career overseas is no doubt a significant and substantial transition. Not only are you switching from student life to work life while becoming fully independent – which alone is a big enough life event – but this is compounded by the cultural shift of moving to a foreign country. And it has been amply demonstrated that international assignments are challenging due to culture shock, homesickness and loneliness.

Yet this is a growing trend: there are more and more international further education options offered – especially in Europe – such as Erasmus, EU-funded mobility programs, Leonardo da Vinci, business school international alliances, and more. Those students who opt for international studies are more likely to want an international career, and there seems to be an increasing number of young graduates who are keen to start their career abroad. We could be looking at a new breed of young global professionals, which Robin Pascoe, a journalist who writes extensively about expatriates, calls the "Hidden Expats": "Unlike many of their older counterparts, the new younger breed of global professional will move at a moment's notice and have no dependents to worry about. They are so eager for international experience they are willing to be hired as 'locals', which just happens to coincide with business needs to cut expensive expat packages to the bone. But the trip isn't all plain sailing."[13]

This is probably good news for companies, which are well-known for their handling of the dual challenges of attracting international talent and managing the international mobility of their internal talent. The question is, are they taking advantage of this new breed of global professionals?

What is striking with the four subjects we interviewed is that – apart from Richard, whose global career was managed by the companies that recruited him, from one assignment to another – the other three were self-starter expats. This means that they received less support from their employer in terms of relocation, on-boarding, logistics and career management.

As we understand our subjects' journeys, we can more easily discover whether this transition of moving overseas at the beginning of your career makes you better off or not, and to what extent companies are taking advantage of it.

Does the family, social, or educational environment influence the willingness to work abroad? Looking at our four subjects, we see a split. Gabriel's and Richard's background did not necessarily set them up for this. But in the case of Lily and Romain, it is clear that early life experiences and family environment gave them a taste for international adventures.

Our observations of the reasons why they wanted to live and work abroad are confirmed and further elaborated upon by Corina Cristal, author of a master's thesis on this topic, as she writes: "the findings proved that young graduates would embark on a foreign assignment due to predominantly intrinsic motives. Their international educational background determines a higher willingness to expatriate, but the factors which have an impact on the decision to relocate are the same as in the case of young graduates who have studied in their home country only."[14]

From a young graduate's perspective, the motives for international mobility can be varied:

- Seeking change, adventure, exploration, travel
- Improving social competencies: self-confidence, independence, problem solving, cross-cultural skills, language skills, communication skills
- Gaining a better understanding of another country, culture and people – from both the living and working environment
- Increasing career opportunities in home country and internationally

The motivation to increase career opportunities is well supported by a recent Erasmus Impact study: "on average, Erasmus students have better employability skills after a stay abroad than 70 percent of all students. Based on their personality traits, they have a better predisposition for employability even before going abroad. By the time they return they have increased their advantage by 42 percent on average."[15]

It's hard to know if our four subjects possessed this intrinsic motivation from birth, or if it was nurtured. It is clear in Romain's case that his family environment – full of travel, exploration and foreign languages – and his international education gave him an early taste of the faraway and naturally led him to embrace an international career. For Lily, who grew up in a family of expatriates, it was her parents who dictated that she should go and complete her secondary education in the UK. However, she is the one who then decided to stay in the UK to find a job. Gabriel's decision trigger was likely a combination of using his knowledge of his reluctantly learned, but useful, Chinese language skills, seeking change, and his response to a friend of a friend's hint about an internship opportunity in China. In the case of Richard, whose family environment and expectation were 100 percent New Zealand centered, it was his curiosity, language ability, and a desire for action and adventure that drove him out of his native country.

As we unfold our subjects' stories, we see a broad range of circumstances, influences and motivations to start a career abroad. We can safely assume that personal characteristics – such as extraversion, openness, curiosity and cultural flexibility – have also played a role here. And in comparison to more traditional expatriates, who tend to relocate at later stages in their career, it is fair to say that our younger subjects were less constrained by spousal or familial concerns; nor were they stimulated by the financial incentive of a rich expat package.

How did they find their first job overseas? The path to employment was not a straight line. It did not necessarily follow the usual (or perceived as such) process of seeing a job ad, sending a resume, going to interviews and so on. For Romain, who had already completed an internship in Asia, it was a family link who connected him to his future employer. The two-step route of internship to employment worked nicely too for Richard and Gabriel. Like Richard, many young graduates who want a global career smartly target companies such as Schlumberger which are famous for providing international assignment opportunities, or even better, lifelong global career management. Of our four subjects, Lily followed the most traditional route to obtain her position at KPMG. But even here, she was following a route that was classical in her adopted country; if she had stayed at home, her job-hunting would likely have followed an entirely different process.

At first glance, given our observations of our young global graduates' personal traits and eagerness for international experience, we should logically believe that their transition is easier than that of their older counterparts. But is that really so?

Younger expatriates do not escape their own brand of culture shock. We recognize in the stories of both Gabriel and Lily that the famous expatriate adjustment life-cycle somewhat hit them both. In the case of Gabriel, it looks as if his honeymoon period lasted from his first stay in China until his return to France. Only when he returned to China did he experience a true culture shock. Lily equally experienced a smooth transition when she first came to the UK to study, possibly as her excitement and busy schedule didn't allow her to be homesick. But on entering KPMG, it became clear to her that she had been relying on her Asian friends. Her shock came on realizing that she didn't have any real British friends. Fortunately, this awareness was quickly turned into change and action on her part.

Lily's experience is insightfully reflected by Margaret Malewski, a Canadian by birth, who completed her university education in her ancestral Poland, worked in Geneva and the Middle East for P&G and wrote the book "GenXpat", in which she examines the phenomenon of young global professionals.[16] "On the surface, GenXpats have lots of friends, go out every night, and have great jobs. But on a deeper level they are lonely, have no sense of roots or community, and can be lacking in depth and continuity in their lives as they bop around from airport to airport and city to city", she says. Indeed, being a young expat professional is not just about working abroad but also involves living abroad. As Malewski adds: "The challenge is really about creating a balanced, fulfilling, sustainable lifestyle." And then there are the age-related, developmental challenges which don't vanish with relocation, such as finding and maintaining a relationship. Romain's story indicates that finding true love will impact his future life and career plans. Thus, paradoxically, by not having a stable romantic partner, young expats are both free to move literally anywhere in the world, and challenged by coping with the transition and sustaining their stay abroad.

But while single, unaccompanied expats of all ages would likely identify with that challenge, it's doubtful they feel the burden of the second issue Malewski highlights: "Since they are often hired as locals, young people don't receive any of the usual support which goes into an expat package like relocation, language or cross-cultural training. They are like a 'hidden' expat, facing financial and cultural challenges at the same time", she believes. Gabriel's experience of moving to China starkly illustrates this point. His unpreparedness and lack of language skills and housing made it a depressing episode.

The Voice of Companies: Globally Accessing the Top 10 Percent

To talk to a company that positively encourages and facilitates early careers away from home, we met with Erik Juhl, the VP of Talent Acquisition at Criteo, which is a rapidly growing global leader in digital performance advertising. Erik explained that their needs are different from those of traditional economy companies: "We are a tech company and … we have a different structure. The talent model is flipped on its head. The skills needed are limited because we are at the top of innovation. Plus, the technology adoption life cycle is fast, so skills become quickly outdated. The name of the game is how to access the top 10 percent."

Erik added that, on top of the high-achieving profile, other specifics are needed, such as being multilingual and possessing a knowledge of big data, other specific tech knowledge and emotional intelligence… To hit the goal, Criteo needs to open up to the global talent market.

Criteo's environment is dynamic, and doesn't fit all personality types. Those from a large company background might find it hard to operate, or even hate the environment. "You have to like exploring and being outside your comfort zone. In a tech company like ours, there is no mindset of employment for life", says Erik.

How Criteo sources candidates appears to be different from most traditional companies. Erik points out that they recruit equally through LinkedIn, direct applications and employee referrals, with a strong framework for evaluating the candidates, and a system built in to eliminate selection biases.

International candidates are evidently highly appreciated, and language competence is a key factor, even though there is no requirement to speak French. There is also much attention paid to creating a positive, family environment for the international employees, including support such as housing, training and spouse coaching. Building a sense of community is indeed important for the newly hired. "People tend to hang out together quite a lot", according to Erik, "it is a strong component of our culture."

When asked about the higher cost of recruiting and employing in this international way, Erik comes back with a swift answer: "We look at it as the 'cost of doing business'. We know it is logistically hard but that is the level of talent our business requires. Also, we're asking more of these people, so there is higher value than your typical employee. Since high velocity is the reality of our tech industry, there is only an 18-24 month expected employee life-cycle. It makes retention planning, on-boarding, training, and employee engagement essential to maximizing the return on investment. This can allow us to build the virtuous circle."

Some success stories include the current Irish VP of Engineering, who is based in Paris and gets along well with everybody, and a French female manager who spent time in Japan for the company before going on to London. A notable failure was an American team member who struggled with working across all time zones.

Erik provides valuable advice for other companies on how to succeed at hiring international talent: "You need a commitment to make them successful. This commitment has to be reflected at all stages of the process: selection, interviews, flying the candidates out. You need to build a whole system to help make that determination real. You also need to invest in them. In the end, it pays off." While we know that not all organizations have this enlightened approach, it is heartening to see that new economy companies have embraced the borderless workplace as far as rules and regulations will allow.

We know that getting the formula right with global talent is critical for corporations as the world shrinks and the global market grows in complexity. Dickman and Harris, in their 2005 Journal of World Business paper, tell us more: "developing leaders who can manage the increasing complexity of running global organizations is a high human resource priority for many organizational leaders. Managing global talent and career paths is therefore a critical challenge in many multinational organizations... An integral part of a majority of organizations' global management development approach is the international assignment (IA)."[17]

According to Terence Brake, prolific author on the future of work and partner in TMA World, a global leadership training consultancy, "The world is going through a highly volatile period when the building blocks of the post-World War II global economy are being challenged. Global and regional economic and political institutions are under threat as new nationalist movements gain support. Does this mean that international experience and cultural intelligence should be lower priorities when developing talent? That could be a fatal business mistake. If anything, we must increase the exposure of talent to different countries, and ensure that the knowledge they gain is sophisticated rather than stereotypical."

But sometimes, reality is different. Not all companies value international experience, as Dickman and Harris explain: "The link between an IA and the development of individual career capital in a global setting is not a certainty. International work is generally seen to develop the global competencies of the individual. However, any global competencies gained may not always be of direct use to the individual. First, international work may enhance the know-how of assignees – but it may also result in skills that are not transferable to the home context by the individual, either through a lack of applicability of the skill in the home organization context, or through the inability of the individual to translate this learning into practice." Gabriel's struggle to find a job back in France illustrates this contention beautifully.

Research on expatriation consistently finds that companies confronted with high costs, high failure rates and repatriation problems, need to improve the process of selecting international managers. For unclear reasons, though, the belief that older expatriates tend to perform better seems to hold, and companies by and large are not targeting the younger segment of the candidate pool as a viable alternative.

If we examine more closely corporate international assignment (IA) strategies, we find that the decision to send an expatriate is essentially justified by two different types of logic. The first is that of filling a position that a subsidiary cannot adequately fill with local talent. This logic includes expat categories such as the "troubleshooter" (i.e., the seasoned executive charged with turning around a failing subsidiary), the "expert" (i.e., the SAP specialist from HQ), or the "watchdog" (i.e., the trusted CFO guardian of good local practices). These assignments require talent that combines experience with trust from the parent organization.

The other logic of international assignment is that of development. Here, assignments are deliberately used as a means to accelerate the growth of an identified high potential. They act as a test of that person's ability to adapt to a different and sometimes adverse environment, and a catalyst to broaden or strengthen soft skills such as intercultural understanding, influencing skills, strategic thinking, resourcefulness, initiative, and so on. There again, companies usually prefer to expatriate individuals whom they know well enough before investing in a costly, and risky international assignment.

While understanding the reasons for these practices, we contend that young graduates – especially those with international educational or early career experience – should constitute a distinct target segment for employers. The lack of work experience may be considered a disadvantage, but there are other traits that make a young candidate desirable for an international assignment: they bring new, untested ideas to the table; their status as single, childless individuals has a positive influence on the decision to go abroad; the personality characteristics they developed while living abroad, such as flexibility and openness, indicate a global management potential. This point is strongly echoed by Richard, who laments the lack of leaders with experience frequently adapting to new and uncomfortable situations, which is precisely what can be achieved by living and working abroad in early corporate years.

As we have seen through the stories of our subjects, young professionals working abroad do not typically receive much support from their organization. One could argue that this is a crucial part of the experience. Jean-Marc Hachey, author of "Big Guide to Living and Working

Overseas", believes that in the long run, it may be important for the development of a young professional to experience actual challenges, live in less than desirable parts of town, and be forced to mingle more with the locals than their elders do.[18] "There's almost a need for that lack of a safety net", believes Hachey, who speaks and consults regularly on the young global professional. "It's part of the growing and development process and will, in the end, serve the young person well by giving him, or her, the experience of dealing with challenges." Nevertheless, there may be a reasonable compromise between jumping into unknown water without a lifejacket and receiving luxurious housing allowances and free local club memberships.

We are delighted to observe that global mobility management is evolving in the right direction, as companies increasingly look for smarter ways to manage expatriates. The long-established dilemma between expensive expatriates and locals has since been replaced by more complex questions. Over the past ten years, many companies have moved from one-size-fits-all policies to more segmented policies designed to meet the requirements of ever more different types of assignments and expatriates. These have included using the "Local Plus" approach – a compromise between using pure local approaches (which could hinder mobility) and costly home-based expatriate packages – which is gaining maturity, and could signal the shift towards making international assignments more attractive to junior talent and more affordable for companies. We hope and trust that this will encourage more companies to hire young professionals with a view to using their aptitude for mobility.

How to Make the Transition Happen

Each of our subjects had to make substantial adjustments when they started working abroad, with the level of adaptation required largely dependent on how big the cultural difference, or gap, was, as well as how prepared they were. Mostly, the adjustment was simply accomplished by themselves through observation, experimentation and trial and error, as we saw with Lily's discovery of beer, rugby and music. Similarly with Gabriel, who received a bit of support from his manager while the rest was initiated and led by himself, and with his efforts in language and social life paying off richly.

In the end, there appears to be a point at which young expats either start to thrive in their new life, or else conclude that it isn't right for them and decide to leave, as was the case with Gabriel after his second time in China. Thus we can conclude that they mostly have to fend for themselves in managing their transitions, and this works best when they keep on open mind, are willing to try new things, and possess or develop a capacity to reflect on and learn from their experience.

All of them learned in the process, and it has been useful to hear their reflections on their experience and discover what sort of advice they have for future young expats. The table below summarizes advice from the young expatriates we talked to and from research on this topic.

7 Tips for First Time Expats

1. **Start early** – travel, explore the wider world, look for internships and summer jobs abroad

2. **Study internationally** – find a university with exchange programs, take international courses

3. **Learn the language** – learn as much as you can before, during and after your stay

4. **Be open** – challenge your assumptions, go beyond your comfort zone, take risks

5. **Immerse yourself in the culture** – get out and socialize, make local friends, get used to "the local way"

6. **Understand your emotions** – most expats go through these stages: honeymoon, culture shock, adaptation

7. **Seek support** – ask your company for a cross-cultural program or find a buddy, mentor or coach

One of the takeaways from our subjects' stories is that in order to successfully navigate your transition, you have to have both the ability and the willingness to challenge yourself. In her advice for Chinese students, Lily is clear on this last point when she advises them to "get uncomfortable, and extend their comfort zone". This becomes a virtuous circle. By being open to learning and experimentation – which Lily modeled wonderfully – individuals continuously increase their adaptability, which in turn makes them less threatened by new situations and more eager to discover, which opens up new opportunities for them, and so on.

This whole mindset and change ability is well embodied by Richard when he talks about "a willingness to go anywhere and do anything, to get far beyond your comfort zone" and advises those contemplating a similar path to take risks young, with the encouraging comment that if it does not work out, you have the time and space to recover.

In the end, do the initial expectations of young expats compare to the reality actually experienced? We hear again from Corina Cristal: "… the results show that the expectations young graduates set in regards to expatriation are only partly realistic. While correct anticipations are made upon cultural shock or training conditions, less accurate opinions were expressed in connection to task-related problems and social networking."

Next, we want to gauge: Did they change? And what do young global professionals learn? We know that the French say "travel shapes youth", and as far back as Seneca, it was believed that: "travel and change of place impart new vigor to the mind", so we think we are onto something here. In 2014, Erasmus conducted an impact study looking at the effects of mobility on the skills and employability of students. The study identified a set of factors which employers would consider desirable, such as curiosity, tolerance of ambiguity, and decisiveness. The results show real impact: 80 percent of mobile students with Erasmus stints experienced an improvement in these particular factors. Those that increased the most were (from the top): confidence, curiosity, serenity, tolerance of ambiguity and decisiveness. While the results are experienced by international students, we can reasonably expect the same impact for young professionals starting their career abroad, with or without international studies prior to that.

But the change also operates at a deeper level. Beyond developing specific skills or personal attributes, some of our subjects reported more profound personal growth. Lily told us that her values have changed, notably in that she has developed a more long-term point of view and an openness to others that were absent from her life previously. As she was reflecting on this, she acknowledged how much this gave more meaning to her existence. As Saint Augustine pondered: "the world is a book, and those who do not travel read only one page".

While a number of the above-mentioned qualities – such as confidence or comfort with ambiguity – can be learned in other circumstances, perhaps the skill that stands out as most distinctly gained through international work experience is intercultural management. It is clear to us that what has set Richard apart from his peers and supported his brilliant career at Technip FMC are his intercultural team management skills and his ability to bridge U.S. and French cultures.

10 Attributes You Will Develop
(That Make You More Attractive to Employers)

1. Agility (intellectual, cultural, social and emotional)
2. Comfort with ambiguity
3. Confidence
4. Cultural sensitivity
5. Curiosity and openness
6. Global mindset
7. Independence, self-reliance
8. Resilience
9. Self-awareness
10. Willingness to take risks

Now we ask: "What's next for them? Stay or repatriate?" When we consider what might be next for our subjects, we find a lot of contrast. From Gabriel, who returned to France (though he may later decide to go overseas again), to Richard, who has enjoyed his entire international career and has become a true global citizen, few seem to be untouched by the experience, even in the broader group. There may well be other periods of life away from "home" later in each of their careers, as the situation fits. Richard, however, does not really have a national "home" any more.

The future is more uncertain for Lily and Romain, as there are complex status and personal issues at stake. Lily wants to obtain full UK residency, which requires a few more years on British soil, so she will be devoted to that above and beyond her career progression. Romain is aiming for a stake in the company he works for, and will no doubt define much of his immediate future as a function of what he is, or is not, offered. There are typically increasingly conflicting priorities as the expat (current or former) ages and advances in his or her career. Richard has managed these by close collaboration with his wife and daughter, with whom plans for the next stop have always been thoroughly discussed and decided.

So, does an initial experience outside their home country increase young professionals' employability? Is this rewarding for their career? The jury is out on this important question. While some are positive – and most of our examples demonstrate good reasons to be on the optimistic side – others are less enthusiastic.

Let's start with the positive view. Recent research confirms a strong correlation between international experience and graduate employability. The most comprehensive survey of global employers – the QS Global Employer Survey 2011 – asked hiring managers and CEOs whether or not they "value" international study experience.[19] The report is unique among recent research because it is based on an exceptionally large pool of responses from 10,000 respondents in 116 nations. It found that 60 percent of respondents said they do value an international study experience and the attributes that the experience may confer to mobile students.

Many of the individual career stories we have covered also demonstrate that the benefits of starting your career abroad are real: Romain is obliged to fend off calls from headhunters and is confident about his relative advantage compared to his French peers. The most vivid example of a successful career in our stories is that of Richard, who for the past twenty years has continued to advance within FMC Technology with postings in Germany, the U.S., Norway, France, and now back to the U.S., where he is a member of the executive committee of the company.

But two cases spring to mind which lend credence to the negative view. Gabriel realized that his China experience wasn't valued by the French labor market, so much so that he had to compromise by taking a bridging job. This definitely flies in the face of our "happy endings" elsewhere, although the bridge led to greater satisfaction at Capgemini subsequently. Similarly, Thomas, one of our readers, commented:

"Going back to one's home country is a challenge as, at some point, you might be perceived as a foreigner and your international experience might not be valued as you believe it should be in your home country, as Gabriel's experience in your article illustrates. In my own case, my desire to come back from my last assignment overseas to France HQ resulted in a job offer in the same company but... in London... while returning to France is still on my mind. Expatriation at the beginning of one's career is challenging and rewarding but bears the risk of being labeled as only useful for overseas assignments. I believe ... you will need some time to come back up (on return), as you build back your network and visibility."

It is of note that the two "negative" testimonials above, while true, happen to be from France, where "atypical profiles" are sadly seen as undesirable. France is a land of formal structures and conformity. Expats can be seen as anomalous people who have lost touch with their country

On balance, then, is a first experience abroad a good thing or not? Perhaps the following research, from a 2016 paper by Georgakakis, Dauth and Ruigrok in the Journal of World Business provides the most complete answer: "We postulate that (...) the relationship between international experience and time to the top follows a U-shaped form. Initially, the acquisition of international experience speeds-up executives' career progress until a threshold where the social-network costs of cross-country mobility out-weigh the human-capital benefits." This finding certainly aligns with our results.[20]

Travel Shapes Leaders

Overall, we feel that the early expatriation experience leads to positive results, even if it is not universally manageable or appropriate. As a result, there is great hope that with leaders like the happier cases we have described here, businesses and economies will move forward with speed and agility, bringing people together with what they have in common instead of dividing by difference.

There are, no doubt, some significant barriers to making this kind of move, including the "right to work" or visa/work permit issues of any given country. What is more, few university careers services are encouraging their graduates to move into a first job overseas, and therefore information needs to be dug out by the individuals, who are certainly the exception rather than the rule.

However, despite the barriers, we see that the more exposure a young person has to travel, to difference, to risk and challenge, the more likely he or she is to seek more adventure in his or her professional life. Travel and expatriation are one of the simplest ways to acquire all of these and more, and our subjects took to it with varying degrees of motivation and success.

Companies would do well to understand the value of what can be achieved while in another country and culture, and to encourage greater risk taking for their high potential talent. As these stories indicate clearly, the benefits of jobs far away from home are numerous, far-reaching and long-lasting.

We believe that the advice given by our subjects is valid, and that all those seeking not just career success, but also a great, engaging and satisfying life, should take the plunge and ensure they get "far away" early on in their careers.

Further Reading and Information

▎ BOOKS AND STUDIES

"Career Integration : Reviewing the Impact of Experience Abroad on Employment", edited by Christine Anderson, John Christian, Kimberly Hindbjorgen, Carol Jambor-Smith, Martha Johnson, and Michael Woolf, Learning Abroad Center and CAPA (2015)

"The Erasmus Impact Study : Effects of mobility on the skills and employability of students and the internationalization of higher education institutions", European Commission (2014)

"GenXpat: The Young Professional's Guide to Making a Successful Life Abroad", by Margaret Malewski, Intercultural Press (2005)

▎ ARTICLES AND BLOGS

"The Double-Edged Sword of Overseas Experience" by Matt Palmquis, in Strategy+Business, July 14, 2016

"How valuable is international work experience?" by Janina Conboye, Financial Times, November 6, 2013

Notepad Blog – The blog section of NetExpat, a global leader in expat assistance
www.portal.netexpat.com/index.php/resource-center/net-expat-blog

The Expat Expert – Robin Pascoe's source of wisdom on expatriate families
www.expatexpert.com

ExpatFocus – An online community that started small in a single country to
become one of the world's largest expatriate websites with a global audience
www.expatfocus.com/expatriate-articles

Chapter 3

Stadium
to Corporation

Making the Leap from Sport to Business

We idolize great sporting stars, seeing them as forever young. But we tend not to wonder about what the future holds for them beyond their last Olympic podium. Memories of these athletes stay engraved in our minds, at their peak performance age, and we give little thought to their next chapter in life. However, for most of them, there must be a next chapter once their bodies are no longer able to keep up with the demands of top-level training. The transition into this phase is seldom managed well, as we discovered, in talking to four former elite athletes who transitioned into the world of business.

Eric

Eric grew up in the U.S. Virgin Islands, and his pioneering spirit in sport and work no doubt derive from the driven and adventurous family environment in which he grew up. His family of high achievers were all involved in equestrian sports, so it was only natural that he ride with his older brothers and sisters from an early age. His father had been a member of the U.S. Olympic team, and was now involved in the local federation, along with his mother. As he says, "I was steeped in it from birth".

He enjoyed riding so much that he pushed himself, finding success first in junior show jumping and then in three-day events. He carefully planned his choice of university to allow him to continue pursuing his sport, and luckily his journey took him to the wonderful Ivy League school of Princeton. During those undergraduate years, he excelled in his riding, qualifying for the world championships during his final year. He chose not to attend, though, in order to ensure his academic success.

Upon leaving the world of classrooms and coursework, Eric was able to focus more exclusively on his sport, and he set a clear agenda for himself. If, after a defined period, he was not in the top ten in the world, he would retire, and set a different target. His progression was spectacular, and he joined the team for the Pan-American Games in '87, followed up with a slot in the '88 Olympics. However, after achieving only a 35th place in the Olympics, it was strikingly clear that he had not reached the threshold he had hoped for. He says that he realized he was "good, but not extraordinary". It was time to act on his agenda and leave his sporting career behind him.

According to Eric, most who transition out of equestrian sports do so while still fairly young, especially as it is not a high-profile, sponsored sport that "pays the bills". Despite all of his family connections with the Federation, he received no support at all from them upon leaving. He looked instead to family and friends who were already well connected to companies and individuals in the City of London and in other big international markets. Along the way, he received advice to try to join a graduate training scheme of some kind, in the hope that this structured development would open up opportunities for him in the future.

While Eric says that being an Olympian certainly opened doors for him, once the door was open he was completely on his own in trying to persuade future employers to take him on. He had a lot more "chats" with companies than he received offers. He also was suffering from not really knowing what he wanted to do, as he had been so focused on his sport until then. In a stroke of luck, he was invited to join the graduate training program at General Electric, and was able to try on lots of different hats for a few years. While the pure corporate environment he was in likely did not suit his entrepreneurial spirit all that well, he received the basic training and the "mainstreaming" he had needed, and felt encouraged to develop himself further by taking an MBA at Wharton.

After Wharton, Eric felt the call of the entrepreneurial wild. His summer job between the two years of his MBA was working in the former Czechoslovakia. One of his clients was the Slovak wine industry, inspiring him to start a company to import wine from Eastern Europe. Due to quality control issues, he refocused his energies towards importing South African wines, as this was a market from which the U.S. had just lifted economic sanctions. This ability to spot opportunities and run with them is one we found to be perfectly constant throughout the people we interviewed for this chapter.

From this first initiative, Eric has moved on to multiple entrepreneurial activities, sometimes as founder, sometimes as early employee. In either position, he thrived on the energy and dynamism of this area. During a stint of several years at National Geographic, the less spirited environment he found there eventually tired him, however wonderful the brand.

His most recent venture is in partnership with a former classmate from Princeton, in a company that still feels like a start-up despite being 30 years old. He loves the possibility of "contesting the field to win", and finding the vision and resources to be number one in their field. But Eric is not a constant thrill seeker. As he says, "I am not always looking for new or different challenges, but I am definitely inspired by pursuing to its logical end whatever I undertake".

Eric's number one piece of advice is to create and use networks to the hilt. In his case, the family environment helped him to be relatively well-connected from the outset, but he has continued to knock down doors and build authentic relationships wherever he goes, making him a popular manager, colleague and fellow businessman.

He also has strong words on the "typecast" roles that are so frequently offered to sportspeople as they retire: sport commentators, brand ambassadors, etc. While these may work for some, there is no guarantee. And it is an awfully exposed way to fail, if that is the outcome.

Andrew

Andrew was probably a little too young to be offered a typecast role when he "retired" from the British ski team. While he had good connections and some experience from his own entrepreneurial initiatives, he did not have a classical pattern of study and work in business. Luckily, he had a big brain and a lot of natural resources that carried him through his transition.

Andrew also came from a family of entrepreneurs and successful business people; his father having created a merchant bank in Edinburgh, built it into a substantial size. So from a young age, he was encouraged to think about how a business works and what defines success. This helped him as he entered the sport of skiing by a fairly chilly route. Weekly, he and his older brothers and sisters boarded a bus to go and ply the slopes in the nearby Cairngorm hills with the local ski club. Although he was good at and keen on many other sports, it turned out that Andrew had a gift for skiing and was already competing at high levels by the time he was in his early teens. Both parents had a philosophy of pursuing excellence, and Andrew followed their lead, pushing himself to ever-higher levels.

The first test of his resilience came at the age of fifteen, when he broke his back. Ironically, he was not even training at the time, but "messing around" off-piste, "probably showing off to a girl", when he was caught out and fell badly. An injury is a terrible thing for anyone, but even more of a challenge for a young person used to being highly active all the time. The recovery period was long and trying for Andrew, but as he reflected on the state of his life, he decided to return ever more determined once he was better.

Shortly after this, he was given the opportunity to "go pro", and inspired by the unusually stellar performance of the British ski team at the time, he pushed himself further and further. When it came time to decide whether to take up the place he had won at Bristol University, he deferred it: once, twice, then a third and final time. While he valued academia, his focus all that time was on reaching the peak of his performance. One of the big challenges for Andrew was that there are not many university campuses based on Alpine hilltops.

Andrew's rankings soared, and he started to make money from the sponsorship and product endorsements that accompanied his position on the UK team. He narrowly missed qualifying for the 2006 Olympics, and this was another call on his resilience – especially with the additional embarrassment of his family having booked to go and watch him compete in this event. However, he was able to move on quickly, and focus on how to use the next four years to achieve the Olympian objective.

In the build-up to the 2010 Olympics, Andrew's qualities as a team player and a natural leader were called upon in a way he would never have expected. Four weeks before the opening ceremony, it was announced that the Federation had gone bankrupt, and there would be no further support for the skiers on the team, either financial or logistical.

As one of the older members of the team and a natural action-taker and motivator, Andrew recalls contacting sponsors and logistics suppliers, in the hope of salvaging something from the situation. This called up every resource he had, including a high resistance to pressure. He also developed an understanding of the functioning of a team more intimately, describing the situation as: "an ambitious group of people, with intrinsically individual motivations, but who needed to function as a team." Curiously, this clarity of mind was useful not only then, but also in his future career at the notoriously competitive strategy consultancy McKinsey.

After the Olympics, and recognizing that his performance had not been as strong as he had hoped, Andrew was feeling more than a little disappointed. It did not take much for him to sense that it was time to move on. This time, once again, it was family and friends who saw him through it, offering material and emotional support.

The strategic planner attitude that we see throughout our sporty subjects came to the fore. With advice from his father, Andrew mapped out a five-year plan, bearing in mind that though he did not have a degree or any obviously relevant work experience, he wanted a serious job in business. What he needed was an opportunity to demonstrate to his colleagues his transferable skills and competencies.

Using connections, and having sat for his GMAT, he found a first role in a venture capital company as an unpaid intern. True to type, he read, took courses and applied himself far harder than most would have during this time. Then followed almost three years of full-time, properly paid work in both venture capital and private equity, in which he learnt, stretched himself, and devoured every opportunity that came his way. Importantly, he also identified and found a new support network.

In 2014, despite not having the academic qualifications required, Andrew persuaded the selection committee at INSEAD to admit him to study for an MBA. This was a giant breakthrough for him. The early weeks and months were a challenge, with him attempting to combine academic and social agendas in an effort to both achieve his goals and expand his network.

Though he promised his girlfriend before going to do his MBA that he would not go into strategy consulting due to the long hours and emotional strain, it was ironic – though somewhat inevitable – that Andrew would be attracted to this collegiate but competitive elitist profession. Like Eric, he found that being an Olympian opened a lot of doors for him, but as he said, "I had an awful lot of 'chats' that led ultimately to nothing."

Career Transition Navigator

ENGAGE

It has been a short while since Andrew joined McKinsey, and he is excited by the speed, the challenge and the strong team spirit. He says of his new career: "It is like pressing the reset button and going back to ground-zero. There is an incredible amount to learn, and relearn, but I'm hugely enjoying the expectation of excellence." He also enjoys the autonomy that is afforded him, allowing him to find the individual motivation that he derives from his sporting background.

One final advantage that Andrew feels he has brought with him from sport is his ability to create and build significant relationships. He sees that he is more experienced and effective than his peers in this area, and is comfortable building rapport with clients. He describes this as a result of his being "somewhat all-rounded with life experiences to draw upon". At this point, he is ready to fly ever faster through the ups and downs of this challenging career choice, safe in the knowledge that his earlier years will continue to serve him far into the future.

John

John had a more solid career plan than Andrew, and is a veritable goldmine of advice for younger athletes. But this did not prevent him from having an emotionally difficult transition out of his sport, rowing.

Like the other two, he chose his sport early, and enjoyed immense success even as a young schoolboy. By the time he began his education at Cambridge University, he was already a national champion at schoolboy level, and had tremendous experience in different racing conditions all over Europe. By his second year at Cambridge, he was a member of the British team, as well as of the "Blue Boat", and felt increasingly dedicated and fulfilled.

One thing John learned to handle fast and early on was speed – and not just that of a beautiful sleek boat slicing through the water. He had risen swiftly, and found the momentum helped him to feel thrilled and honored at every new opportunity.

Having foregone the opportunity to compete on the national team during his final exams, John went on to combine his career, first in the city for a merchant bank, and then in the civil service, with full-time training for the national squad. With increased sponsorship for the team available, he made rowing the priority in his life, combining it with postgraduate study in economics, leading to a master's degree at LSE. He uses this experience to recommend to all young athletes that they keep their options open through ongoing study. Some of the rowing coaches encouraged John in this decision, although ultimately it was his to make.

The economics degree had really turned John on to international development issues, especially international debt, which at the turn of the millennium was at unsustainable levels for many low-income countries and was the subject of a major international campaign. The experience of traveling around the world to compete had opened his vision even further, so it was a natural step to turn in this direction when he finally gave up his sporting career.

It is clear that John, of the three of our interviewees, had done the most planning. Perhaps because he was just naturally suited to that, or perhaps because his career was longer than both Andrew's and Eric's. He recognizes that 99 percent of elite sportspeople are so focused on their performance goals that they cannot see past these to a future career, and was pleased to share with us that the British Olympic Association is starting to build initiatives in this direction, to establish links and mentors for the members while they are still young and not yet keen to think about such things.

However, despite the planning and the clear interest and knowledge that John had for the next stage in his career, the transition was tough. After his third Olympics, in which he had been somewhat less successful than in the second, he felt the time had come to get down to more "serious work", and stopped rowing suddenly, as many do. This abrupt change was a challenge to manage in terms of identity, even if it was not so difficult professionally, as John managed to find various roles, including for a small business, for local and central government and currently in a return to international development.

The initial switch was tough emotionally and psychologically. John missed the excitement and "special" nature of traveling to compete in international sporting events. He says that it felt strange to switch to introducing himself as "I'm John Garrett, and I work at...", as opposed to what he had become used to, introducing himself as a medal-winning rower. Friends and family were important in helping him shift to the new life.

He also managed to continue his rowing activity and links to some extent by being an umpire for The Boat Race and by rowing in veteran crews from time to time. Indeed, the rowing world allowed John to meet his wife.

On balance, John feels that although there was no systematic support from his team or federation, he certainly was helped through his transition by his clear professional plan and by encouragement from his rowing coaches, family and friends. He recognizes that this transition is difficult for all, and is particularly keen for more athletes to receive help. His primary recommendation for all of them, however focused they might be, is to stay interested in other areas at all times. Not only does this help a competitor deal more effectively in emotional terms with injury or setbacks, but it can also offer a path forward after the period of competing.

Kavitha

Our final subject, Kavitha, is a Canadian who grew up with a supportive family and played tennis on the ITF and WTA tours for several years. She also managed to obtain a great education at both Princeton and Oxford University. Kavitha competed at junior grand slams such as Wimbledon, the U.S. Open and the Australian Open, and reached a junior career high of around number 40 in the world.

Like each of the others, she got an early start, and expresses a great deal of passion and enjoyment for the sport. She, too, had older siblings who played the same sport, and who inspired her on every front. However, what shines through in this particular story is the bond of the family. Kavitha spoke with great fondness of how they trained and played as a family: "We did tennis together – it was a family thing."

As she reached the status of four-time junior national champion in Canada, Kavitha took the decision to put education first and to follow her sister's path to Princeton University. There, like Eric, she was able not only to learn from brilliant professors, but also to train with the superb athletic program on campus. It was here that she really discovered the camaraderie of being part of a team, despite playing an individual sport, and enjoyed the close-knit community of her tennis clan. During this time in college sport, she reached number 13 in the NCAA, which reinforced her conviction that her next step was to "go pro"; so on graduation, she made the transition to pro without so much as a thought of a career in business, beyond the "planes, trains and rackets" of the international circuit.

On discovering how much playing on the circuit was a labor of love, Kavitha realized that "she was a grown-up" all of a sudden, competing around the globe. Managing the pain and occasional loneliness became another challenge she learnt to handle. However, the pleasure far outweighed these niggles, and she is thankful to have played as part of a great community in extraordinary and occasionally remote locations and big name tournaments.

Her proudest moments include being coached by sporting legend Louise Gengler, training with Martina Navratilova as she was making her comeback, and playing in the pre-U.S. Open WTA event the Rogers Cup. Wisely, Kavitha sees her exploits in tennis as being about the hard work and discipline required to excel and "more about the experience, and the stages you get to play on", than about pure win or lose. This attitude has no doubt set her up well for her more recent career in business.

Like the others, Kavitha used academia as a transition out of sport, pursuing a master's degree at Oxford. While writing her dissertation, she was introduced to the Tata Corporation and was offered a role in their consulting division. She started in the management leadership and training program, and subsequently evolved into a business development role at a Canadian subsidiary. After almost three years at Tata, other career opportunities beckoned, and she used an MBA at INSEAD as leverage to go and find them.

The INSEAD year was the "most uniquely challenging" she felt she had ever experienced. She realized that her relatively small experience of the business world left her exposed compared to some, so she immersed herself fully in the learning all around her. Kavitha received much support from the Careers Service and defined her search carefully, eventually landing a position at Coca-Cola Refreshments Canada Company whose products she had always loved. She has been at Coca-Cola in various roles since, putting her top three transferable skills into action: discipline, equanimity (or "tomorrow is another day"), and globally aware adaptability.

Kavitha mentions one likely liability for many sports champions: their intensely competitive nature. She can see that some former athletes may find it difficult to be "reasonable or moderate" about their competitive streak once they move into business. Fostering a team environment that is conducive to success is not necessarily compatible with the desire to win at all costs. She believes that she has made the transition easily because of her natural constitution, and that it was no coincidence that she sought out team tennis. Her transition has been a great success, and she says, "professionally I am so happy, doing mind-opening and valuable work. I am passionate, proud and privileged to be at Coke." This feeling is key to the transition, and is based on the advice she gave to herself and would give to others wanting to move out of sport: "Be equally excited and passionate about your work every single day".

What's Going On? A Transition Seldom Managed Well

Even Pelé and Muhammad Ali at some point had to retire from their sports. We know that almost no sporting stars stay in sport, though a few will evolve towards coaching, federation roles or media positions, researching and reporting on "their" events. If they do not remain in the sporting world or periphery, we must assume they do something else, whether they retire on their prize money – which is rare – or seek other professional activity.

While we know that some sports stars have dazzling success after the track or field – like Björn Borg in fashion, Venus and Serena Williams in design and sports teams, or George Foreman with his grill business – we also know of several former Olympic champions who only manage to scrape by with occasional gigs as personal trainers, or who have even slumped into depression or worse after their career was over.

According to a 2009 Sports Illustrated article, 78 percent of NFL players are either bankrupt or commit suicide within two years of retirement, and an estimated 60 percent of NBA players go bankrupt within five years of leaving basketball.[21] Our four subjects' stories highlight an obvious gap in considering how people transition from sport to business: one in which many hundreds and thousands of former sports players sit, having failed to make the shift.

There seems to be ample evidence that this transition is rarely managed well, and we aim to find some inspiration, in the hope that fewer tragedies occur, and that both athletes and corporations may benefit.

Much stems from the question of points of origin. Our subjects were not in sports by chance. They started from an early age, and generally inside an encouraging family environment. John chose his sport early and was hugely successful even as a schoolboy. Eric followed his family tradition of equestrian sports. Kavitha's family tennis practices and games were just part of the fun of growing up in her household. It came naturally, but it was not easy. They all moved to competition level as a result of intense practice and competitive spirit: more of both than any of their siblings. These people enjoyed their sports, but they also pushed themselves to greater heights than the others. Nature, as well as nurture, was coming through here.

The majority of our subjects attended university, often in top global schools, and this allowed them to keep their options open later. This is, again, a clear indication that the family environment, as well as the genetic mix, is probably strongly at play here.

Having options is of advantage if you are leaving the sport at any stage, but even more important if you leave before you expected or hoped. Eric withdrew from his career having not attained the level he had defined as decisive. Andrew moved on from the slopes when his performance disappointed him. Both recognized that it is difficult to make a living out of sport, and this fact influences the choice to retire. Not only have years gone by with no or little income, but the opportunity cost of those years, with relation to salary and seniority, is even greater in most cases. The pain, sacrifice and occasional loneliness are not the greatest concessions that must be made to enjoy a successful sporting career.

While our subjects mostly planned their transition deliberately and well using five year plans, family connections, school links and so on, we remain cognizant that most others do not fare so happily. John reckons that almost all elite sportspeople are so focused on their performance goals that they cannot see past them towards a professional future of another nature. Sometimes luck plays her role, but mostly the transition is just painful and lacking in support.

Recent reviews of career transition literature reveal that between 15 and 19 percent of athletes require considerable emotional adjustment when retiring from sport. Pascale Witz, a French international track and field team member and now director of several boards after an executive career at companies like Sanofi and General Electric, tells her story: "The recovery process was long and painful. I quickly realized my dream of competing in the Olympics was nearly impossible. With a bitter sense of underachievement, I knew I wouldn't be able to perform at the same level. I decided to leave my athletic career after almost ten years competing. At the time, I was devastated."[22]

Transition "out" is often deeply unpleasant for those who have become used to being in the limelight, just as John described earlier. Winning accolades and spending time in the company of other high fliers can be somewhat addictive, and the stress of giving up the winning drug adds to the tensions shared by most other career transitions. The stressors range from financial to social, psychological or physical, and they can have traumatic effects. None of this is helped by the lack of preparation for life after sport, either.

A 2004 study by Saša Cecić Erpič and other academics highlights that on a psychological level, athletes face difficulties associated with identity crisis, loss of self-worth, low self-esteem and substance abuse, and on a physical level, they experience challenges with injuries, health problems and difficulties de-training.[23] There is also likely to be a drop in financial income, or at the least an increase in living expenses as subsidized and sponsored accommodations disappear from the horizon.

We begin with the challenge of identity change and loss of recognition and admiration. While we can probably all somewhat remember the experience of moving from being a big fish in a small pond to being a small fish in a very big pond, we need to remember that these athletes have been very big fish in gigantic ponds. In a 1986 study, Ogilvie and Howe concluded that the degree to which athletes derive their identity from their athletic roles will strongly determine the intensity of the identity crisis they will face at the termination of their careers.[24] Those who develop a strong athletic identity may be prone to more severe and frequent psychological difficulties as well as more problems in organizing their post-sports career life. And finally, Anderson and Morris suggest that because of the joy, identity and love which athletes experience through participation in sport, the thought of leaving it is emotionally distressing.[25] We saw John experience a strong case of this syndrome, and can assume that the more stratospheric the achievement, the harder it may be to return to earth.

Next, we see that because sport has become a way of life for them – sometimes from age two – de-socialization from sport can become difficult for athletes. This may result in negative beliefs regarding a sports career and post-sport life. These characters have often experienced a socialization process that exists almost exclusively within their own athletic environment, and thus have been inhibited in developing certain life skills. The sacrifices, commitment, single-mindedness and grit required to reach the pinnacle, and the consequent reduction of time and energy spent in other social roles, lead to the formation of a strong athletic identity, which is related to a risk of experiencing difficulties after the transition.

We have seen that there is typically little help or support in the preparation of the transition from the sporting environment. This simply has not traditionally been included in the list of duties for most coaches, team leaders or federations, as both John and Eric told us emphatically. However, we must wish that some progress be made in this direction, as, like repatriation, the "end" is often just as difficult as the beginning – if not more so.

Fortunately, for now, family and friends appear to be most supportive. From their stories, it is clear that none of them would have been able to travel the path of the transition so well had there not been support of a material, emotional and socio-professional nature. Once again, the background or pedigree of our champions meant that the kind of family help they received made it much more likely they would find a new path than other athletes with less fortunate socio-economic situations. However, even with introductions, as Andrew and Eric so bitterly experienced, being a former athlete opens doors but does not ultimately lead to guaranteed results. If it was difficult for our subjects, how much more is it so for those less well born or connected?

The Voice of Companies: Mutual Benefits

Fortunately, a growing number of initiatives from corporations and other organizations have emerged to support athletes' careers, giving them a future beyond the stadium.

The International Olympic Committee (IOC) Athlete Career Program (ACP), in cooperation with Adecco, has been supporting athletes through their career transitions since 2005. This program provides resources and training to enable the athletes to develop their life skills and maximize their education and employment opportunities. The ACP helps to bring athletes and companies together. Morgan Tracey, who is part of Team USA's bobsled and skeleton team, has been part of the ACP program since 2010. She was looking for not only the ability to put training first, but also the opportunity to apply what she had learned from three years of law school. Having worked for GE as a Legal Assistant for several years, Morgan spoke highly of the program: "The best thing about working for GE through the ACP is that I can work it around my training and pursue my Olympic dream."

GE, one of the IOC's top sponsors, has extended its support by giving employment opportunities to athletes. These positions allow athletes to train and work, funding their careers while keeping training and competition at the center of their flexible schedules. This way, companies like GE gain access to world-class employees who combine an accumulation of extraordinary traits and skills with the determination to excel in whatever they do.

Other companies have created their own programs to attract and develop sporting talent. The French railway company SNCF was the first in France to recruit top athletes through integration contracts in 1982. For more than 30 years, SNCF has been committed to supporting these employee-athletes throughout their career, allowing them to combine their professional and sporting lives. The program includes flexible working arrangements, leaving time for training, competition and the opportunity to discover the group's business activities.

In 2017, 35 elite athletes participated in this program. Stevens Barclais, a Taekwondo fighter who won a bronze medal at the 2013 world championships in Mexico, is communication project manager in Paris and says: "It's difficult to train 5 to 6 hours daily, including Saturdays, and at the same time go to work. This contract has helped me regain my stability. I'm less stressed, and can visualize my goals much better." Another benefit of the program is the incredible support given by all SNCF employees to their champions. Sébastien Mobre, a wheelchair athlete and sales agent at the Aix-les-Bains railway station, expresses his gratitude: "I am thankful to all my colleagues who encourage me throughout the year. I have received congratulations from SNCF agents I don't even know from all over France. Thanks to them, we can fulfill our dreams and bring them dreams as well."

Whereas SNCF mostly targets athletes who are still dedicated to their competitive sport, the insurance company Allianz France also addresses retiring athletes: those who have enjoyed elite sport but are looking to fully transition into corporate careers. Why did Allianz launch this initiative? What does insurance have to do with sport? A section of Allianz's recruitment website explains their rationale: "The creation of the Athlete and Careers program enables Allianz to diversify the profile of its future workforce, and you, top athletes, to join a company that recognizes and values your talent. The performance culture, drive, perseverance and 'mindset' of elite sportspeople are essential qualities to succeed in our business." As noble as it may appear, the diversity argument goes along with a simple and practical motivation: to hire great sales talent in a country where this is in short supply, despite relatively high unemployment figures. Of the hundreds that Allianz France recruits every year, they aim to hire 5 percent with a sports background. The company has set clear selection criteria: "The athlete must have a culture of performance, love numbers and know how to negotiate by introducing a relationship of trust over time." So beyond the number of medals won or competition levels reached, the competencies and aptitude are what count.

To facilitate the transition, Allianz's Athlete and Career program is designed as a tailor-made occupational retraining scheme. It includes 16 weeks of training, a one-year assimilation period which might include various job rotations, and specific follow-up in order to ensure "win-win" success. Since its inception in 2013, the program has attracted over 50 athletes from a wide range of sports – from cycling, swimming, basketball, trail and rugby to the traditional Basque pelota.

The stories shared by the athletes who joined the ranks of Allianz France highlight the challenges and opportunities related to the recruitment of high-level athletes in the company as well as the mutual benefits of this collaboration.[26] They confirm that a special support system is necessary for these candidates to allow progressive integration into a corporate environment. They also reveal the richness and added value of the high-level athlete in situations within the company where a professional trait such as adaptability, resilience or teamwork is required.

Should these special hiring initiatives be limited to Olympic medalists or equally successful professional athletes? The professional services firm Ernst & Young (EY) took the approach to a different level. In 2013, EY conducted a global online survey of 821 senior managers and executives, of whom 40 percent were female. The findings revealed powerful insights: nearly all female senior managers and executives had played sports at some level. Overall, 90 percent of the women sampled had played sports either at primary and secondary school, or during university or other tertiary education. Among women currently holding a C-suite position, this percentage rose to 96 percent. When comparing C-level female respondents to other female managers, a far higher proportion had participated in sports at a higher level, especially at university or as a working adult.

Thus, EY teased out some of the links between women's participation in sports at a personal level and their success in the corporate environment. While a strong sports player doesn't automatically translate into a strong corporate manager, it is nevertheless clear that sport can play a positive role in developing the leadership skills of female executives. As a result, EY launched the "Women Athletes Business Network" (WABN). The goal of the WABN is to inform, empower and create an environment that supports female athletes who seek to develop their leadership potential beyond their sporting careers. EY does this through their Facebook group, advice from some of the world's top female athletes and business leaders, research on the connection between sport and leadership, and a unique mentoring program.

Created in partnership with the International Women's Forum (IWF), the mentoring program pairs up to 25 female athletes each year with top business leaders from IWF's network of senior women executive mentors. If you are interested in hearing from these extraordinary women, we recommend you check out the interviews about these athletes who have successfully transitioned to a new career.[27] Gender equity is not happening fast enough, especially at the leadership level. These inspiring women provide good reasons to be hopeful.

The opportunity is there today for anyone who finds themselves working with these people to help them develop their exceptional skills for their own well-being, the benefit of the companies they work for, and in some cases, for the good of the whole world. We look forward to further developments of this kind, and encourage all companies to explore the possibility of setting up initiatives to engage with and hire these athletes.

How to Make It Happen?

We have seen that it is monumentally difficult to make this transition well, and all the more so if one has received little to no advance advice about how to make it easier. The following summary will prove useful for anyone embarking on a sporting career, and should be considered and kept as a reference for frequent consultation.

Advice on How to Successfully Transition Out of Professional Sports

- Keep your options open through ongoing studies
- Develop an alternative career plan while you are performing as an athlete
- Look for a business career that will make you equally excited and passionate
- Be prepared to lose adoration and to develop a new identity
- Get expert advice and personalized counseling to prepare your transition
- Involve yourself with and seek help and support from your family and friends
- Build early awareness of your transferable skills
- Grow and leverage professional networks
- Once you have transitioned into business, channel your competitive nature towards teamwork and collaboration

As for keeping options open by studying, this sound advice from John allowed him to create a career based around his study area, even though he already had a degree from Cambridge. What is more, the advantage of creating additional time through study is huge, and gives the opportunity to plan what is coming next.

John also recommends that all athletes develop and maintain interests in other areas at all times. The balance that this creates not only helps during lulls in the sporting career, but also creates possibilities and a path to follow once a competitive career has ended and the shift becomes necessary.

Passion and enthusiasm have been easy to find for the athletes as they build their sporting prowess, but are less obvious to include in a future career that is hard to find and define. Kavitha's comments about teamwork being part of her makeup are particularly pertinent here, as are her clear, bold statements about her pride and privilege at working at Coca-Cola. Pascale Witz also makes this link in her Fortune article, stating, "to my surprise, track and business actually have a lot in common – generally speaking. For instance, they share common values: respect, teamwork, and optimism."

Networks are crucial in any field, but they are particularly vital in this retirement phase. Whatever the athlete's background, there are opportunities to build relationships of comfort and trust with any and all of those surrounding them, whether those be family connections or sponsors and suppliers. Eric's advice to use these networks to the hilt is of clear value before, during and after the shift.

In order to leverage the whole range of transferable skills in a new career, the individual must build early awareness of these. The list usually looks something like this:

10 Transferable Skills Athletes Bring to the Corporate Table

1. Speed, energy and dynamism
2. Self-motivation, reliable autonomous performance
3. Focus, discipline and dedication
4. Passion and determination
5. Flexibility and adaptability
6. High resistance to pressure, resilience
7. Strategic planning
8. Pioneering spirit, ability to spot opportunities
9. Teamwork and collaboration
10. Relationship building and networking

Andrew's initiatives taken with the suppliers and sponsors were demonstrably a reflection of his autonomy and self-motivation, as well as his survival instinct when the team was under threat. His strategic planning abilities were also of acute importance as he mapped out his five-year plan. What he lacked in professional knowledge, he certainly made up for by using this dogged and visionary technique.

While not all athletes may be outgoing by nature, they are all called upon at some point to work as part of a team. Individual sports such as swimming or ice skating may well be performed in isolation; but even then, the athletes compete as teams in championships at home and overseas. All must learn how to collaborate with one another, as well as build strong relationships with trainers, administrations, and more. The challenge of traveling overseas to participate in competitions is also helpful in this area, as change, culture shock and so on will propel the individual towards new ways of looking at the world and new interactions with others. This aspect undoubtedly smooths the path for their futures after retirement from sports.

It may be obvious to mention discipline, but this is such a crucial part of success in any area. Kavitha reminds us of this several times. Any organization should be happy to welcome a former athlete for this aspect alone. Well channeled into a new activity, the assiduity and rigor will bear many fruits.

Once we have considered all these transferable skills and appreciated their value (if well-used), we may reflect on how the former athletes adapt to their new lives, and how they enjoy their new careers.

Andrew reminds us that it is akin to pressing a "reset" button and going back to playing with building blocks. He is learning with the enthusiasm and application of a toddler, using his thirst for excellence to propel him onward.

There is a contrast between the individual motivation to succeed that derives from sporting careers and the difficulty some have in dropping the uncompromising competitive streak that is crucial to becoming a world champion. Once in the field of business, the team environment becomes subtler but remains essential, and the transition is not easy for all.

We see once more that the transition will be facilitated by the smart company which fosters a sense of collaboration between organization and athlete. Judith Schladitz, a career management specialist and HR consultant, comments: "…former athletes quite often experience initial problems due to the lack of specific, measurable goals and immediate feedback. Knowing what progress is needed, how to achieve it and, indeed, seeing the purpose behind what they are being asked to do are all things they have taken for granted during their career. Far too often workplaces don't provide these and the adjustment for a former sportsperson can be challenging."

It may be the case that it is as much about the person they were psychologically and socio-economically before their sporting career, as it is about the transferable skills nurtured by sport. In other words, if you were going to go to an Ivy League college anyway, in addition to excelling in your sport, you were probably going to have a good chance of success in business too. So, we are aware of the bias this chapter presents.

Moving Smoothly On

While we see that our athletes did not, themselves, get much help in their transition, our later research demonstrates that there is increasing momentum in this area. Dozens of organizations have openly showed off such recruitment programs, while many more are considering the prospects of hiring sporting talent for their transferable competencies.

It is evident from our stories that it is the nature of the basic and acquired competencies in these impressive characters that allows them to move successfully on to this next stage in their lives. This collection of invaluable abilities is developed in greater proportion than in their sedentary peers, and if these are put to good use by the companies they join, they can rapidly develop into extraordinarily successful businesspeople as well. There is no limit to the extra performance that can be derived in this way.

Celebrities with a Sports Background

- The first female head of the International Monetary Fund, **Christine Lagarde,** was a member of the French national synchronized swimming team
- Former IBM CEO **Sam Palmisano** turned down a trial with the NFL to pursue a job in sales
- Former First Lady and U.S. Secretary of State **Hillary Clinton** played several sports, including basketball, soccer and softball
- PepsiCo CEO **Indra Nooyi** played cricket in India and later baseball in the U.S.
- Mondelēz International CEO **Irene Rosenfeld** was a four-sport athlete in high school and played basketball at Cornell University
- Whole Foods Co-CEO **Walter Robb** was a soccer star at Stanford
- The co-founder of Marvell Technology Group, **Weili Dai,** played semi-professional basketball in China
- DuPont CEO **Ellen Kullman** played college basketball at Tufts University

Further Reading and Information

▎ BOOKS AND STUDIES

"Beyond the Finish Line: What Happens When the Endorphins Fade", by Krista Guloien, Influence Publishing Inc., July 2016

"From elite female athletes to exceptional leaders: For all the places sport will take you", by EY, 2013

▎ ARTICLES AND BLOGS

"Transition to retirement can bring emotional turmoil for elite athletes", by Lori Ewing, The Chronicle Herald (The Canadian Press), 15 June 2016

"3 lessons executives can learn from athletes", by Pascale Witz, Fortune, 30 April 2015

"Why Athletes Make Great Entrepreneurs", by Richard Branson, LinkedIn Blog, 17 August 2016

▌ WEBSITES

Athletes in Transition (USA) – A talent acquisition firm specializing in placing professional and Olympic athletes with employers
www.athletesintransition.com/services

IOC Athlete MOOC to benefit Olympians worldwide – The online platform of the IOC in cooperation with the IOC Athletes' Commission (AC) and Entourage Commissions
http://olympians.org/actions/projects/37/ioc-athlete-mooc-to-benefit-olympians-worldwide/

Women Athletes Business Network, powered by EY – WABN's goal is to inform, empower and create an environment that supports elite female athletes who seek to develop their leadership potential beyond their sporting careers
www.ey.com/womenathletesnetwork

Athlete Career Transition ACT (UK) – ACT was created through a combination of the career transition experiences of ACT's Founders, retired Welsh International Rugby Union brothers Andy and Steve Moore
www.actpathway.com

Chapter 4

Battlefield to Boardroom

Creating Success Beyond the Military

"It seems as if violence is everywhere, but it's really on the run.... yet, historically, we've never had it this peaceful." A recent Huffington Post began in this way, explaining how the number of violent deaths per capita globally has declined dramatically over the past decades. And yet this is not the feeling most of us get when yet another tragic massacre or coup d'état bombards our screens. Sadly, it has not yet been possible to eliminate armies and national service, and thus the need to recruit bright minds into the military. But are we managing what happens when these brilliant people are leaving the battlefield? This chapter aims to explore, via the stories of five former military men and women, exactly what the transition feels like, with more or less support, and seeks lessons in making it more effective and manageable from both sides.

Devendra

We start with Devendra, who was one of three brothers in an Indian "army family". He grew up with a sense of duty and tradition, saying he just made the "logical shift" at sixteen to the military academy, from which he would graduate with flying colors. His career thrived, and Devendra rapidly progressed through a military career, combat roles and peacekeeping missions in Africa with the UN. This early exposure to other geographies would prove to be significant later, and certainly set off a spark of interest for worlds other than the military one. In 2004, as a young colonel, Devendra was asked to raise a new unit, which he now compares to a start-up business with venture capital funding. After he was given the command, he and his unit went straight into intense combat operations; he felt he was a father-figure to his troops, responsible for anything and everything.

On successful completion of command, increasing specialization in project management, confronting huge logistical challenges and more, Devendra realized he had a sense for business. The questions started to float around. Was he being challenged sufficiently in his army role? Was there more to discover, learn and develop outside? Should he stay or go? Most of his colleagues stayed on beyond the obligatory 20 years, as it is comfortable to do so, but Devendra decided to take the leap of faith in 2007, despite having a wife and small son. For him, the critical question was: "When was the last time you did something for the first time?" When he did not find a ready answer, he knew it was time to move on.

The few courses that Devendra was able to benefit from on leaving the army were well-intentioned, but more focused on a transition into retirement rather than on a renaissance as a business leader. He was conscious of needing to acquire skills, and decided to take the GMAT in order to assess his abilities to go into further business education. He felt confident that progressing towards an MBA was the correct next step.

With a fine score in hand, Devendra applied to and was eventually offered a place in the MBA program at Boston University. In the meantime, he was also offered a "great break". He became head of projects in India for an infrastructure company, and rode out the 2008 crash over the following few years, developing some early management experience and hands-on expertise in handling major infrastructure projects in India. Yet the MBA was still calling him, and just before his GMAT score became invalid in 2012, he chose to embark on a dual MBA program from Tsinghua and INSEAD. It was a special course, and he describes this as the "best decision I ever took".

Finding himself in a totally different platform and among a totally different peer group, as well as being forced to question himself on all fronts for the first time in a decade, was a stimulating situation, and he took it in his stride. He told us "the higher you go in the army, the lonelier you get, whereas I now have a magnificent network of supportive buddies just a phone call away". Although he was much older than the rest of the students, he felt rejuvenated by the experience, and moved confidently on to greater promotions and more senior roles as a result.

The military strengths that set Devendra apart from others in his current role as CEO of a French multinational are based on his unique combination of analysis, quick solutions and implementation. He sees this as a unique viewpoint, in which one can see the loopholes of implementation, but has no fear of advancing. "We are not scared of the outcome." In talking about business plans, Devendra states that a lot of optimism is built in, whereas in the military world, the "everything could go wrong" attitude makes him conscious of being willing to accept the setbacks. It is "losing money versus losing lives and limbs, and resilience is built into our thought process."

While his financial and client service understanding was lacking, Devendra believes the rest of his "superior" skills taught him to overcome the gaps quickly and humbly upon arrival in the civilian world. He was conscious of what he did not know, and sought to learn it. The MBA classroom was the right platform for him to talk and derive benefits. He is now a happy and successful CEO who is clear about the mix that has facilitated his success and lucid about the barriers that face so many who do not have such a simple transition. For Colonel Devendra, "active combat roles may be over, but as a corporate warrior, he continues seeking and surmounting new challenges".

Ton

Ton, on the other hand, had a transition that was painful and confusing, despite great success in his military life as a Platoon Leader in the Royal Dutch Military Police, and as a Captain in the Air Force. He had joined up as an 18-year-old as part of the obligatory national service imposed on young Dutch men at the time, but pursued a medium-term engagement in the hope of better understanding leadership. On the fall of the German wall, he found himself relocated to the Netherlands, and was clear he did not wish to proceed as a career soldier, deciding to become a civilian once more.

Ton simply handed in his gear, and left, letter of gratitude from the Queen in hand, to find a new life. He moved to a town that he picked for its comfort and proximity to those that counted for him, but with little idea of what he would be doing. Over 150 application letters later, he was pretty clear that most companies were not keen on hiring former officers. Indeed, he had not been invited to a single interview. The rejection reasons were all about "lots of impressive leadership experience, but no business acumen".

Career Transition Navigator

EXPERIMENT

Realizing at this point that the void needed to be filled, Ton signed up for university, studying Organization and Labor Psychology. He also started volunteering with a crisis hotline, similar to the Samaritans, learning non-judgmental listening. Both the study and the empathic listening would later be critical in building his success as a coach, but for now, he needed work in a more traditional company.

On arrival in his first executive leadership role as "head of change" in a large construction company, Ton discovered the real reason he had been hired: he was to take charge of a massive company restructuring. He used his military experience to "keep his cool" and to be first in last out on the work floor, all day every day, with "the men". Things got tough, but he held his ground, as he had learnt, and gained a great deal of respect. Throughout, he consulted with colleagues, sought opinion sincerely, and tried to figure out inclusive solutions. This was noticed and richly rewarded, not only with further and rapid promotions, but also with the sense that the change had been as painless as possible, thanks to his work.

In the next few years, Ton became clear that his calling was as a coach. He had, in fact, been functioning as team, individual and organizational coach in his corporate roles (and even before), and that had excited and fulfilled him. He trained, and started practicing, building on his contrasting contextual experiences to create a practice of empathy, leading to solutions.

Ton's wisdom from the military includes the notion that you must "walk your talk" and be a leader who can be trusted. This goes through to his profession today, in which without trust, he would have no clients. He also believes that showing people you care about them, whether in combat or while you are giving them bad news about redundancy, is crucial. Either way, their life is "in my hands". He also talks about "going the extra mile" and never giving up, his mantras in both military and subsequent careers.

Fearlessness is the final quality he believes the military trained into him: "I have been an executive coach for over a decade now, and the one thing I notice time and again is that most people are afraid. Afraid to be judged, afraid to give or receive feedback, to ask for help, or to lose their job. Apparently this is the system we have built for ourselves." As a coach, he can help this fearful majority through the worst challenges, and to focus on the good and important stuff. He sees that generally, bosses remain bosses and do things in a bossy manner. "That's not leadership, that's just a lazy and unprofessional attempt to fool others that you are a leader."

As a coach with a big influence on many companies at board level, Ton crusades for more recruitment of former military staff. He believes companies should challenge their assumptions about the military, looking for the positive and constructive aspects of an individual's experience. Business skills and knowledge can easily be taught, while character cannot, and that makes all the difference in this world.

Priya

Character is something that Priya was endowed with naturally, and developed further early on. From another military family in India, she played on tanks and was surrounded by "olive green" while she was growing up. Moving to a new, generally small, location every two years made Priya flexible and easily able to fit into new situations, make a range of new friends, and to appreciate each new place for what it was, regardless of the perceived hardship. During her years of high school, she was fascinated by the possibility of joining the army, but at the time, the only route "in" for a woman was by being a doctor, and she was too impatient for that type of study.

Having negotiated her way out of parental pressure towards studying Economics, and into a degree in Hotel Studies, Priya found herself beginning a career at Marriott. But she was soon enticed away by the news that there was a single opening in the lady officers' special entry scheme that required a hotel management graduate. Her boss encouraged her to attend the selection tests, and she was successful. The grueling training made her doubt her choice several times, but she found strength, adapting and drawing inspiration from others. Her difference was both a hindrance and hardly noticeable. On several occasions, with her short hair, newly skinny frame, and darkly tanned skin, she was stopped at the ladies' toilets and directed elsewhere. Her parents despaired, swinging from laughing at her appearance to begging her to return home.

Her first posting to Leh, a remote outpost in the Himalayas, was lonely and isolating. She was not only the youngest, at 21, but also the only female. The next youngest person there was a 45-year-old lieutenant colonel. This meant she "got to do a lot". While this stretch was a great pleasure in that it developed unexploited talent, she did find it difficult to get the "men" to accept her. Taking advice from her father, she showed them tangible strengths, such as running faster than them, and used her prowess, with a mix of feminine empathy and supportiveness, to weave relationships of trust and confidence.

The time in the mountains allowed Priya the opportunity not only to learn to ski, but also to be selected for the Lady Officers' Skiing team, in preparation for the winter Olympics. Unfortunately, she broke a rib and was unable to compete; but the honor was important nonetheless. The attainment of elite sporting status added to her will to excel in all aspects of her military career and aided Priya when she decided to leave the Army after the five years she had planned. She attended IIM, a top business school, on a highly selective program for exiting officers. During this course, she realized how substantial her knowledge gaps were, and read fervently, in addition to mastering data analysis, and so on. Job offers flowed in, and she spent an initial handful of years at Prudential and at another corporation before getting back in touch with her old boss from Marriott, who immediately invited her to return.

Priya says that HR in hotels is different from more sophisticated sectors: grassroots activities, basic level staff and hectically unpredictable – similar to the army. She has managed to excel by building strong relationships and ensuring continuous learning. She is shortly going to be given an opportunity to move to operations in preparation for a general manager role one day. She sees that her company rewards interest and initiative: "They take a chance on you, and you run with it". The strongest wisdom Priya offers covers her whole career: "It all boils down to how you treat people. My father was full of humility and took care of his people. That is what I tried in the Army, and what I do now. You mentor others, so that you are free to develop yourself. Success breeds success."

She sometimes wonders whether she should have stayed fifteen years in the Army, or whether she should have taken an MBA. This pondering points to a desire to work overseas that is not yet satisfied, though at her speed of development, it should come soon (at time of publishing, Priya had just moved to a big role in HR at Qatar Airways, based in Doha). Priya knows that investing time and effort in herself has paid off, and recommends that other exiting officers "leave their high horse behind", focusing instead on reading and building information. "The more you know, the more you can engage in interesting conversations, wherever you are."

Tom

Tom received his education in institutions known for being the best, building his academic capacities before deciding to join the British Army. Having been in the military cadet corps at school, and undertaken obligations while at Cambridge University, Tom decided to follow his instincts on graduation, and not allow himself to be distracted by a corporate career for which he was not yet ready. He did not like the idea of "spending his twenties behind a desk", and sought the military alternative, a more outdoors life, as well as adventure and a chance to travel. He got this, and more.

Life as the commander of a unit of Gurkha Engineers in the New Territories of Hong Kong (before the regiment disbanded) was a series of substantial and fun challenges for Tom. He was soon to be married, and managed to balance his own working life with his future wife's, thousands of kilometers from their home. He felt inspired by the need to lead by example, having always enjoyed staying physically and mentally fit, using self-discipline as his devise. As a British subject by birth, with his early life spent in Southern Africa, and a British education, Tom was already adept at handling linguistic and cultural differences. The experience of commanding a number of Nepali soldiers while based in a Hong Kong that was shortly to be "returned" to China was a stretch of those skills, but a significant one in contributing to his abilities upon leaving the forces.

When the Berlin Wall came down in 1989, the UK government started to talk about "peace dividends" and cutting the Army's budget. This led to extremely low morale, so much so that some training had to be curtailed. This was the point at which Tom decided to leave, knowing that he would feel increasingly frustrated at the situation and that he had much to offer the corporate world in terms of teamwork, man management, planning and executing projects, and self-discipline. At the time, there was little support offered to a departing officer, and he shouldered the risk alone, resigning his commission before lining up a corporate alternative.

It was hard for Tom to accept that few, if any, companies he applied to would recognize his five years experience, and so he was forced to apply for graduate entry level jobs. He recognizes that he might have avoided this fate if he had known more about networking, and how to use that to work his way into a higher-level job, where his experience could be recognized. He may also have undersold himself. In the end, he joined Schlumberger, and while it was a blue-chip company, he had entered at the same level as the fresh graduates with whom he joined the "boot camp".

It was not difficult for Tom to excel at Schlumberger, as he had so much more team and management experience than his peers. Less than 75 percent of those who had joined the boot camp actually passed the training, and Tom found that the resilience that he had developed in the Army was of great value beyond his engineering skills and his ability to manage a team under considerable levels of stress. He told us that he "once worked for 36 hours straight without sleep, and the Army was good training for that". Subsequent years have included the rite of passage through a business school MBA, so as to obtain easier access to high level roles. This led to senior roles at the International Finance Corporation, and most recently as President and CEO of the International Council on Mining and Metals.

Tom has strong views on how things can be improved for those transitioning from a military to corporate life, while recognizing that many companies and militaries are now taking proactive positions on the subject. He cites Goldman Sachs as innovators, as they run an interesting "internship" program for veterans, which allows them some time to find a fit. He also recognizes that if he were leaving the Army today, rather than twenty years ago, he would have received much more support.

As for the initiatives that an individual can take, Tom talks much of networking and not underestimating your skills. Military life tends to encourage a humble attitude in the best commanders, and this can be too prominent once a change is underway, hindering the kind of self-belief required to penetrate the bastions of corporate life. Building and nourishing a network of varied friends, contacts and acquaintances will be useful at any time, and should be encouraged.

George

George is someone whose life is now dedicated to ensuring that this sort of transition be easily made by the individuals concerned, and valuable to the corporations who may welcome them to their world. He started a military career young, with, as he admits, the "cliché
d" desire to get more experience and travel. He was looking for something that would offer him personal and professional challenges while also providing a long-term career and stability.

He had a long and distinguished career in the Marine Corps, in which he saw action in some of the most intense battles of the late 20th century, as well as supported and trained his Marines who have fought in the many intense battles in Iraq and Afghanistan during the last decade. His service and experiences include intelligence, HR, operations management, training and talent development of all kinds, and George has become devoted to ensuring the best possible transition for former military staff into their new corporate lives. He has now founded Veteran Coaching LLC, which provides career transition coaching to veterans and employers of veterans alike.

Like many others, he decided to make his own exit once he had reached the pinnacle of success in his particular areas of expertise. With little left to develop, he was moved to retire and look for further challenges in the corporate world. Having planned and anticipated this transition, certainly aided by his experience in the HR and talent development field while "inside", George worked hard on networking and gathering information before he left the Marines; and although he did not actually have a career lined up before he exited, he had planned ahead financially in order to be able to support himself during the transition.

His take on the attitudes he encountered while seeking his next role is that he experienced reactions based on familiarity with the value of military experience, as well as total ignorance on this front. He believes that the key is to be able to tell and sell your story in terms that a potential employer will understand. It may be significant here that George left the military only in the last year, while our other subjects have been out for some time. Times are changing.

In his work as a coach, consultant, speaker and veteran expert, George now advises corporations and individuals on how to maximize the positive impact of not only the transition, but also the future value that can be added to a corporation by integrating former military staff. His work is sometimes discreet, and other times highly visible. He is notably working with the Macy's Corporation in their Military Executive Development Program, allowing those privileged to be involved to develop understanding and complementary expertise, so as to be able to contribute at a strategic level to the future value of the company. He believes that mentorship and continuous learning are the keys to future success, and recommends that every company have at least one person on their HR team who can not only understand the value of welcoming former military staff, but also be able to support and facilitate the necessary transition with empathy and vision.

What's Going On? Courage Under Fire

A career in the armed forces, wherever it occurs in the world, and at however high a level, is something quite unique. As the British General Sir Michael Rose said about military personnel, "no other group in society is required either to kill other human beings, or expressly sacrifice themselves for the nation".[28] So what is it that draws talent to the military in the first place?

From our five subjects' stories, there appear to be two main factors explaining why they enroll in the armed forces: family reasons or personal reasons. Devendra pursued the path that was not only logical but that also fit his family's expectations, while Priya felt drawn to the only social environment she had ever known, despite the challenges of being a woman in that context. They both followed a somewhat predestined route, and they both seized the chance to make the most of it.

The other three made more of a personal decision, driven by self-motivation and optimistic expectations of what the army would bring to them, such as an outdoor life, adventure, travel or simply a stable career. Ton wished to understand leadership principles and action, Tom could not imagine the constraints of being stuck behind a desk, and George was seeking travel, adventure and stability. All three had already had a good taste of military life by the age of 18, and consciously chose to pursue it.

Overall, it is fair to say that a career in the armed forces brings opportunities and risks. According to a 2007 report, David Gee asserts that: "benefits include challenging work, discipline, physical fitness, self-development, a sense of identity and belonging, plus global travel. Risks include the 'culture shock' of changing to a military lifestyle, bullying, career dissatisfaction, and serious injury or death."[29]

"Intense" is the adjective that first comes to mind when we look at our subjects' experience during their time in the army. As we would expect, they have gone through the familiar rite of passage that most military personnel have to endure. For Ton, the transition was "painful and confusing". In Priya's case, the grueling training and huge social gap with her former situation made her question the sanity of her choice more than once.

The intense and sometimes hardship nature of their experience has had a huge impact on building skills, as well as character: the stretch that Priya experienced in the Himalayas, or the complexity of the situation Tom found himself in in Hong Kong, caused a dramatic shift in abilities, confidence and competence.

The army also brings a huge diversity of experiences: different roles, geographical postings and challenges. Devendra tasted combat, peacekeeping in Africa and more, while George's roles ranged from intelligence to HR. To list the range of challenges all our subjects tackled would take a chapter of its own, and this volume of versatility is significant.

Further, there is an opportunity, specific and almost unique to the army, which is the chance to take on people management roles early in one's career and progress rapidly through the ranks: all five of our subjects found themselves in situations of risk and responsibility far beyond that of their non-military peers of a similarly young age.

The effects of this stimulating early career growth are heady: the rites of passage and the intense experience, coupled with the hardship, add up to a strong sense of identity and belonging. This contrasts dramatically with their subsequent life beyond the military, with a frequent sense of having left behind a lost paradise. In a 2015 study in the U.S., Abrams, Taylor and Kennedy note that 64 percent of veterans state that they had a greater sense of meaning and purpose before leaving than they do in their new careers, while 83 percent of them claim that having purpose is crucial to their career satisfaction and success.[30] This is a large and worrying gap.

The decision to retire was a deliberate, conscious one for all of our subjects. This came mostly due to the realization that they had "done their time", mixed with a hint of frustration in some cases, and the idea that they had potential in their career which the military no longer supported. Devendra was looking for more challenge, and a chance to use his obvious talent for business, and risked the financial and social stability of his family to make his move. Ton was keen not to get stuck as a career soldier; when the sparks of the excitement of foreign postings died down, he knew his time had come. Priya, on the other hand, had predefined a five-year window for her military years. And both Tom and George made their decision to leave at moments when they could see, strategically, that their value and potential would be better used outside.

For each one, the question arose of where to go, and each situation was different. For Priya and Devendra it was part of a plan, and they dove quickly into further education, entirely focused on reorientation. George's anticipated exit allowed him to build a career and business based on his experience, while both Ton and Tom were willing to make an unprepared transition, with the real (and experienced) risk of not finding the right new challenge easily or quickly. This sort of mix is reflected in the David Gee report, which examines the trends of why military personnel leave, though these include further, less lofty, aspects such as the pay gap with civilian careers, workload, limitations of freedom and opportunity, and poor accommodation.

The journey out of the military was not smooth for any of them, and the degree of support provided was quite varied. The minimal support received by Tom and Ton forced them to learn the hard way that military experience wasn't understood or valued… George's financial preparation demonstrated his clear understanding that he would encounter much ignorance too.

For all of them, sooner or later, further education helped to smooth the transition into the business world by bridging some knowledge and skills gaps, as well as by creating a powerful way to take stock of what they learned while challenging their assumptions and building their network. Ton used his fascination with leadership to choose his study focus, and combined this with volunteering to create a fine career as a coach. Devendra found he needed to eschew the traditional courses, which were focused on the move towards retirement, and to take the initiative to seek out a unique experience for his progression. All of them took some measures, in the few years after their departure, to shift their focus and abilities through study.

It is important to realize that our five subjects are among the "happy ones". We chose them more for their example of success and fulfillment than for their representation of a broad sample. Their stories may not reflect the bigger picture, and the reality for other military professionals can be drastically different

Firstly, we need to recognize that, by their nature, jobs in the military are dangerous and can lead to injury, trauma or worse. Some research demonstrates that this can make the transition much more difficult: Haynie and Shepherd focused their research on the mechanisms of career progression and studied the extreme case of soldiers and Marines disabled by wartime combat.[31] Their study highlights obstacles to future employment that are counterintuitive, and stem from the discontinuous and traumatic nature of job loss. Effective management of this type of transition appears to stem from efforts positioned to formulate a coherent narrative of the traumatic experience and thus to reconstruct foundational assumptions about the world, humanity, and self.

Secondly, and more generally, a major hurdle in finding a job in the civilian world stems from the misunderstanding of what the military can bring to the corporate world. This leads to more "omission" of past facts and achievements than would seem likely or desirable. The 2015 Abrams, Taylor and Kennedy study tells us that more than a quarter of veterans downplay or avoid drawing attention to their service in the military. Veterans of color are more likely than their white veteran counterparts to have altogether avoided telling people that they were in the military, while 30 percent of veterans with a service-connected injury or disability have not disclosed it to their employer.

And finally, there is the irony that many former military people find no problem at all in obtaining jobs, so long as those jobs include the same constraints as their former career. Many, including one of our readers, Bill, tell us that they left the military to spend time with their families, but despite hundreds of job applications in their home country, they find themselves forced to accept roles many time zones away from home. He says, bitterly, "getting a job may be easy for a vet, but getting the job you want is difficult, especially for a mid-level leader".

The stories from our five subjects suggest that while their integration was not all that easy, they nevertheless managed to adapt well to their new work environments and bring value to their jobs and employers. Naturally, the landing is softer if the workplace bears similarities to that of the military. This was the case for Priya, who says that the hotel industry is similar to the army in many ways.

But even in newer and more different environments, our ex-officers have built a unique ability to adapt. Devendra's well-honed skills allowed him to fill the gaps quickly and subtly, while Ton was able to go well beyond the initial scope of his first job to manage a restructuring and apply his people skills and composure. In the case of Tom, there is even a sense that he came with a competitive advantage, having built team and management experience that others of the same age, let alone those fresh graduates with whom he joined the company, would not have gained in a corporate or academic environment.

Our subjects' stories admirably illustrate their agility in applying military skills to civilian careers. Devendra's story is particularly striking, with the bundle of analysis, quick solutions and implementation setting him apart and on track to the C-suite. His relative clarity about risk, gained from perspective on death and lost limbs, was critical also.

Many aspects of military life are seen to be critical in shaping who these leaders have become today. In a 2016 interview in Wharton Magazine, Alex Gorsky, now CEO of Johnson & Johnson, recalls his "happily uncomfortable" time in the military. Before beginning his business career, Gorsky spent six years in the military. He went to Ranger and Airborne school, earning the rank of captain while serving in Panama, Europe, and the United States. "It taught me not to care about things like how high the wall is or how far across the river you need to swim – you've just got to figure out a way to solve the problem," he said. "And you never have enough resources; things always happen that are unexpected."[32]

Gorsky credits the military with helping him to develop resilience, one of the most important characteristics needed in the role of CEO today. "Because, frankly, whatever organization or company, the reason that you're there as a leader, is to manage through challenges and seize opportunities", he said. "You need to be comfortable with being uncomfortable, to be able to face a series of challenges and crises at times, and to do it in an inspiring, non-robotic, real way. You need to maintain calm when there can be a lot of anxiety; to maintain perspective."

6 Highly Desirable and Distinctive Transferable Skills from The Military

Fearlessness – "losing money versus life and limbs"

Resilience – "you can never feel as bad as when you lose a comrade, so it is easy to get back up and recover from the failure of a project or initiative"

Character – "it is easy to train up business skills, but impossible to train up character"

Self-discipline – "I survived remote, isolating and exhausting postings by reminding myself of the value for my nation of this hardship"

Cool – "I managed this situation, by keeping my cool – just like I had in the midst of heavy combat"

Caring – "it is all ultimately about how you treat your people – and humility and empathy count above all"

Perhaps the most remarkable, distinctive skill that ex-military officers develop and sustain is people management and caring for people – skills often in short supply in the corporate world. Ton talks about people's lives being "in my hands", while Priya reminds us that "it all boils down to how you treat people."

We are conscious, however, that the success stories we are sharing here should not hide a more difficult situation, as is the case in the U.S. Abrams and Taylor Kennedy's study of 2015 finds that many veterans are stalling out once they enter the U.S. workforce. Skills that translate into a workplace setting are often being left on the table. Twenty-nine percent of veterans feel overqualified for their current position. As Julia Taylor Kennedy, co-author of the study, says: "Veterans feel under-utilized and under-appreciated. No wonder the veterans we surveyed 'checked out'." Evidently, veterans from all levels of the military can find the transition difficult. In terms of career placement, the most senior officers to young vets can "feel like they're being demoted", says Patty Sauka, a career coach with VA for Vets.[33] She estimates that about half of the veterans she coaches take whatever job is available just to get their foot in the door. The other half will not take anything less than the position level they held in the military.

The Voice of Companies: Paying a Tribute and Creating Opportunities

Johnson & Johnson is a great example of an American company which is committed to hiring more veterans. CEO Alex Gorsky has made this a priority for recruitment, as many are looking for employment and find it hard to translate their military skills into what big business is looking for. In a 2016 CNBC article, Abigail Johnson tells us that of the approximately 45,000 employees that Johnson & Johnson has in the U.S., over 5 percent are veterans.[34] The process includes ensuring all employees are trained and developed to understand the backgrounds of those in the military, creating a welcoming environment with mentorship and coaching, and being able to translate what was done in the military into a business situation.

Another more recent example is Starbucks. In August 2016, the coffee company committed to hiring at least 10,000 veterans and military spouses by the end of 2018. An obvious additional plus in this case is the

PR boost, with a dedicated page on their news website illustrating how Starbucks is "paying tribute and creating opportunity for people who've served and sacrificed for their country".

Amazon is another example of a growing number of U.S. companies that are taking advantage of vast numbers of well-trained officers and enlisted men and women transitioning out of the services. A 2012 Fortune article by Adam Lashinsky shows that Amazon's work in hiring veterans actually began unintentionally, but in the 1990s they became conscious of having hired a number of former officers to run its warehouses, where logistics skills are highly sought, and by 2010, they had formalized their veteran hiring program.[35] Today, executives at Amazon have embraced veterans because of their logistical know-how and "bias for action," and as a result, 25 percent of their new salaried employees in 2011 were ex-military. Young former junior officers are particularly attractive to Amazon because they are well-educated and (literally) battle-tested.

Jaguar LandRover address their aspiring ex-military recruits in the following respectful tones of recognition: "Discipline. Teamwork. Calmness under pressure. Many of the skills you honed within the military are exactly the qualities we need in our production environment and across our business. Joining us could be the perfect route into a successful civilian career." The company provides "resettlement training courses", designed with service leavers in mind, to give them the best chance of success in the civilian job market.

Many employers in the U.S are striving to become more military-friendly, particularly as they realize the long-term benefits of hiring and retaining veterans. Procter & Gamble, The Home Depot and GE are just a few other companies with military-friendly reputations, as are employers who are members of the "100,000 Jobs Mission".

But are these well-intentioned organizations leveraging the former military skills in an optimal way? Sadly, this does not yet seem to be the case, with the best will in the world… "Any company can hire a veteran but not many are successfully utilizing the immensely valuable skills and experiences that veterans bring to the table" says Mike Abrams, U.S. Marine, and co-author of the previously cited study. "Companies that identify the key barriers that are inhibiting veterans in the workforce can unleash the innovation potential from this unique and diverse workforce."

According to the Abrams and Taylor Kennedy study

- Nearly 40 percent of veterans say that senior leaders are not capable of seeing their full potential.
- Nearly 30 percent of veterans feel overqualified for their current position, with many under-utilized skills, including: social media, language fluency, computer programming, statistical analysis, transparent decision-making, relationship/stakeholder management and team building.

What can companies do better to help ex-military officers ease into their world? A UNC study relates that it may take a little more time to acclimate newly separated military personnel to the civilian workplace, but it appears to be worth it.[36] Employers who hire veterans find that it is a win-win situation for all involved. HR and talent managers interested in launching a program dedicated to hiring and retaining veterans in their organizations can begin the process with the following steps:

- Get support from senior leaders
- Use existing resources to find veterans
- Welcome veterans into your organization
- Offer flexibility, enhance employee assistance programs, and establish veterans' employee resource groups

Tom, who regretted he didn't receive much support when he transitioned, also acknowledged that things have improved. Companies certainly have become much more proactive and creative. As he mentioned, several U.S. banks have been innovators. Launched in 2012, the ten-week Goldman Sachs Veterans Integration Program (VIP) provides service men and women exiting the military with an opportunity to develop their professional skills, strengthen their understanding of financial services and prepare for future careers in the industry. Similarly, JP Morgan Chase & Co, which has hired more than 10,000 veterans since 2011, offers a 12-week program which includes guidance by managers and mentors who are committed to their success.

7 Do's and Don'ts for Companies Looking to Recruit Former Military Staff

Do

- **Find the right person** for the right job - if they have operations experience, put them in Ops

- **Value the leadership track record** they have, however young they are

- **Empower the new recruit** to close the gaps in his or her knowledge – quickly

- **Take advantage of loyalty** – this is innate

- **Be flexible** in the first few months: it can be a difficult transition

- **Challenge your assumptions** about the military when recruiting

- **Remember that business skills can be easily taught**, while character cannot

Don't

- **Be impatient about knowledge acquisition** – a former officer learns faster than a fresh graduate

- **Put them in jobs** where they are overqualified

- **Worry about losing them** - turnover of ex-military staff is low

- **Worry about focus and discipline**

- **Be surprised by excellence** – a Korn Ferry study showed that veteran CEOs deliver higher returns

- **Hold back on giving opportunities to lead**: men, projects, and so on

- **Hesitate to support them** with further training and stretch projects

It makes intuitive sense to think that former military men and women will be more successful in business sectors which share similarities with the military environment. This might be based on the products (think defense industry) or the core capabilities (think logistics companies). Recent research provides valuable insights and helps us understand how military experience at the most senior level may bring an advantage, depending on the industry or the type of business situation or function.

A report titled "Military Experience and CEOs: Is There a Link?" by Korn Ferry International looks into this phenomenon, and has come up with some compelling numbers on how well veterans are performing as CEOs.[37] The report's major findings include the fact that military officers are well-represented among the ranks of CEOs (8 percent, as opposed to overall male population who served in the military). What is more, ex-military CEOs seem to be concentrated in the consumer (non-cyclical) and utilities sectors. By contrast, ex-military CEOs are under-represented in the consumer cyclical and technology sectors. And finally, CEOs with a military background are more likely to deliver a strong performance. The study found that companies led by military veterans as CEOs delivered higher average returns than the S&P 500 index over one, three, five, and ten-year horizons.

However, a 2009 study by Efraim Benmelech and Carola Frydman shows that service in the military leads to lower corporate investment in both capital and R&D.[38] Their evidence also suggests that CEOs who serve in the military perform better during industry downturns. "Taken together, … results show that service in the military has a causal effect on managerial decisions and firm outcomes."

How to Make the Transition Happen

The first imperative to making the transition happen is to identify your transferable skills and evaluate how they can be best put to practice in the corporate world (see the box above). This is the time to take Tom's advice to put away your humility and not to underestimate your skills.

Next comes the importance of further education. All of our subjects took measures to increase, deepen or diversify their experience with further learning, both inside and beyond the classroom. Due to the early entry system common in military service, it is sometimes the case that no formal university qualifications are obtained during service. At the same time, the individual is busy racking up experience of the kind outlined above, creating a significant gap between capabilities and perceived entry level in companies. One of our readers found success only in the less-structured economy of Hong Kong, having struggled to gain any recognition or offers in the UK after seven years in the elite Parachute Regiment. This also led him eventually to pursue other education, choosing to do an MBA at thirty, whereas the last time he had taken any formal exams had been at fifteen.

There is also an argument that organizations can do a better job in attracting this high-potential population. One coach who responded to our article on this subject felt that most ex-military know they will miss the structure and the camaraderie of their former environment, as well as a connection to a mission and purpose. As a result, they tend to develop preconceived notions which unduly keep them away from the corporate world.

Those leaving should therefore be encouraged to reset their expectations and to allow their assumptions about the corporate world to be challenged. The aforementioned study by Haynie and Shepherd takes on a greater significance here, nudging them to reconstruct all their assumptions: not only about companies, but also about the world, humanity and the self. With their assumptions reset, it will be easier to enact future-orientated career strategies, with those most able to distance themselves from past trauma likely to be most successful in moving toward a future career, finding meaning and purpose through work.

In all this optimism about the transferability and relevance of military skills and capabilities, it is important to recognize that not all of them may just be copied and pasted into a civilian career. Sometimes there is some "unlearning" to be done as well. Co-creation is a skill that is flagged as hard to find in high-ranking military people, and this makes sense – in tense situations, there is no time for consensus-taking. As one of our readers commented: "Yes, there is potential with veterans, but careful assessment and match is the key". The need to unlearn and adapt lie with the veteran, and there may be a need to outline this more explicitly in the support he or she is given during transition. Priya recognized this when she mentioned the need to get off the "high horse", and focus on building a new self and new knowledge. However, not all may have this insight.

7 Do's and Don'ts for Former Military Officers

Do

- Prepare and educate yourself all through life – knowing that leaving military life is inevitable
- Network and connect with all kinds of people, learn something from anyone you meet
- Travel – explore the world via different angles and cultivate your cross-cultural sensitivities
- Leave the negative sides of military life behind
- Recognize that you have certain skills and attributes others will never have (decorations, etc.)
- Identify quickly what you need to learn for transition, and acquire it even more quickly
- Learn to tell your story in a resonant and relevant way

Don't

- Underestimate your skills and their transferability
- Tell your new colleagues about everything they are doing wrong
- Wait for promotion – no more batch promotions
- Expect the others to understand all you have done in the past
- Negotiate too hard on offers – you are just getting started
- Focus too much on yourself – see things from the point of view of your potential employer
- Hesitate to ask for help from friends, family, experts, and coaches

Finally, we should not forget the importance of networking, as almost all our subjects mentioned it as being crucial. The military world is quite isolated from the rest of the world, and one's social and professional connections inside become a given. However, on the outside, not only are connections not a given, but the individual that has spent ten years "inside" has also missed out on ten years of building external and useful links with a broad range of people. Tom felt this lack particularly acutely, but George had recognized its importance and gone to extra lengths while still in the military to strive to avoid this problem.

Right Foot Forward

It is encouraging to see that a broad range of steps is being taken both within companies and by consulting organizations to make more positive value out of this kind of transition. We are particularly optimistic about the growing numbers of companies taking the initiative to tap into this previously neglected talent pool. It is equally reassuring to know that military organizations worldwide are beginning to see the value of helping the "leavers" gently out, even if progress here still seems somewhat slow. The various educational institutions relevant to such leavers could possibly learn from this trend, and do more to be active in encouraging veterans to join them in order to speed up and smooth out their transition.

What gives hope, however, is that there is still such a way to go in terms of leveraging all this extraordinary and unusual talent, and that so many different stakeholders are tackling it with gusto. When this is properly achieved, many more remarkable individuals will be making positive contributions to the future success of a greater number of organizations.

Further Reading and Information

▌ BOOKS AND STUDIES

"Mission Critical: Unlocking the Value of Veterans in the Workforce", by Michael Abrams and Julia Taylor Kennedy, Center for Talent Innovation, 2015

"From the Armed Forces to the Workforce: Why Veteran Hiring Is Both the Right Thing to Do and a Smart Move to Make", by Robin Erickson, Bersin by Deloitte, May 2015

"Ready to Serve: How and Why You Should Recruit Veterans", by Chris Hitch, UNC Executive Development, 2012

"Military Experience & CEOs: Is There A Link?", Korn Ferry report, 2006

▌ ARTICLES AND BLOGS

"Companies look for creative ways to bring veterans into their workforce", by Sarah Halzack, The Washington Post, November 10, 2013

"How Amazon learned to love veterans", by Adam Lashinsky, Fortune, May 7, 2012

▌ WEBSITES

J.P. Morgan US Military Veterans Internship Program
http://careers.jpmorgan.com/student/jpmorgan/careers/military/us

Starbucks Career – Military & Spouse: Serve With Us
www.starbucks.com/careers/veterans

Veterans Jobs Mission – Find military-friendly employers in the U.S.
www.veteranjobsmission.com

Chapter 5

Consulting to C-Suite

Becoming a Business Leader

While former management consultants represented only 5 percent or so of CEO transitions over the past ten years, evidence from a recent study by Spencer Stuart would suggest that consultants are more than worthy of consideration for a role at the top.[39] When they did take the helm of a company, they tended to improve the condition of the company over the course of their tenure more often than other leaders — 71 percent of the time versus 42 percent for those without management consulting backgrounds. This does not necessarily indicate that all consultants should transition to CEO or that all CEOs should be former consultants, but it certainly makes it worth examining a variety of stories in order to explore the characteristics that lead to this kind of shift and to discover the factors for success or failure. In this chapter, we do exactly that, looking at the story of four different characters, all of whom have been successful consultants as well as highly effective leaders.

Thomas

Little had prepared Thomas for his transition into consulting, when he found himself a 30-year-old junior consultant at McKinsey & Company, having already operated as sales director, finance director and even member of the executive committee in a French steel company. This was a time when McKinsey was moving towards more work in implementation of strategy, so Thomas' strategic mindset, top MBA and deep experience of a significant industry was of great interest to them. As he crunched numbers and carried out market analyses in the early months, Thomas repeatedly asked himself, "what on earth am I doing here?"

However, as clients became aware of his existence, they started demanding to work with him, as he was the one who had real experience, as opposed to most of the other career consultants. The enjoyment he derived from challenging thinking and improving the lot of some of Europe and America's greatest CEOs was tremendous, and he found it highly intellectually stimulating. However, he realized that it is easy to tell such leaders what to do, but far harder to make it happen. He was missing the implementation!

So, influenced by the frequent calls of headhunters who pointed out that five years of operations and five years of consulting was the "perfect storm" for another powerful change, Thomas decided to take up the next challenge presented to him. It came in the form of one of his clients, Polychrome Corporation, whose CEO offered him the following comment for a month's consideration: "If you are so darn smart, come and implement this strategy for me." It took less than that time for Thomas to decide to accept the challenge, and he was delighted to return to a world of operations and implementation as Polychrome's VP for Europe.

He had also calculated that if you leave consulting before you have made it to Partner, you can be hired as a VP, but if you wait to leave until you have reached Partner status, you can only become a CEO, and there are far fewer opportunities for CEO roles floating around. Thomas wanted to become a CEO, and after effecting a total turnaround of the European operation over five years, his ambition became a reality. He moved to New York to take an appointment as CEO.

The power relationships Thomas enjoyed in this role were of great excitement. Knowing that he could get the head of any significant investment bank to take his calls, or that he could chat with and influence a board member of any Fortune 100 company, was something he took great pride in, even though he recognizes that he missed the pure intellectual stimulation of consulting. He found it important to learn change management and to learn how to deal with people by building a coalition, empowering individuals, leading by example and communicating effectively. This challenge no doubt became the substitute for the missing intellectual side of things.

After five years as CEO in New York, Thomas and his family wished to return to Europe, having had a "great ride" across the Atlantic. It was relatively easy for him to find a new role as CEO, and he had a brush with posts at Arjo Wiggins and others before accepting a place at one of the companies that eventually merged into steel giant ArcelorMittal in the early 2000s. This return to his first sector was a logical one; he was able to combine the strategic vision with his leadership abilities to aid a company in huge flux to remain at the top of its performance.

At this point in his career, Thomas has chosen to live with a portfolio of activities. Upon "retiring" from CEO life a few years ago, he had the freedom, financially, to slip into golf and travel. Instead, he has chosen to combine teaching a self-crafted strategy course at business schools and inside corporations with running an olive plantation, and acting as managing director of his business school's local alumni association. He is firm in his belief that in this epoch, "there is no more retirement", and continues to use his unique combination of skills to add value across the board.

He describes his activity today as "tremendously exciting", and perhaps sees a parallel between the change he has brought about in his own professional activity and the change he managed in his earlier roles. While he recognizes that consulting taught him a sense of urgency, he knows well that he needed to learn about how to enforce change in those who (typically) do not want it, and this was something he could only develop by doing. His portfolio career allows many to continue to benefit from this balanced view, and we hope to continue to read about and learn from him for many more years.

Rupert

Rupert's transition out of consulting was an easy one. An Australian, in consulting "for the usual reasons, of variety, experience and interesting colleagues", he had always wanted to make something for himself. The thrill of creating was attractive to him, and he took the time he spent doing his MBA at INSEAD to reflect on his wish to create capital value.

Career Transition Navigator

EXPLORE

After a few more years of consulting in London, Rupert had become highly aware of the damaging lifestyle involved in his profession, and talks with candor about those colleagues "on their third wives, and traveling endlessly". With ten years of consulting behind him, he decided to buy some time and money by accepting a role at HSBC, so as to be able to create a company of his own within a few years. He had become disenfranchised and bored with consulting, and felt motivated by the possibility of controlling his own destiny while creating value. The difficulty for Rupert lay in actually realizing that he had made the decision but had not yet acknowledged it. Once he did see it, however, it was "blindingly obvious", and the only option was action.

By the late 1990s, Rupert had started his first company, based around coffee. He has tirelessly reworked his business model to hone an organization with a turnover of several million, that serves and has served coffee, to corporate employees, to British Airways passengers and to millions of others. What did he miss when he first left the consulting and finance world? "The regular paycheck, of course. But more significantly, the power and brains of a team." Rupert now sees and admits that in those early years of entrepreneurial activity, he wasted a lot of time. He was indulging his desire for the freedom he had so sorely missed, and could have done things faster and better had he chosen to. The realization that time is money hit him later than it might have.

Consulting methodology has helped Rupert in his "modeling up" of the coffee industry and his creation of a whole new metric not frequently used in the sector. He has used sophisticated techniques to become a "big player" and to approach both clients and suppliers with increased confidence and credibility: "My clients are serious board members of large corporations, who are blown away by my stakeholder analysis of their situations. The faith they have in my professionalism derives directly from my consulting work. I am absolutely rigorous with regard to transparency on both performance and metrics, and I could not be that way without having done so much this way in my previous work."

Reflecting on the differences between the two worlds, Rupert is eloquent. He talks about how he hopes one day to hire more consultant types, but sees the financial constraints of a medium-sized business as being good for identifying capabilities differently. He is immensely proud of his people, and enjoys developing the best in every one of them. He has had to "unlearn" consulting jargon, of which he admits he was the king. After a period of frequent quizzical looks, he realized that simple terms, explained clearly, would work better in the café industry. These days, he is more often discussing "like for like" performance than "NPV", "CAGR" or a "deep dive".

Enjoyment and gratitude fill Rupert's life these days. While he admits that his business does take up more than the "one day a week" that he likes to pretend, he feels tied to his business, and states that his mood and outlook are necessarily linked to the fortunes of Caffe Kix. When asked whether he would return to consulting, his position is unequivocal: while he is happy to share his experience for the benefit of others through board and advisory roles, he has no interest in going back to the executive world. He has enjoyed his journey, however lonely, prolonged and full of the unexpected it has been.

A big shift in mindset has helped. He has let go of a typical consultant's tendency towards OCD by "getting comfortable with being uncomfortable, letting go of some things I would have liked to control, and accepting that a day has been 'good enough'." Rupert has engaged fully in his life as an entrepreneur, and if it were not for his sharp intellect and crystal-clear thinking about his industry and position, it would be difficult to imagine that he was ever immersed in the corporate world, let alone consulting.

Christina

Christina also underwent a huge shift in mindset as she joined one of the largest family-owned companies in Europe. This was not a change she had particularly expected to make, as her vision of professional life had been one of loyalty to Boston Consulting Group, her firm for the twenty-two years since she first started out in consulting. As a partner with many high-powered clients and rewarding internal roles, Christina was not a likely candidate for exiting consulting. Though she had occasionally considered the option, she had never found a role that was sufficiently attractive to make her consider the jump. She enjoyed the intellectual stimulation, rarefied atmosphere, flexible working conditions and interaction with significant leaders across industries and cultures that her consulting job afforded.

After a chance encounter with the chairman of this company, she was flattered and surprised to find how attractive it was to be desired for her own unique combination of skills and abilities, and to be offered a board level position. She was also given the chance to make a choice between two different business units, and she decided to take the more challenging one, in the automobile business, about which she knew little. Thus began a lengthy and admirably complete transition period. Christina read more than thirty books on the industry, and quizzed all her former colleagues who had made similar exits. She took the time to obtain coaching on both the industry and leadership angles of her new role, and ensured that her family and herself were able to settle well in the new location, far from where – and how – they had previously been living.

While Christina had had a high-level interaction on bringing her into the company, she made the common mistake of assuming that she would continue her privileged relationship with the chairman once inside. Partners at consulting firms become accustomed to having CEOs and chairmen on speed dial. This assumption proved embarrassing to Christina when she wrote to the chairman for advice and guidance and he firmly steered her towards her immediate boss. She has quickly learned that as a sector non-expert and an outsider, management via keeping your mouth shut and being modest is a good way to survive.

Being an outsider is something Christina has had to get used to, as she is different in background and makeup to her new colleagues. While this felt uncomfortable at the outset, she now realizes that it is an asset. She can use her difference to get things done in an environment where speed and dynamism are not the norm. The other main challenge Christina has faced is that of entering a company that was actually doing quite well and did not need "fixing". Figuring out what she can actually change is an ongoing challenge, and one she struggles with occasionally. She has learned to have a short-term and long-term view of what and how to change, with different rationales behind them.

Although it was difficult to leave BCG after almost a quarter of a century, Christina says that once she had "smelt" the opportunity, she knew there was no way she could stay. However, she did use the BCG philosophy about its alumni to her advantage. "Once a BCG-er, always a BCG-er" is their motto, and this has certainly helped her both during her transition out and as she works in her new operational world. Coaching, references and other information and opinions have been of great value to her all along the way.

Her old (and still active) networks can never be matched by what she builds from here on in, but they are still useful, so she takes advantage of that however she can. Would she go back? "Absolutely not". But Christina does seek ever-greater opportunities to learn and develop, so while she finds her current challenge sufficiently complex for now, she may well be tempted in other directions subsequently. At this point, she is learning to identify and integrate into the "soul" of her new company, and using her difference to effect whatever appropriate change she can.

Graham

Unlike our previous three subjects, Graham, a British former general practitioner turned influential change guru in the UK's health policy, fell into consulting by accident. Although he had done an MBA (incidentally in the same class as Rupert), he had done so in search of self-development and happiness. He had not looked with any seriousness at the possibility of becoming a strategy consultant as so many of his friends at INSEAD had. Graham spent a short period managing a team in a healthcare reform think tank in the U.S. during the Clinton administration, gaining early experience in significant research and paper-writing, after which he followed his wife to Boston, where she was to study and he wished to find work. What better employer than the Boston Consulting Group?

A self-confessed "non-Dean's List" student, Graham had not envisaged this possibility, but was encouraged to join by an enthusiastic and supportive senior partner. He was immediately heartened to find himself in the healthcare practice, surrounded by driven, energetic and international colleagues, all of whom were doing interesting things. What was harder for him was to find himself back at the bottom of the pile, carrying out analyst tasks, when he actually knew and had good relationships with many of the CEOs in U.S. healthcare, both current and non-clients. He found himself assigned to a variety of projects, many of global scale, and fell quickly into a frenzied routine of travel all week, every week.

As he describes it, there was one weekend in which all of Graham's ideas crystallized. He and Sarah, his wife, had travelled to the West Coast for a two-day BCG healthcare conference, from which they arrived home at 1 a.m. on Monday morning. Four hours later, Graham was on his way to the airport to attend client meetings in Germany. When he returned two days later, and his wife, who was pregnant at the time, told him that she still felt tired from the weekend, he realized what an absurd feat he had just accomplished and seriously questioned his sanity. With this foremost in his mind, he realized that he wanted a "proper" job again: one with a more reasonable lifestyle, and also budgets, staff and implementation.

A return to the UK seemed logical at this point. Graham took a role which came up in the National Health Service as CEO of a region of the country. The change was, as Graham describes it, "like going from flying to landing in treacle, and then learning to swim". Nevertheless, he got a great deal done, and moved on to a second role as COO and then CEO of a large teaching hospital.

Once again, the alumni network management of these consulting giants came into play, and his former BCG colleagues invited Graham to rejoin in order to co-lead a new initiative – fourteen years after he had first joined. At that point, he refused, saying he was still happy introducing all kinds of new policies and actions, and living a manageable lifestyle to boot. However, six months later, he had fallen out with his chairman, and tentatively asked if the offer might still be open.

BCG welcomed Graham with open arms, allowing him to negotiate his own terms. He is no longer part of the consulting hierarchy, and acts, in his words, "as a partner-like buddy". He does not work more than half time for BCG, and has just recently shifted his status to self-employed. In this way, Graham manages to keep the aspects that are important to him, such as business building and "seeing things through".

Graham, now holding several non-executive directorships, has entered "serious portfolio career territory", and has learnt to be happy with whatever he is doing at the moment. Unlike some of our other subjects, he has no clear map for the future, but feels confident that his will be a good one. He has a clear set of criteria for new opportunities which he shamelessly imposes on whatever might come up, so he knows that he will make good. He also has a simple attitude to the less attractive aspects of his past career, and a strategy about how to avoid these in the future. Suffice it to say he will be spending more time with his family and on good health, and less on impressing others and being overly competitive.

While we have talked about four successful and happy former consultants, it is worth noting that many consultants never make the transition, and in some cases, the failures have been significant and painful. We know of one example whereby a senior partner from a prominent strategy consultancy joined a large pharmaceutical company as head of strategic planning, reporting directly to the CEO. Within a short time after joining, he had launched a series of initiatives, creating confusion and chaos in an organization that was already riddled with complexity. He demonstrated few skills in communication or empathy, and thus alienated the majority of his team and peers, and did not endear himself to the CEO either. To top it all, ironically, he ended up dramatically increasing the spending on external consulting, which was the opposite of the intended effect. By this time, the CEO had lost patience and asked him to leave.

He has since returned to the world of consulting, but this time on his own. Fifteen years later, his debacle is still vividly recollected with a mix of horror and humor by those inside the healthcare company, and we can only imagine that the episode does not figure in the most glorious moments of the consultant's life either. Not all of those cut out for great careers in consulting are destined for equal success out in the "real world".

What's Going On? Is the Myth to Be Believed?

If we look beyond the myth, there is much to learn about this transition. For starters, there is a widely held belief that consulting is a clear and sure path to CEO positions. Fabrice Desmarescaux, a top headhunter based in the Asia Pacific region, has much to say on the subject:[40]

> "At campus recruiting events, the top consulting firms pitch themselves as CEO factories. Join us, and accelerate your career to become a CEO, they say... The logic goes like this: firms like McKinsey, Boston Consulting Group, or Bain always hire the smartest graduates from the best MBA schools around the world. Over the next few years, these consultants learn to structure complex business issues, perform sophisticated analysis, manage inter-disciplinary teams of associates and clients, and communicate their advice to a senior audience of CEOs and board members."

This would undoubtedly attract significant numbers of ambitious future leaders, and has proven to be the case over past decades. According to a 2013 study by Duff McDonald, "A few years ago, more than 70 past and present CEOs of Fortune 500 companies were McKinsey alumni, and in 2011 more than 150 McKinsey alumni were running companies with more than $1 billion in annual sales."[41]

All that heady rise to the top looks pretty good, but we are less convinced that it is still really true in 2017. Fabrice's search firm recently conducted a study analyzing the December 2006 McKinsey partners' cohort, consisting of 81 bright men and women in their early to mid-thirties. They then asked: "Where are they now, after 10 years?"

- 55 percent still work in strategy consulting: 35 still work at McKinsey and 11 have moved to competitors.

- Some 10 percent have pursued a variety of fields outside of consulting or corporations, including private equity and academia.

- 35 percent work in corporations, of which 6 work in strategic planning or similar roles in corporations, and only 23 (28 percent) have become senior executives (in non-strategy roles) at corporations. Nine of these (11 percent of the total) have titles of CEO or President.

So, the truth may be somewhat less glossy and glamorous today than it once was. We have seen the claim by Spencer Stuart that CEOs from consulting tend to improve performance significantly more than those from industry, yet the shift is not happening as much as that evidence would deem logical.

It is worth examining what exactly attracts professionals to consulting in the beginning in order to understand what triggers a move out. While Graham claims to have "fallen into consulting by accident", there are without doubt numerous reasons why consulting is attractive, and leads young talent to line up for a seat at the table:

- **Challenging work environment** – A chance to prove one's brainpower, shared by all our subjects.

- **Variety in work engagements and clientele** – Learning from the clients' environment, as Christina did, not only inspires, but also creates an expertise that can lead to being invited into that same environment.

- **Working with smart, interesting colleagues** – Rupert and Graham are adamant that this played a substantial role in their choice, and the chance to be surrounded by interesting, stimulating colleagues is a common reason given by those attempting to enter consulting.

- **Great training and learning of best practices** – Building core skills and viewpoints, such as the ability to look at the big picture of an organization and see how all the parts fit together, as well as to synthesize large amounts of data into an effective presentation in a short period of time.

- **Power relationships** – Thomas reminded us of how exciting it is to be able to get important corporate leaders on the phone at the drop of a hat. Christina too enjoyed the power.

- **Better pay** – It is well known that starting salaries, as well as later remuneration at the big consulting firms, tend to be well above those of other areas, (apart, perhaps, from investment banking). While none of our subjects mentioned money as being the most important factor, we do see that Rupert used his income from both consulting and banking to create security in his jump out.

- **The ability to travel** – The jokes about being called back from a holiday to go to an engagement at McKinsey exist because of their reality. The work is intense, and travel, as related by Graham, between continents without much consideration for the carbon footprint, is commonplace. For those who love being up in the air, and relish the challenge of different cultures, situations and markets, this is a huge attraction.

- **Keeping career options open** – While becoming an experienced consultant, one learns a great deal in all the ways already mentioned, and this allows for keeping doors open. A consultant who develops an ability in healthcare, for example, may move in and out of consulting as he or she likes, and this is exactly what Graham did.

However, it is clear that for many, some of the thrills upon entering consulting pale, sooner or later, next to the frustrations thereof. All kinds of ideas fill the minds of those wondering about a change, and it might in the end be a single reason that triggers the move. We look at some possible catalysts below:

- **Career aspiration** – Thomas had his heart set on becoming a CEO, and created a plan for this to happen. Rupert wanted not only a "proper" job again, with budgets, staff and implementation, but also the excitement of creating something significant.

- **Negatives of consulting** – Frustrating, repetitive tasks, number crunching, market analysis, and so on, can take their toll, as can the long hours, the stressful internal environment, and the heavy travel. Graham's questioning of his sanity is a great example. There is also a concern about how much impact the engagements really have, as Thomas observed: making recommendations is the easy part, but making it happen is altogether something else.

The relentlessness of it all undoubtedly does not leave much time and energy, thus hastening the level of negativity once the doubt creeps in.

Once the doubt is there, it probably does not often disappear, and once that is the case, it only takes one trigger to make the move likely. The trigger can take different forms, with varying pertinence for each individual:

- **Thomas** was influenced by the incessant calls from headhunters; so it was no surprise that he finally decided to take up the challenge offered to him by one of his clients, to "come and implement the strategy he had recommended".

- **Christina** had a chance encounter with the chairman of the company, and was desired for her unique combination of skills and abilities; she was also given the luxury of a choice between two business units.

- **Graham** and his wife's realization that they were living an absurd lifestyle led to him wanting a "proper" job again.

The challenges when moving to a corporate role are many and varied. Former consultants can feel and look like extraterrestrials compared to their new colleagues. In no particular order, the obstacles include:

- **Being an "outsider"** with a different background and makeup than new colleagues can be uncomfortable, but it can also be an asset; one can use one's difference to get things done, as Christina did.

- **The need to "unlearn"** consulting jargon, and to realize that simple terms, explained clearly, would work better in the café industry.

- **A change of speed and dynamism** from high to lower, though this does not always apply, especially if moving into a startup as Rupert did.

- **It's no longer about "fixing"** a company, as Christina realized; there is a need to learn that to figure out what can be changed is an ongoing challenge – with both a short- and long-term view.

- **How important it is to learn change management**, as Thomas observed, and to deal with people by building a coalition, empowering individuals, leading by example and communicating effectively.

- **Assuming a more modest position** and being a little slower to speak up: a common mistake once inside is that of assuming continued privileged relationships at the top. Christina learned this the hard way when she was strongly referred to her immediate boss.

- **Thinking longer term,** beyond just your next consulting engagement: "Having myself recently left BCG to become a CEO of a newly formed company, I can relate to many of the observations. The change of time horizon was the hardest for me to overcome." (François Chirumberro, CEO and co-founder at 82).

Perhaps because of – or perhaps in spite of – all these challenges, not all great consultants make great CEOs or C-suite members. The Spencer Stuart study gives us some resounding examples of how the transition might fail. First, consultants who are gifted at analyzing complex problems and identifying a range of possible solutions, but lack the drive to implement those solutions, do not make strong chief executives. They do not make the full shift from recommending to doing, and that is a fundamental weakness that can never be made up. Second, strong "people leadership" in a consulting context may not necessarily translate; leading teams of highly educated, motivated MBAs in the "up or out" environment of most management consulting firms is different from leading an employee population with a mixed set of skills and backgrounds.

When this goes wrong, it can go very wrong indeed, as we found in our earlier example of the ex-partner who took on the head of strategic planning role in a large pharmaceutical company; he was severely lacking in communication and empathy skills, and thus alienated the majority of his team and peers. Finally, it is less risky to advise than it is take direct action – those consultants with the courage to be the decider and to accept the personal risk of those decisions are more likely to be great CEOs. Each of our subjects find themselves in the category of those who "make it", but many do not.

The Voice of Companies: Handle with Care

When we spoke with Peter Goethuys, the Chief Talent Officer of Sanofi, we managed to understand more concretely some of the challenges we had learnt of in our studies of the individual subjects. Peter began by confirming that the company had never had a particular strategy for hiring former consultants, although this had changed slightly with the arrival of former CEO Chris Viehbacher. Under his guidance, a former McKinsey consultant was hired as Head of Strategy. Similar hires happened in both business and organizational development departments. Peter underlines that it is ad hoc: an openness to consultants exists, but there is no formal path for this to happen.

The company is now facing a need for more strategy-savvy people, and feels that consultants would be a good source for the more complex parts of their business, where high intellect and problem-solving ability are assets.

The experience with consultant hires has not been all positive. A typical struggle was the one they faced when they hired a former strategy consultant and investment banker in a highly visible top position. From the beginning, it was uncomfortable for both sides, with the onboarding rife with mistakes. "He came in like a consultant, tried not to behave as a manager, focused on the wrong things and burnt almost all his bridges within six months", recalls Peter.

When asked what the major challenges are for former consultants, he gave us a few:

1. **Connecting with the organization** – Consultants are used to working with the top of an organization, with extremely smart colleagues. They focus on the most powerful people and don't connect as well with more "normal" people.

2. **Limited knowledge about how to manage a team of managers and experts** – If they have been in consulting for a while, they often work more as individual contributors, using their great conceptual and problem-solving abilities rather than managing people to deliver a task and get results.

3. **Can be overbearing** – They tend to tell people what the issue is instead of really understanding what's going on and working together to get to a solution.

4. **Occasional lack of accountability and delivery** – Their model is that of giving advice and moving on. They can get bored easily, so tying up loose ends is not their focus.

And what pluses do they bring?

1. When they have real leadership abilities and strong emotional intelligence, it can be amazing.

2. The short-stay consultants are often more successful – those on whom the specific consulting culture has not had too deep an effect, though even with the "notable exceptions", communication style can still be a challenge.

3. One of the strengths they do bring is a focus on developing people. They are generous with giving others opportunities for development.

Peter advises consultants contemplating the move to business to come well prepared for massive change in the type of work, the environment and personal contacts. Shifting their ambitions to a more reasonable level initially, and coming with a substantial dose of humility and willingness to listen can also help.

Equally, his advice for companies who bring in consultants is to take a series of precautions to guard against rapid failure and upset. This includes doing formal EQ (Emotional Quotient) testing and evaluating leadership traits and potential; looking at the values and career purpose; and also assessing accountability. "It's no longer just about being able to do great analysis, manage projects and give slick presentations. You are really responsible for the people you lead and the results you have to bring in", adds Peter. And finally, the onboarding requires much support and encouragement towards the right behaviors for success in the new environment.

Overall, Peter is in favor of hiring people with consulting experience in big companies like Sanofi, as they have a lot of elements that leaders in a complex business environment need to have to be successful. As always, you need to pay a lot of attention to making the "right fit" between the individual, the company, the boss and the colleagues so that you can make sure you have the right person in the right place at the right time.

7 Do's and Don'ts for Companies Hiring Former Consultants

Do

- Support your incoming former consultants.

- Understand that these people are different.

- Be open to exploring and implementing the changes these people recommend.

- Help them to manage the parts they are not used to, like administration, expenses, less glamorous travel, etc.

- Find a way to derive value from the high-level relationships these men and women have.

- Expect to engage at a different level.

Don't

- Assume that just because they are smart they will not need backup from you.

- Make a big deal of the difference. Instead, help them to fit in and feel valued.

- Resist it – after all, you brought them in to shake things up, right?

- Begrudge them the extraordinary lifestyle they had before.

- Put them in a box, like all the other new staff at that level.

- Push back due to relative lack of seniority.

How to Make the Transition Happen

There are two big questions to be considered if you are thinking of making the switch at all: when and where? Both count and neither is easy to fathom, as there is no conclusive evidence in favor of one universally successful approach. However, there are interesting and unavoidable aspects to consider if you are contemplating it.

With regard to "When?", a career in consulting that confers all the skills and attractive abilities previously mentioned will have a different value at different stages, and it is obvious that aspiring to a C-suite position after only a few years is unlikely to be realistic. However, once the level of senior consultant, engagement manager or partner is reached, there are conflicting items to think about when considering the timing of your leap.

Thomas had calculated, in a typically "strategic" way, the right time to leave. He did not want to wait around for the scarce CEO roles, and felt a jump earlier, before achieving partnership, would be more advantageous to him. Hindsight shows us this was a perfectly calculated strategy in his case. However, based on the Spencer Stuart research, "leaders who have worked at the partner level for a top strategy firm appear more likely to succeed. This makes sense given that they have probably worked most directly for CEOs of client companies and therefore appreciate the issues and levers of the top executive. They also are likely to have had deeper experience tackling some of the most complex and important challenges organizations face."

Bruce Raines, in his article, "The Fork in the Road to CEO", is less optimistic about the chances of consultants: "If you want to be a CEO of a mid-sized to large company, know that the majority of chief executives' backgrounds have common links. Almost all of these CEOs come from one of two worlds: they either trained in a big corporate organization, or they started the company. Period."[42] If he is right, this would explain the smaller numbers of transitions made in the past few years, and serve as a warning to many of how difficult it can be to transition from consulting to C-suite.

For Raines, coming from a background in the large corporate world can give you a number of advantages that other companies can't. These include scale, international scope, state-of-the-art processes, training and mentoring (the chance to work with and learn from the top personnel in the company) and ultimately the chance to implement real-world strategy. In addition, there is the excitement of promotions and raises, less risk, more security, and visibility, skills transferability, and recruit-ability. All non-negligible reasons to believe that the consulting route is not always going to be successful.

Famous CEOs Who Worked in Consulting

Name	Position, Company	Consulting Firm
Akio Toyoda	President and CEO, Toyota	Strategy& (formerly Booz & Company)
Emmanuel Faber	CEO, Danone	Bain & Company
Eric Spiegel	President and CEO, Siemens Corporation USA	Strategy & (formerly Booz & Company)
Erik Engstrom	CEO, RELX Group (formerly Reed Elsevier)	McKinsey & Company
Frank Appel	CEO, Deutsche Post DHL	McKinsey & Company
Greg Case	CEO, Aon plc	McKinsey & Company
Indra Nooyi	CEO, Pepsi	The Boston Consulting Group
James McNerney	Chairman and CEO, Boeing	McKinsey & Company
James P. Gorman	Chairman and CEO, Morgan Stanley	McKinsey & Company
Jeff Immelt	CEO, General Electric	The Boston Consulting Group
John Donahoe	CEO, eBay	Bain & Company
Kenneth Chenault	CEO, American Express	Bain & Company
Mario Greco	CEO, Zurich Global Life	McKinsey & Company
Meg Whitman	CEO, Hewlett Packard	Bain & Company
Nancy McKinstry	CEO, Chairman of the Board, Wolters Kluwer	Strategy & (formerly Booz & Company)
Oliver Bäte	CEO, Allianz	McKinsey & Company
Tidjane Thiam	CEO, Credit Suisse	McKinsey & Company
Vittorio Colao	CEO, Vodafone	McKinsey & Company

As to the question "Where?", we look once again to Raines, who tells us: "For large companies, almost any industry can provide an excellent career for the management consultant. Of course, if you had an industry specialization as a consultant, you have a decided advantage going with a major player in that field." This is what Christina, Thomas and Graham did. This looks like a good clue as to how to make a success of the move.

However, it is not necessarily a given that a move to a client company is the best choice. It seems perfectly natural that clients who have benefitted from the work of a consultant will be keen to hire him/her, since they have had a chance to test drive them in situ. This is certainly the case of Thomas and Christina. Duff McDonald, in his article "The CEO Factory", commented on the likelihood that Brian Salsberg, who made the move from McKinsey to Avon, was not "walking through the $11-billion-dollar company's doors for the first time". According to him, the chances are that any consultant who obtains a sweet corporate role has previously worked with that organization as a consultant. Another example of an appointed CEO who had previously been consultant to the corporate organization is Frank Appel, now CEO of Deutsche Post DHL and formerly a McKinsey partner. There are no doubt many more, though client confidentiality issues may sometimes prevent us from observing the link.

On the other hand, the Spencer Stuart research suggests that it does not seem to matter whether the consultant has done work for the company doing the hiring. That relationship is not evident. "There are certain industries where deep knowledge and expertise are needed, and consultants working in the industry are therefore more compelling candidates. However, it was not the case that consultants simply crossed over from serving a specific client to being that company's top executive."

A final piece of advice from Raines alludes to the "consultant-friendliness" of corporations, and recommends a focus on those which have a track record of promoting management consultants. He is firm and clear on the idea of never taking a job with a company that has never engaged with a major management consulting firm. This is where you would feel most like an alien.

There appear to be three main paths to the C-suite and the top. These can help to understand which position to take:

- **Strategy** – A strategy position often leads to a promotion into a functional or general management line position in an operating unit, or into a more senior, corporate role. These include strategic planning or business development roles.

- **General Management** – Positions in operating units of large companies are attractive, although sometimes harder to obtain. They provide real management and P&L experience. Occasionally, the starting position might be as the assistant to a CEO, "Chief of Staff", or other central position, usually reporting to a senior corporate leader.

- **Functional Management** – Positions such as marketing, finance, or operations director or vice president are excellent jumping-off points into general management or senior functional roles.

As for the context in which to take on the new position, we can see that crisis can often present the biggest opportunity for impact and that "outsider" status may well provide a huge advantage. Many of us remember the remarkable turnaround of IBM effected by former McKinsey partner Lou Gerstner. He was successful principally because he was not saturated with IBM's corporate culture, and was able to see a turning point that was of crucial strategic importance. He referred to this culture as "insular and balkanized", and worked to consolidate both people and process, saving the company and building the foundation for its continuing progress today.

The Spencer Stuart research confirms this, showing that when former consultants take the helm of a company, they tend to improve the company's condition more often than other leaders – 92 percent of the time versus 70 percent for non-management consultants, and even more so when the company's condition was classified as "Crisis" or "Challenged".

What are the key skills, techniques and competencies that an ex-consultant can leverage in a corporate role? We know that consulting methodology, including modeling, has allowed Rupert to take a totally new approach to his chosen industry, and to create a whole new metric that is hardly used elsewhere in that industry. His rigor, transparency and analytical skill amaze his clients, and he tells us that he could not do this without having spent time as a consultant.

With all the great techniques in the world, however, it is not possible to make a successful shift without a significant change in mindset. There is an adjustment to be made to a new corporate environment, whether as a company creator or shaper. Rupert's sense that he needed to become comfortable with uncertainty and discomfort, and with accepting the "good enough" rather than being a perfectionist, is a great summary of one enormous challenge. Christina was stretched to the core as she leapt from the frying pan of twenty-two years of fanatical loyalty to BCG and into the fire of a large family-owned company. She armed herself for the change in typical consultant style, reading up extensively, getting coaching and support, and quizzing anyone who would listen. She also thrives in the BCG alumni network, from which she derives support, coaching and ideas. The path is not easy, but she finds it rewarding, and she is grateful for the opportunity to make the shift.

Do's and Don'ts for Former or Soon-To-Be Former Consultants

Do

- Take time to research your new industry and role with care and get some coaching.
- Use your consulting methodology to bring added value and dimension to your new role.
- Bring your analytical brain and try to fix things.
- Bring energy and dynamism to your role and expect to change things.
- Be modest in coming in to the new role.
- Take pleasure in the slightly less frantic lifestyle.

Don't

- Assume you can play off of only old skills and relationships.
- Expect that you will find the same freedom to "do your thing" in industry.
- Think that it will be as fast and open to change in reality.

- Believe that you know it all and can fit in because of that.

- Take too much time enjoying the freedom, or you may never catch up.

- Think that something is obvious to all, or that your new colleagues are lazy.

There is a further aspect to consider beyond the immediate time of the transition. We also need to understand what happens afterwards: do these movers gain satisfaction in their new careers and lives? There is often a lifelong loyalty to one's consulting firm, with strong ties, an active alumni network and more. The BCG devise, "Once a BCG-er, always a BCG-er" helps Christina still, as it did during her transition. This sort of support and allegiance are common, and to be taken advantage of, wherever possible. With the BCG "power" behind her, Christina feels cautiously confident and empowered to continue her rise in the organization without looking back.

Even Graham, who has "gone back", has done so only on special terms: when BCG invited him to rejoin, he first refused, then eventually rejoined outside of the consulting hierarchy, allowing him to preserve his sanity and to maintain a path of balance and happiness. Conversely, the unsuccessful partner who had joined a large pharmaceutical company as head of strategic planning has since returned to the world of consulting, but this time on his own.

Onward or Upward

Since we originally interviewed our subjects, things have certainly progressed, and there is an increasing consciousness of this kind of transition and the opportunities and pitfalls it implies. What is clear is that a certain proportion of former consultants positively thrive on this kind of liberating transition out, and some of them even manage to recreate that kind of freedom if and when re-entering the world of consulting. What we still need is more data on the successes and failures. With the many mistakes that a high-level consultant may make on transitioning into operational roles, the more these can be understood and anticipated before making the transition, the more likely it will be a success. This is something that can be worked on from both sides – individual and organizational – and that is an area of opportunity for improvement.

If we return to the hypothesis touted by the recruiters that consultants are mostly CEOs-to-be, we must remember that those individuals who decide to stay are, by contrast, far from being failures. They have, for the most part, become senior partners: they make a decent living, and continue their work serving interesting and prestigious clients globally. The world of consulting has expanded in scale, scope and sophistication, and is now a profession in its own right.

"The stakes are great both for the management consultancies, where a culture of 'up or out' implies that the future-former consultants are the firm's clients of tomorrow, and for the organizations that choose to on-board former consultants in leadership roles." This comment from Kevin Barrett, founder and CEO of an outplacement firm in Paris, sums up the complexity of the transition, and provides a suitably sophisticated warning to handle it with care.

Further Reading and Information

▌ BOOKS AND STUDIES

"Confessions of a Management Consultant Turned CEO", by Anita Simonton, Georgeanna Kiser, SPC Press, Inc.1997

▌ ARTICLES AND BLOGS

"Is there life after consulting?", by Fabrice Desmarescaux, LinkedIn Post, 13 September 2016

"Is Your Next Great CEO a Management Consultant?", by Gretchen Gavett, Harvard Business Review Blog, November 19, 2013

"The CEO Factory: Ex-McKinsey Consultants Get Hired to Run the Biggest Companies", by Duff McDonald, Observer, 10 September 2013

"From Management Consulting to CEO: The Fork in the Road", By Bruce R. Raines, Consulting Track, April 2012

▌ WEBSITES

McKinsey Alumni – McKinsey's alumni page
www.mckinsey.com/about-us/overview

Once a BCGer, Always a BCGer – BCG career website
www.bcg.com/people/alumni/default.aspx

Chapter 6

Profit to Purpose

Making a Success of Making a Difference

A transition into non-profit from the profit-driven corporate world is something that more executives are making these days than did ten or twenty years ago. Some aspects of the change are obvious, and others more subtle and unexpected, with a broad set of dynamics at play, which reflect many of the issues of the shifting terrain of careers today. It would be tempting to believe that all or most executives working in non-profit today are and always have been driven by the passion to save the world – or whatever aspect of the world it is that they are so keen on. However, while this may sometimes be the case, it is not always so, and many of our interviewees repeated phrases such as "it was never on my radar screen" or "I did nothing in particular to seek out opportunities in the non-profit sector. It just fell into my lap."

Ramon

What does emerge, however, is that once they are "in", the cause becomes one of the main drivers in their professional lives. Ramon, however, has been cause-driven since early childhood.

Ramon's motivations for being involved in the world of purpose spring logically from his background and his natural tendency to reflect deeply on the world. He was born in the Dominican Republic, into a modest family, which emigrated to the U.S. when he was five years old. He distinguished himself early on by becoming the first member of his clan to attend university (an Ivy League, at that), which triggered an uneasy immigrant Catholic guilt at being a success while his elder brother was not making the same progress in his new life. During his time in university, Ramon noticed that there were "not many brown or black faces" around him, and started to question what kind of system could have brought this about. He was highly sensitive to his environment, and deeply aware of things not being quite fair.

Fate struck to underline Ramon's feelings, as he spent his first week in his first job after graduation at Pepsi. As the Twin Towers fell, he heard a subtle voice in his head asking him if he was truly doing what he should be doing – he had heard Steve Jobs's legendary commencement speech earlier, and it had left its mark on him. Having left Pepsi, Ramon found makeshift ways over the next four to five years to contribute more.

Eventually, while at business school in Spain, he met a small but crucial group of like-minded people. As part of their coursework, they created Emzingo. This social enterprise is part of a massive shift in the social sector, and creates transformational learning experiences in developing economies for its clients and participants. Emzingo has managed to disprove the false dilemmas of suffering and being poor in order to do good.

Anabel

When examining the motivations for some, it is clear that many did not have a conscious calling, but that the signs were nevertheless there all the time. Almost all speak of some sort of need for a test or a sense of dissatisfaction with the status quo before moving into non-profit. Sometimes even subject of study, focus of project work and one's own charity giving can be strong indicators of a change at some point in the future. The shift may come from a different initial motivation, such as the chance to "step up" in terms of stature, size of organization, and so on, as it did for Anabel.

According to Anabel, she had little experience in non-profit work, apart from a short project in Sierra Leone during her degree work in Human Sciences, as well as volunteer work in the UK with underprivileged children. She is perhaps too modest, as many of us have done far less than that.

However, perhaps what Anabel means when she says that purpose work "was not on her radar" was that she did not see it as a legitimate means of making a living. She had spent ten years building a massive capacity as a leader and motivator of teams at world-class companies such as Virgin and Carphone Warehouse, and so had developed a taste for being challenged and stretched in this kind of context. What was different this time was that she was looking for another sort of test, and so much so that she left her job to search for an international role in an organization that was challenging the status quo.

After a brief foray into a start-up company, into which she was invited via her MBA network, she was told of an opportunity to become the COO of Save the Children. When she looked into this, she found all kinds of positive points, including a sense of pride at the work, and the opportunity to step up in terms of responsibility, as she would be a member of the Board. While it would mean a cut in salary, she took the plunge when offered the job.

The quality of people at Save the Children and the challenge of working with them is something about which Anabel talks with great enthusiasm, just as she enjoys the variety of backgrounds from which they come. She speaks with reverence about how many of them are at the absolute top of their fields, whether it be in technical or fundraising areas, or in marketing and communication. She has come to understand deeply the need to manage and motivate different groups in separate ways, and so she has developed an ability to engage in a variety of ways, according to context and audience.

A recognition of her fundamental strengths is what keeps Anabel lucid about future plans. She derives great pleasure from running a tight ship, so certainly does not see herself moving into politics or government, preferring the simpler dynamic she works with now. Her lasting statement is "I would encourage more people to do it – you learn a lot".

Dondi

One crucial aspect all of our interviewees spoke of was how to bring the staff and others they work with "on a journey". Few, if any, traditional relationships of hierarchy and power exist in non-profit structures, particularly when you are dealing with volunteers or sometimes unwilling partners or collaborators. When the old model does not apply, the leaders have to learn new and at times uncomfortable behaviors. This was a particular challenge for Dondi, whose background in traditional business in the Philippines meant that he was used to calling the shots with no questions asked.

Five years ago, Dondi decided "it was time to tackle the causes of poverty, as opposed to Band-Aid solutions". He abhors the corruption and poor governance which directly contribute to the poverty of the Philippines. The decision to weigh in was not at all difficult, although he knew that he would be putting himself at odds with politicians and "pseudo-leaders".

It took about a year to settle into his new "calling", but almost five years to learn to "engage for change" rather than to "just battle away".

As for the skills that Dondi has derived from his work in the non-profit sector, he speaks of patience and engagement, underlining the fact that he "listens more". He has become more adept at persuasion alongside the authoritarian CEO approach that is particularly prominent in the Philippines, and feels that the work he does with the different organizations is stretching his talents in all aspects of communication.

Dondi lives in a country with a short-term approach to political thinking (though don't we all?), and at the same time a particularly resistant attitude towards change. He says "as a businessman, these things just bug the hell out of me." The satisfaction of developing his capabilities in listening, problem-solving, strategic planning and organizational development is tremendous, and he knows he is rounding off his stature as a leader and a businessman. He feels that his EQ has grown immeasurably, as he has learned to motivate volunteers, the business community, stakeholders and government towards change, however painful that movement might be.

There is no question in Dondi's mind about whether he will continue his non-profit work. At the time we spoke with him, he had just spent a few weeks volunteering at a foundation run by friends, helping street children to find a new life. He may be "only" at 30 percent of his time just now, but as he and his wife find themselves empty-nesters, and as his need to build more financial security recedes, it is patently obvious that we will see more of Dondi in the pursuit of purpose than profit. This is a man with a mission, and he will continue to marshal the resources necessary to achieve it.

Nick

The path towards getting things done and done properly in non-profits is one that leaders recognized as being bumpier and more unpredictable than in comparable corporate contexts. Nick, a former cost-cutting and re-organization expert in the strategy consulting field, tells of the interesting ride he has had.

When Nick joined Cancer Research as director of strategy, he soon discovered that he had hundreds and hundreds of different stakeholders to get to know and to "take with him on a journey". This image is one he uses a great deal when describing that there is no longer any "top-down" driving in his professional life. He observes acutely the challenge of bringing people on board when they are not naturally won over by analysis or logical arguments, and in a consensus-driven culture where top-down management is not the norm.

Passion and emotion abound in the non-profit world, as all our interviewees have observed, but Nick is the most candid on this question. As he puts it: "I have never seen so many tears. People are being themselves and much more genuine than in the corporate world, and it is so much easier to get excited about cancer survival rates exploding than it is about increased profits." However, he is quick to balance this with his view that emotion can be a roadblock to change, as others have stated. People get attached to the idea of doing good, whatever the strategic arguments that may surround them. The new skills derived from working smartly within this environment are tremendously powerful.

One concern shared by almost all those we interviewed, at least before they actually got into their roles, was: "Will I have to compromise my standard of living to a degree I find uncomfortable?" And what we observe is that the reply is almost universally "no".

There are various ways that the transition can be made palatable, and sometimes the gaps between former and current salary are not as large as we might imagine. In addition, there are some crafty ways of managing the difference. Ramon and Nick both experienced this.

Ramon and the other founders of Emzingo took a particularly intelligent approach to the start-up phase of their business, each one holding onto his previous role (and salary) for some time before making the leap. They staggered who took time off and worked for money, to maintain the momentum, even though this occasionally led to some precarious juggling. All three of the founders are now in the business full-time, and while their bank accounts are not as sizable as they once were, they have created an equilibrium through contributions to society that offset any small pecuniary discomfort they might still feel.

Nick experienced an innovative approach to remuneration while he was working as a "partner" of Save the Children. BCG worked in partnership with Save the Children to send consultants on missions across the world, with a dual contribution to a reasonable (but reduced) salary. This meant that there were few if any barriers to a consultant going off on this adventure, and no single party suffered unduly.

None of those we met were able to speak of an improved financial situation as a result of working in the non-profit sector, but equally not one of them complained of suffering in this respect, either. Tabloid papers may make currency of this kind of thing, but there must be a fair trade-off in this area as much as anywhere else. If you want to attract and retain a great leader, you must collaborate to find a solution that is comfortable for all. If that means six figure salaries, then it is the job of the organization to work towards even greater surplus, so as to be able to pay that salary and gain the greatest value.

Even if sometimes salary cuts can be the less fun part of making a move to the non-profit sector, it is important to remember, as almost all of our interviewees did, that it is not a "one-way street" into this field. The need to stop separating corporations from non-profits was vividly advocated by Alexander Friedman, chief investment officer of UBS Wealth Management and former CFO of The Bill & Melinda Gates Foundation, in a 2010 Financial Times article: "These days, it has become something of a trend to demonize capitalists and praise philanthropists. But if we are to make true progress in tackling our most pressing social problems and live up to our moral obligation to help those in extreme poverty, these two seemingly polarized groups need to come together in fundamentally new ways."[43]

As we start to see that the skills and talents developed while inside a non-profit are increasingly valued and sought-after, we can imagine this making it easy to contemplate a return to the profit sector after some time.

Diana

Diana understands clearly that these two worlds need to come closer to each other. Having done "incredibly well" in the private equity field, and reached a "plateau that was less interesting and exciting than the climb up", she found herself CEO of a highly prominent firm before forty, and feeling that the second half of her working life should be different, make more sense and be a kind of "setting to rights" to make up for all her success in the first half.

Career Transition Navigator

EXPLORE

To this end, Diana returned to school at Oxford and literally shut herself away for a year, hoping to figure out her new destiny, with a strong sense that she could not and would not fit into the non-profit world. So when a friend called her and asked if he could introduce her to the head of the Clinton Foundation, she was intrigued, given the stature of the man, but still felt this was not a professional opportunity in which she would be interested.

Within 20 minutes, she was hooked on the fact that this was a world of mostly private sector people, solving global problems with a market-driven outlook. Gone were her entrenched fears of not fitting in – and the rest, as they say, is history. For five years, Diana worked in a number of senior roles at the Clinton Foundation, including running all country operations in Africa/Caribbean/Europe and all global teams.

After the Clinton Foundation, Diana became aware of the CDC Group, a UK Development Finance Institution, which had a rich and proud history, but which had become criticized and somewhat beleaguered. It was an opportunity to combine her experience as a commercial investor in private equity with the knowledge she'd gained about development at the Foundation. She has now been CEO for several years. When asked if she would return to a purely for-profit role, she says that it is difficult imagining fulfillment without a development angle now. The challenge at CDC is so rich and multidimensional that she believes just toiling in order to deliver an improved P&L would feel a bit empty.

Many of the leaders we talked to were bullish on the prospects of moving across, among and around what is known as the "tri-sector" area – the cross section of profit, non-profit and government entities. Anabel told some extraordinary stories of projects to get a mouthwash from a big pharma company used in an innovative way in Africa on the umbilical cords of new-born babies, and the massive effect this has had on infant mortality rates. She also spoke of government campaigns regarding the importance of hand washing, in partnerships with Save the Children and a soap manufacturer. Each party could not have delivered such results singly. The collaboration is crucial, though still quite unusual, and Anabel is fiercely proud of being part of such powerful initiatives.

Chris

Another leader who is clear on the power of the tri-sector area is Chris, the CEO of Whale and Dolphin Conservation. Chris not only claims a mixed background combining military service, marketing, and now the leadership of a substantial global charity, but also recruits across sectors as much as he can. He believes that the boundaries are breaking down between sectors, and those who can collaborate across the private, public and social sectors will increasingly be valued.

He says: "What some in the non-profit sector have to accept is that it is not a one-way street: people move in both directions, you know. The traditional belief was that older executives 'retired' into the non-profit sector, but, thankfully, this has been dead in the UK for at least a decade."

Chris recognizes that the leaders that they are discussing have not only transferable skills, but also contextual knowledge and experience that can be critical to success. He adds that "they also have networks that allow a new form of legitimacy to be accrued to the entities that employ them. For the companies that engage with these tri-sector leaders, there can be significant rewards."

How to Make the Best of This Growing Trend?

So, why do we see this growing trend towards non-profit areas for senior leaders? One factor is undoubtedly the increasing questioning of current economic models, fueled by the global financial crisis of 2007 onwards. Arguably, things have never really quite recovered, despite what pundits might try to posit. In this environment, even the most hard-headed executive is more likely to find reason to ask him- or herself some tough questions about career, purpose and contribution. As a result, a significant body of leaders is either considering making the transition or has already made it.

Ironically but usefully, the economic overdrive that preceded the crash is what created a group of leaders who now have the financial and vocational security to contemplate more broadly their options. What is more, the non-profit sector is increasingly embracing the sophisticated approaches of the private sector, making it more attractive as a working environment for a second career. And many non-profits look towards private-sector leaders to implement the change involved.

The range of motivations that drive such people to non-profit roles is huge. We go from the "calling" early in life, like Ramon, to "giving back", to "ditching dissatisfaction, and finding purpose". We have read the stories of those in these main categories, but there is another one which is pure serendipity. Sometimes, changes just happen because of a little coincidence that takes on outsized importance, as in the case of Vanessa D'Souza. She came to her role as CEO of SNEHA, a large Mumbai-based NGO, having volunteered there casually during a career break from investment banking. She did not seek out the role, but was offered it, having impressed the right people on the board. We suspect that the number and diversity of reasons will continue to grow as we see greater numbers moving in this direction, and look forward to discovering more and more varied stories.

Surprises, both positive and negative, abound in this relatively uncharted territory. We note that most of our subjects were not as disappointed by their new salary and working conditions as they had expected to be, and this is a plus. While non-profits range hugely in their ability to pay comparably to corporations, there is scope to find a well-paid non-profit job if this is so desired. On the other hand, the challenge of getting things done fast and properly can be a killer, and ruin the happiest of salary arrangements if not well managed.

Other frustrations include the gap between job description and reality, with the comment "this is not the job I signed up for" remarkably common. And finally, culture and people idiosyncrasies make for a huge complexity to navigate, and significant obstacles towards achieving set goals. Vanessa shared that she felt she was almost in another world, likening the different cultures to apples and oranges, and Nick struggled hugely with the contrast in his new role, but both have decided that the fortitude required is worth finding.

Once one is "in", it is difficult to ignore the cause, and it tends to become a significant driver in one's professional life. Anabel found particular stimulation in the quality of the people, while Diana cannot imagine feeling fulfilled without a development angle. Dondi is avid for more non-profit experience, and has since become an honorary consul, and Vanessa feels her life has changed dramatically. As they learn and develop themselves inside the non-profit world, the overall quality and professionalism of the environment increases: a win-win. With regard to the development likely within a non-profit environment, here is a list of transferable skills that often stretch:

- Patience – volunteers are not paid employees, and it's a different covenant
- Making the dollars and pounds stretch
- Innovation springs from the need to find solutions with little resources
- Influencing multi-stakeholder environments
- Listening and not imposing – taking the people on a journey

A growing EQ and ability to engage more diversely are often quoted as the most gratifying developments, and a more "journey" based approach to motivating the various stakeholders seems to be a commonly agreed-upon success.

And finally, we see that not only are there the "two-way streets" that Chris referred to, but there is also a tendency to end the separation between corporation and non-profit. Not only do we get the extraordinary innovation that comes from tri-sector collaborations, but also we get

Fortune 100 leaders like Alexander Friedman of UBS talking about the need to stop demonizing the rich and praising the philanthropists, and instead to find new strategies to bring the two together, however polarized they might be. For true progress, "we need fundamentally new ways".

In these challenging times, it is encouraging to see this growing energy, and we must hope that the boundaries blur ever further, with altruistic agendas growing, and more good done by more individuals and organizations.

Famous Tri-Sector Leaders

The tradition of making a fortune in industry before shifting interest to philanthropy started over a century ago. In their Harvard Business Review article of 2013, Nick Lovegrove and Matthew Thomas explain: "Tri-sector leaders have been among the most significant and influential people of their time. For most of its history, in fact, the United States has seen a steady stream of people – including Andrew Carnegie, Andrew Mellon, George Shultz, Michael Bloomberg, and Bill Gates – who made their fortunes in the private sector and subsequently turned to government service and philanthropy." In their research, Lovegrove and Thomas have found five paths to tri-sector leadership:

▪ Business First
Some highly successful private sector leaders subsequently become government or non-profit leaders, or both.
Examples: Michael Bloomberg, Bill Gates, Hank Paulson, Steve Rattner, Diana Farrell, Jay Cowles, Aneesh Chopra

▪ Government First
Some distinguished public-sector leaders subsequently develop second careers in the private or non-profit sector.
Examples: Jared Cohen, Jeff Seabright, Bob Hormats, Julius Genachowski, Sheryl Sandberg, Stan Litow

▪ Non-profit First
Some leaders spend their early careers in the non-profit world of community engagement and social entrepreneurship before moving into government or business.
Examples: Barack Obama

- **In and Out**
Some tri-sector leaders keep moving among government, business, and non-profit jobs during their careers.
Examples: Carol Browner, David Hayes, Ian Solomon, Lael Brainard, Bob Kocher

- **Stay in Place**
Some leaders spend their careers primarily in one sector but engage and collaborate with individuals in the other two to address tri-sector issues.
Examples: Muhtar Kent, Eric Schmidt, John Berry, David Bradley

The Voice of Companies: How One Charity Sees It

As this trend of flow between the sectors increases, the challenge of managing the talent in an appropriate way also grows. We had a chance to talk with Elizabeth Sideris, the Executive Director of Human Resources, at Cancer Research UK, who supported Nick through his transition, and advocated for and executed substantial work in encouraging mobility (both in and out) in this area.

She states that "aeration is vital", adding that at least half of the organization's recruits come from outside the charity sector. "Finding people of Nick's caliber is hard, and we really do subscribe to the philosophy of filling our key positions with the right people for our stated direction, which means finding those with the right motivation, skills, drive and impact to create and deliver, in alignment with our vision and objectives." Thus they use whatever methods necessary to find the best people for their strategic needs, taking the time and other resources required to do so, including paying substantial sums to headhunters for the privilege. "We know the investment is worth it, and we have a clear policy of looking outside our field."

Cancer Research is seen as an incubator of talent, and one from which other charities regularly poach, whereas Cancer Research itself typically does not need to poach from others. This demonstrates that the charity is at the top of its talent game, Elizabeth is quite sure.

How do they make working at their organization financially attractive? Their approach is to pay above the median for the charity sector and not too far below the median of the for-profit sector. The aim is that when for-profit individuals enter, at best, their salary is matched, and at worst, there is a small cut. Cancer Research also aim to make the other benefits attractive, so that holidays and peripheral items add to the package. "It's our job to be motivating, as leadership potential is more important than experience."

What about how to handle the culture change? Elizabeth believes that the challenge is probably more about sector than profit or non-profit. She cites her own story, of moving from finance to medical research, with which she had a terrible time adjusting, and of then moving on to Cancer Research, which was much easier. It would seem it depends on where you are coming from. "Nick had already had a taste of the non-profit sector, so his transition was not a shock, even if it was not easy. As Nick came in, he was working with someone who was strategically aligned with him, curious, seeking best solutions, higher performance etc., so it was easy for him, and for us, to acknowledge his performance."

On the key differences, Elizabeth reflects: "We are collegiate, and can take too long, sometimes, to make decisions that would be executed much faster in a business environment, however, it is important in our business to think in a considered way. We have definitely made progress in terms of hierarchical impact, and we are now more evidently a meritocratic organization."

There is much to be proud of, and motivated by, in this organization, that is so visibly setting the agenda for making the best of all worlds. Elizabeth, who herself enjoys the pressure to constantly "up her game", says, "Our charity thrives on the diversity of people, background and viewpoint that we cultivate, and we need to optimize that at all times. We have been a "top employer" in many surveys, and we are proud of having achieved that." The satisfaction of making a difference is less easy to find elsewhere.

How to Make the Transition Happen

There are a certain number of critical questions to ask yourself before making the move to a non-profit role. This is a significant transition, just like any other major professional change, and should be taken just as seriously, if not more so. Here is a list of the main questions and issues that experts in the field, including headhunters, consultants to non-profits, and more (listed at the end of this chapter) commonly refer to:

- **Ask yourself the difficult questions, understand your motivations, keep crystal clear:** "Doing good" might be better achieved by making a contribution to the cause than by your taking a job for the wrong reasons. Additionally, prominent donors' actions are visible, and they set the tone for others to follow.

- **Get a deep comprehension of the players, stakes, economics and constituencies in the new workplace, and consider how changing regulatory environments might affect you:** Assume you know nothing about "their" environment, and start your research and information -gathering from scratch. Some of these entities are gigantic, and just as complex, if not more so, than the organization you will be coming from, with just as much need to learn how to navigate the slippery paths.

- **Narrow your choices and remember that you cannot move from cause to cause without your heart:** In a mission-driven organization, your capacity to take up the cause is of primary importance. Your organization's focus is its raison d'être.

- **Ensure your CV reflects the ideas, issues and causes that you wish to work for:** Highlight the most relevant competencies to your new role, and underline more strongly any previous volunteering activities. Evaluate your transferable skills and think carefully about how to match these to the right role. Of particular interest are financial management for ROI; metrics to measure the impact of programs; and communications and marketing professionals, who can turn intention into strategy, distributing the message across all platforms.

- **Network differently, inform yourself deeply and find out where the leaders and key players in your area meet up:** Find out how those who have already trodden this path are doing, and what they wish they had known earlier. Be ready to explain your motivations and sound solid and convincing.

- **Stay in your old position until you are ready to make your informed and well-thought-through move:** The old adage applies here too – search while in post, and this could take a while.

- **Increase your skills – new tools, approaches and strategies may be necessary:** Take courses, attend conferences and explore new university and other programs that might prepare you properly and expose you to the people you need to meet.

- **Remember the common stereotypes the non-profit people may have about you:** Remember Chris's comment about sandal-wearing hippies? The shoe is on the other foot! You will likely be seen as worthy of resentment and suspicion, not to mention incapable of managing on a shoestring.

Once you have made the transition, you will need to:

- **Take the long view:** Imagine how long it will take to have an impact or turn things around, and double it. Change in most non-profits is slow and painful.

- **Accept a "good enough" infrastructure:** Let's face it – you will probably not get more than that! Keep it simple; if necessary, outsource certain parts of this area.

- **Look on the bright side and seek out those with whom you can engage to help build the future:** Make the right friends and allies from the outset; ensure you bring on board those who have succeeded and have a forward-looking attitude, while marginalizing the unproductive ones.

- **Bring your plans and visions around people and growth:** Be sure to come in with energy and helpful corporate tools, which you can use in a simplified context, to create a process for performance management, with rewards and developmental opportunities.

- **Focus your early attention on the leadership team:** Early time spent with the leaders will pay off. Getting to know them, and how each of them fits in with your vision, will allow you to bring the right ones on the journey with you, and help you be clear about who needs to go in the early months.

5 Frustrations to Overcome in a Non-Profit

1. The need to communicate constantly about what you are doing, or else the money does not come in

2. Lack of process and skills in early-stage organizations can be a brake on growth

3. Surprising competency gaps in the stakeholder organizations can lead to slow progress

4. Getting over the temptation to "battle" as opposed to "engage"

5. Some stakeholders expect non-profit people to be sandal-wearing hippies, but the surprise when they meet "normal" leaders can be used to advantage

Not Yet Smooth Sailing

This is a challenging transition, and one of the least studied and written about elsewhere, so our findings and reflections are necessarily a little more speculative and anecdotal here.

From the vignettes we have presented, we conclude that this is an area full of exciting change, with people at all levels, most especially leaders, able to take advantage of the flux to learn, develop and add value. Most especially when we get the magic tri-sector mix...

There is a way to go before everyone is able to understand and navigate the tri-sector area comfortably, but things are moving in a fascinating direction. The boundaries will continue to blur, and the moves will continue. Will the non-profits begin to look more like for-profits? Or vice versa? Probably not, and thus it is likely that the cultural differences to navigate will remain similar and substantial. However, with good planning and management on both sides, this is a particularly exciting area of cross-fertilization to be developed in future years.

Further Reading and Information

▌ BOOKS AND STUDIES

"The Skills the Nonprofit Sector Requires of its Managers and Leaders", Research Report, Non-profit Leadership Alliance, June 2011

"The Nonprofit Career Guide: How to Land a Job That Makes a Difference", by Shelly Cryer, Fieldstone Alliance, 2008

"Change Your Career: Transitioning to the Nonprofit Sector", by Laura Gassner Otting, Kaplan Publishing, 2007

▌ ARTICLES AND BLOGS

"The Unexpected Challenges of Transitioning from For-Profit to Nonprofit Leadership", by Nicki Roth, Saroga and Kathleen Yazbak, The Bridgespan Group, July 2014

"Triple-Strength Leadership", by Nick Lovegrove and Matthew Thomas, Harvard Business Review, September 2013

"Is the Grass Really Greener? Advice for the Not-For-Profit Crossover Candidate", by Nancy Mistretta, Russell Reynolds Associates, 2008

▌ WEBSITES

The Bridgespan Group – A global organization that collaborates with mission-driven leaders, organizations, and philanthropists to break cycles of poverty and dramatically improve the quality of life for those in need
www.bridgespan.org/Home.aspx

Non-profit Leadership Alliance – An organization whose mission is to strengthen the social sector with a talented and prepared workforce
www.nonprofitleadershipalliance.org

Institut de Coopération Internationale (France) – A non-profit association specializing in support and training for non-profit projects
www.institut-cooperation.com

Chapter 7

Boomerangs

Managing a Return
to Your Former Company

Over the past ten years, the number of Fortune 100 companies that actively run "alumni programs" has ballooned. One of the main results of this approach is that an increasing number of people are returning to their former employer at some later point in time. Those who are part of this growing phenomenon are colloquially known as "boomerangs". In this chapter, we attempt to analyze some of the trends and challenges involved in the return to the fold via the story of six different executives around the world.

Louise
Sometimes it can just be a simple, logical and pleasant process to go back. Such was the case for Louise, who speaks calmly and rationally about her return to a pharmaceutical giant after a multi-year absence.

Following an early start in practice as an MD and a move from Florida to the Northeast, Louise decided to take on a clinical role in R&D at a large pharmaceutical company, mainly because she loved the people and the culture of the organization. After a subsequent merger, the research pipeline diminished in her area of expertise, but she wanted to continue to work in this particular area. So she left, on excellent terms, having been courted by a biotech startup working on an exciting and more relevant development.

A series of happy biotech roles followed over the next several years, though she remained in touch with her colleagues from the old company. During that time, she almost boomeranged a few times, though it never quite worked out for a variety of reasons. However, on one occasion, she was made an offer she found too good to resist, and, despite some questioning from those close to her around the nature of the role she had been offered, Louise returned to the pharmaceutical giant. This time she was in an operational post, rather than clinical, and found she loved the contrast. She has been back for five years, and in that time has enjoyed six different roles in both operational and clinical positions.

Career
Transition
Navigator

ENGAGE

Perhaps the wisest advice Louise received on her return was to "take a good look around for a few months and only then figure out what you want to do". This gave her the chance to explore and reacquaint herself comfortably without any pressure to conform to old perceptions, either of herself, or of the company. She found many familiar faces, but decided to spend time getting to know people once again and finding out "how things are done round here". This was the best investment she could have possibly made.

Louise is not considering a move away from where she is now, and firmly believes that "if you have a good boss and great colleagues, with clarity and effort, and whether in a big company or small, you can take an opportunity and make it work".

Louise has navigated motherhood, tensions with colleagues and oscillating economic cycles, but with her emotional intelligence and strong investment in relationships, she has made a return to a company that she now views as part of her landscape, and which it would probably be difficult to leave. Her colleagues and leaders in the business have played along with her, and now it seems likely that she will continue to find challenges and interest in her work there for the foreseeable future. A tacit contract of complicity has been developed, and neither side feels compelled to deviate. We certainly wish that more boomerang experiences could be this simple and enjoyable.

Can

Sometimes a return can be the start of really massive change — as happened to Can, who has been linked to the BMW Corporation for all of his working life, and whose story shows how environment and challenges can catalyze transformation.

Can started his professional life in a prominent holding company in his native Turkey, as a promising young graduate trainee. He moved in and out of various specialist sales and marketing roles and built a privileged link with BMW in Germany. Thus he became known for his specific expertise, and was relied on as a valuable asset in the company. There was one significant drawback to this situation: Can became impossible to promote or develop, as no one wanted to lose access to their expert. So after a few years, Can realized that he wanted to progress beyond what he could achieve at the company. He left with his family to seek new opportunities in Canada. On exit, Can was careful to be clear in his dialogue, stating his frustration while keeping things friendly and warm.

Several years in Toronto gave Can the chance to work his way up through a large group of BMW dealerships, and finally he gained a corporate role at the BMW head office for Canada — yet again, as the specialist. This time, he realized that he was creating his own problem, and started to make plans to break out. He found coaches and mentors within the organization, and took himself outside his comfort zone. Just as he felt he was on the right track, things changed again.

In 2010, Can was invited to return to his original company, with an offer to explore a new management role bringing together Sales and Marketing. The difficult decision to leave Canada took six months.

Eventually, the family moved back to Turkey with an optimistic outlook, hoping that time and reorganization would have solved some of the earlier problems. Unfortunately, Turkey was still lagging far behind the best practice he had enjoyed in Canada, and it was tough for him to impose or nurture change. He recognized that he was being slowed down by cultural resistance, but felt that he was on a mission.

After being told yet again that he was "too valuable" in his current role, and passed over once more for promotion, Can decided that the only path to take was that of radical change, and self-motivation. As he describes it, he "grew up and changed everything". He stopped blaming his slow progress on others, and started to take responsibility. In the process, he lost weight, gave up smoking, became a better husband, father and friend, and realized that he knew exactly what he wanted in every aspect of his life. He also discovered that he was capable of expressing this eloquently to his management and entourage, and is now able to see when to accept the status quo and when to drive change. He has established a positive relationship with his "family" at work, after years of not really figuring out how to do this, and is finally on the way to establishing his true career path on his own terms.

Olivier

While the benchmarking and special expertise were an obstacle to Can's progress, such knowledge and experience can be used as a significant boost, as Olivier discovered in his journey in and out of French electronics giant Alcatel Lucent.

As a fresh engineering graduate with study experience in both France and Germany, Olivier was attracted by a career in industry, and joined Alcatel with the hope that he would soon be offered an expatriate post somewhere. Sure enough, he found himself working in the U.S. just over a year later. While he found the work enriching and fascinating, and he liked the culture at Alcatel, he found himself experiencing a seven-year "itch", and left the giant for a small internet-based start-up. Two years in this different environment were enjoyable, but the company failed, and he found himself obliged to change again. Although he had a green card, Olivier decided to return to France with his family, feeling that if he did not move right away, he would probably never go back.

He joined the French public finance institution Caisse des Dépôts via a professional link, and enjoyed six years there. He noticed a clear difference in culture and practice, and realized that his preference was really for industry and application, not theory and advice. It was an easy choice, when a person with high-level roles at both Caisse des Dépôts and Alcatel Lucent offered him the chance to return. He had good memories, and despite the company's poor reputation at the time, he had no hesitation in agreeing to the new role.

Olivier's decision to return was based on three separate factors, two of which had applied previously: firstly, his respect and liking for the person who got him back "in"; next that it was a return to "application", and finally a welcome move back to a global environment and culture. It was fortunate that his thinking was this conscious, as the company to which he returned had changed beyond recognition. There had been a big merger, many of his colleagues had left, and he had changed departments too. This was emphatically not a return to his "family", however it was not a negative experience either. Olivier just felt as though he had joined a new company, with helpful people who showed him the ropes. And his own sense of value remained intact also, as he realized that, having seen other businesses, he had a fresh and useful perspective to bring. He describes it as an "external training" experience, which has allowed him to grow his value.

On the subject of whether he feels he will remain, Olivier is more guarded. He feels a certain loyalty and comfort with regard to Alcatel Lucent, but he is also itching for another expatriation. This desire to travel will undoubtedly be the main driver, above and beyond the strong link he has with his company now.

David

David's first stint in Coca-Cola was because he, too, was keen to work overseas. After an initial period in France, he was thrilled to be sent to the U.S., and spent a while working there as an expert on an SAP project. He realized fast that he preferred operational roles, but was not granted the opportunity to get back into this area. So, unsurprisingly, when a headhunter called on him to explore his interest in a role as HR Director for Starbucks, which was setting up in France, he was easily tempted by the idea. However, despite his positive convictions, he still describes as "the most difficult moment in all my professional life" the day he told his boss that he would be leaving his Coke "family". He was close to all his colleagues, and the company was a leader in HR practices worldwide. This was a terrible but unavoidable wrench.

In the five years that he spent at Starbucks, David learnt and developed enjoyably and impressively, but the company experienced slower growth than hoped for. The excitement abated, and on being offered a role at Christian Dior, he was seduced by the brand, and accepted. By the time he realized that he had been brought in to engineer and implement massive layoffs, it was too late, but he knew he had made a big mistake. Within less than six months of entering, he was putting out feelers with friends and headhunters. His overriding sentiment at the time was that "going back would be failure." When the Coca-Cola HR Director, with whom he had remained in contact, used a mix of guilt and friendship to attract him back, he could resist no more.

The return was to a company he assumed would not have changed significantly, especially as he still knew most of the leaders and significant players. But there had been a substantial corporate transformation in the meantime, from country-centric to European, from linear to matrix organization, and so on. This was a totally different entity from what he had known, despite it all looking so similar. He felt powerless to achieve his objectives, and horribly frustrated. However, feeling that the sorties to Starbucks and Dior had not necessarily brought him much glory, he sensed a need to stick it out at Coke and make things work.

After almost three years back, he was offered a European role in London, where he could lead an organization, use his outside experience and knowledge, and be seen as a reference: someone who understands the market and its benchmarks. However, David prefers growth environments, and Coke's business in Europe is becoming more and more about stagnation and cost-cutting; if he needs to seek that growth environment outside Coca-Cola, he will find it easier this time.

Jonatan

As a contrast, we have the story of Jonatan, a talented ballet dancer from Spain. When he finished ballet school, he won a place in the corps de ballet in the Regional Theatre at Linz, in Austria. The conditions were extraordinarily good, though early on, he realized that the company was not really suited to him: he was by far the youngest dancer, and the work was more theatrical than the work he had been used to. However, he was treated extremely well, cast a great deal, and offered a promotion to "Principal" in his second year. At the same time, the director of the company emotionally announced to Jonatan that, in 2013, five years into the future, he would be the one to dance Romeo in a new production of the eponymous ballet. This seemed like an extraordinary promise, but it turned out to be real.

Jonatan soon wished to find more challenges and made the decision to leave. He was offered a role in a German company, which he accepted, despite his director's attempts to make him stay. The new company was more familiar, and this was what Jonatan needed at the time. He was, strangely enough, cast as Romeo, and danced the role to great acclaim. But soon enough, the director at Linz was on the phone, begging him to return, pleading, "Without you, there will be no Romeo!".

Finally, he went back, not least because his wife was from Linz, and would be happy to live back in her hometown. He made the decision on a mix of practical questions and a twist of emotional reaction. The Romeo rehearsals began with excitement and anticipation. However, this feeling was soon to transform into despair, as Ulrich, the Director, was rushed to hospital, seriously ill, and later died, leaving chaos behind him.

The Romeo ballet was unfinished, but it was in that year's program, so the company members developed their own roles as best they could. A new director came in, and fired all but two of the existing members. Jonatan was one of the survivors. In the space of a few months, he had watched his dear director wither away, created his own ballet character, survived a massive company purge and undergone an unexpected divorce. He had returned to Linz for his family and for his director, and now he had neither! Decisions to return based on human factors have the capacity to go disastrously wrong on the turn of a dime.

However, right now, he intends to stay there, as he needs stability and time to recover, and also because the company is now housed in one of the most modern and beautiful opera houses in Europe. It might be easy to attribute the melodramatic nature of this story to its artistic sector, but it is clear that all of us are human and will base our thinking on people and relationships as much as anything else.

Greg

Greg certainly found that the personal relationships and "clan" at a well-known East Coast business school were a constant link, as he wove back and forth, in and out of this great school. His description of his path is quite different to that of some of the others here, as what he mentions most is how there was a lot of serendipity involved in his long career, that "just happens" to include multiple moves in and out of the school.

As a young MBA in 1975, Greg's first job was on the MBA Admissions Committee for his university. He had chosen this role not least because he just could not see himself taking a more traditional MBA route like consulting at McKinsey or trading options on Wall Street. After two years, he was on the cusp of being offered a promotion to head the Admissions Department, but missed out on this for reasons of perceived "difference" between him, his lifestyle choices and the majority of the staff at the school of the time.

For several years subsequent to this disappointment, Greg tried out various companies and sectors. Nothing really fit, and upon being asked to join CCL as head of marketing, he went back to the higher education field with a sense of relief. Thus ensued almost ten years of international activity, of which three were spent in Brussels. When he returned to the U.S. offices, the sparkle had gone, and he decided to go back to a post at his alma mater, in Executive Education this time. He developed this role until 2008, when the management made a large number of generous early retirement package offers and, aged just sixty, Greg happily accepted. He spent the ensuing year playing with different options, but eventually was attracted back into active work in education in the U.S.

A short foray to a regional university kept him occupied for a couple of years, till he came back to his own school again, where he loves the work as Director of Executive Education, Europe. He is inspired by the open, inclusive, and flexible environment around him. He mentions with optimism the fact that one of his colleagues is only just retiring, despite already being 70. The atmosphere is a far cry from that of 1975, and he feels that he is really part of an important and strong clan at the school, where he hopes to stay for as long as he possibly can. Greg is another great product of the wisdom of those managers who invite their boomerangs to step back, take their time, and pretend that "they have never been here before". This looks increasingly like one of the few guarantees of success in making a boomerang work effectively.

This increasing trend is one that gives any boomerang employee and his or her organization a huge opportunity to build on the past, and to create a new future, with some risks, but far fewer than those involved in a brand new recruit. We see some of the pitfalls in these stories, but far more so the possibilities for both sides that the exercise creates.

What's Going On? Why They Leave, Why They Return, and How They Manage it

The term "boomerang", defined as employees who are rehired by their former employers – also called "rehires" – gained acceptance in business lingo a few years ago and has grown in popularity since. We can all call to mind a number of big-name chief executives who have returned to their jobs at the request of struggling companies. This happened at both Apple and Starbucks, which both overcame a struggle to survive and went on to thrive after the return of Steve Jobs and Howard Schultz, their respective founders and CEOs

But beyond these high-profile executives – who are called in crisis and may or may not triumph – what about the millions of professionals who develop more "regular" careers in corporations? Is the boomerang phenomenon a mere buzzword, or a reality that reflects a growing trend?

One of this book's authors, Antoine, started his career in the early 1990s with a leading global cosmetics company. During induction, every newcomer was exposed to the corporate philosophy of lifelong career and was told that entering the company was like joining a religion. If you happened to leave the company, there was no turning back. These times have changed. The other author, Claire, started her career in the late 1980s at Hong Kong's Swire Group. She was sold pretty much the same story, and like Antoine, committed treason by leaving after a few years; however, she is currently discussing a possible return as a consultant. This was unimaginable even a few years ago.

David Almeda and Dan Schwabel completed a 2015 survey commissioned by the Workforce Institute of more than 1,800 human resources professionals in the U.S. which looked at the boomerang trend.[44] Their study reveals a changing mindset about boomerang employees. "You have a better chance now than ever of getting into a company where you formerly worked", says Schwabel. What has changed? According to survey results, nearly half the HR professionals claim their organization previously had a policy against rehiring former employees – even if the employee left in good standing – but 76 percent say they are more open to boomerang employees today than in the past. Another survey by Robert Half confirms the change: "98 percent of human resources managers said they would welcome back a returning employee."[45]

We hypothesize that the growing practice of rehiring former employees might be mostly born out of necessity. It has become an alternative talent acquisition strategy. In this competitive market, many organizations are facing the problem of high attrition. The best talent has saturated, and organizations need to use diverse methods to attract the desired talent, including bringing back former employees.

But what about the professionals themselves? The Robert Half survey found that 48 percent of workers would consider coming back to a previous employer. What motivates an employee to rejoin a company he or she once left? Let's start by looking at the reasons that led them to join the company in the first place. Hearing our five subjects, it appears to be a combination of the usual reasons that motivate someone to take a job (in-line with career plan…) and perhaps a bit of serendipity in some cases.

Louise was attracted to her pharmaceutical company because she loved the people and the culture, while David chose Coke for the international dimension. Jonatan was attracted to Opera Linz for the excellent conditions and fast-track promotion promise. All of this is pretty classic and expected.

However, Can might well have made other choices, as his was based on "a good job" in a prominent holding company, and his affinity, as well as his ability to grow, were not an obvious fit at the outset. Greg ended up in his MBA admissions role more by default than anything else, as he did not fancy a more traditional career path. Both of these look more like serendipity.

There seem to be four different types of boomerangs, which can explain the reasons why they leave their employer (and then decide to return).

Firstly, there are those who leave to advance their career. These are the ones who worked for a company for several years, then saw an opportunity to add skills and progress elsewhere. Can was "stuck" in his specialist role and left to break out of the mold his colleagues had trapped him in. David was moved by the headhunter's call back to an operational role, having realized his preference for this kind of work, and feeling deprived of such an opportunity at Coke. And finally, Greg moved on when he realized that his lifestyle choices were not furthering his cause at the school. The notion of being trapped is at play here, though not necessarily a question of fit. However, in Jonatan's case, his realization that his youth and style did not fit with the company's culture was instrumental in his decision to leave.

Next come those with a career itch to scratch. They have been around for a while; they may have glimpsed an opportunity they could not pass up. Or they are burning to try something different, perhaps by changing industries or following a passion. They thought, "If not now, then when?". Sometimes that works out well, but sometimes it does not. Both Louise and Olivier left to join start-ups, with different outcomes. The seven-year itch is certainly not limited to marriage!

In his study, Almeda identified two other types of boomerangs: those whom a life event, following a spouse, or pausing to care for a sick relative forced to leave; and those who boomerang on purpose, either tactically or strategically. Almeda calls these "see you next year workers". Regular, planned boomerang moves are increasingly popular, particularly with "retired" boomers or interim, seasonal workers who come back and forth.

If we push this last "on-purpose" reason to a more long-term, extreme perspective, and apply it to executives, we may in fact see interesting cases of "the only way up is out", or something close to the Prodigal Son parable. Two executive-level cases come to mind. Alex Gorsky, CEO of Johnson & Johnson, left after a first chapter to join Novartis, where he served successfully for four years as head of the company's North America pharmaceuticals business. At the end of this period, he returned to J&J.

"I always knew I wanted to come back and finish my career at Johnson & Johnson", he said. Similarly, Guillaume Faury had served in various senior management functions at Eurocopter for ten years in 2008. But then to everyone's surprise, he quit and joined the carmaker Peugeot. People close to the situation believe his departure was driven by the limited prospects to take the top job. But then in 2013, he was called back and is now CEO of Airbus Helicopters and a member of the Airbus Group Executive Committee.

Whether the above moves were conscious, deliberate, or perhaps even some kind of "gentlemen's agreement" remains unclear. But in these cases, boomeranging can be seen as a strategic career move that helps ambitious executives find a quicker and more effective way to the top.

We can see the many reasons why boomerangs leave their company. But how does each one experience the departure? While leaving a company might look from the outside as an act of disloyalty, most boomerangs are actually attached to their organization, and seem to experience the decision as a difficult, emotionally challenging process. David likened his departure to that of abandoning a family, going so far as to say it was the most difficult day of his whole professional life. Former GE executive Bob Nardelli wrote a blog titled "Leaving Is Painful. Coming Back Is Amazing" in which he recalls the pain: "I made the choice… with a heavy heart and a lot of emotion, leaving behind great friends, associates and a world-renowned business… my business experience was solely GE. I only knew GE's culture, operating systems and governance."[46]

These boomerangs simply left to organizations and jobs that offered what they were no longer finding in the original company, and that valued their skills and experience. But while they were probably convinced that this was the right move for them at the time, was the grass eventually greener on the other side?

For some, it wasn't, and they soon realized they had made a mistake: David understood the duplicity of his Dior offer, and his mistake in accepting, quickly, but too late. Jonatan left Linz, seduced by the promise of a company that was more suited to his age and talents, but that "sensible" decision was not enough to hold him, so the return to the fold became logical too.

Others, like Louise, went with the flow, continuing to develop in the new organization, but remaining open to other opportunities, including in the organization they had previously left: Louise almost boomeranged several times before actually doing so, and we are back, possibly, to a case of serendipity, which would not have happened if she had not been open to the option.

For many, it appears they had "maxed-out" what they could learn in the other organization and felt keen to move on in search of bigger responsibilities: Olivier was happy to return to a global culture, while Greg looked for more "sparkle" on his return to his alma mater. Bob Nardelli states categorically that his skills were tested at Case Corporation, and his deficiencies honed in areas he did not have exposure to at GE, and this set him up for his bigger role on return.

How did the return happen? Two aspects of the move back seem to be important catalysts for the re-entry: The boomerangs remained in touch with the previous company, and in many instances the offer came directly from, or was initiated by, a former boss or a manager who knew the person well enough to value their return back. This was the case for Louise and David, and Bob Nardelli recounts: "I had to pinch myself when, four years later, Jack Welch and GE's HR Manager asked me to return to GE. We had all kept in touch and they were tracking my successes, and realizing the portability of my skills." Another boomerang we met, Luciana Balduino, on her return to J&J, mentions respect for the leader who brought her back, as well as a strong human element, as being key.

How easy was the transition back in? The stories we hear from boomerangs reveal a paradox: on the one hand, it felt like a simple "coming home", and on the other, most say their transitions were not as easy as they had thought, and did require some adjustments. In some cases, like for Louise, the return seems perfectly straightforward. She says it was "a simple, logical and pleasant process to go back".

But it is definitely not always that easy. Why? First, we should remember that the boomerang phenomenon is not yet that widespread. So the returner might feel some discomfort simply with the idea of going back. In David's case, his overriding sentiment was that "going back would be failure". He finally accepted out of guilt and emotion. The guilt element is also a driver to prove oneself, as Nardelli illustrates: "It's a tribute to Jack (Welch) and his GE culture that he asked me to return, although he subsequently often referred to my time away from GE as the time I 'ran away from home'. I came back to GE determined to prove that his decision was the right one."

The need for adjustment is driven by two main factors. First, while the executive was away, a lot of the organization moved on. Second, they typically re-enter in a different and/or bigger position. David was surprised to find a new organizational structure, a different place in the business cycle, and a new, more inward-facing culture, despite the fact he knew many of the leaders and key players. Olivier realized he was not "back in the family", but nevertheless enjoyed re-learning the ropes, and Luciana Balduino talks about learning and getting reacquainted as being key to her transition.

The Voice of Companies: A Strategic Re-use of Talent

BCG is putting its money where its mouth is with boomerangs. We talked to Nick South and James Kent, both partners at BCG, about how they treat boomerangs and other "unusual" senior hires. They are enthusiastic about this strategy, which is being used more frequently in their firm. We talked about Graham, whom we discussed in Chapter 5, but this time, it was with the idea of how to integrate a returner, or any new, experienced hire, which was hardly practiced at all in strategy consulting firms until a few years ago.

BCG has a philosophy which assumes that quality of thinking is a function of background, and that there is a need for a mix. In recent years, this has played out through bringing in more experienced hires, a move away from mainstream graduate and MBA hiring only. Thus the firm is paving the way towards building its talent pool differently.

The key questions at the outset are: "What's our value proposition to those folks? How can we support them in their adaptation to our idiosyncratic culture?" Hence, we realize how crucial onboarding is.

As with other transitions into and out of consulting, the first thing they have learned is that people need to be given a lot of time to understand how they work, even if they are returning. This might take the form of investing a long time in a first project: observing and learning how the thinking, the client interaction and everything else are done at BCG. They recognize this as a crucial stage, but say they have not yet got it right, though they are putting a lot of energy into it.

There are two main paths for returners: consulting and "expert" roles. Graham was a consultant in his first stint at BCG, though that was fifteen years ago, and on another continent. It was not obvious at the beginning whether he should follow the consulting or expert track, but, typically, BCG took the time to figure it out with Graham.

One of the crucial balancing acts required is that of applying the expertise, and feeling the value quickly from delivering that expertise. Graham returned after a long period away and had even been the CEO of a large hospital, so his skills had diverged a long way from those he had originally derived at the firm. What is more, BCG had brought him in at an immature stage of their healthcare consulting practice, so there was not always the full scope for activity. Initially they used him as a door-opener, and he was highly adept at this. However, once the projects were sold, it was harder to plug Graham's skills and tastes back in. He was frustrated by the "excess" of thinking that he observed, having worked in a large, underfunded health authority, while they found his expertise at the drop of a hat incredibly useful.

Eventually, both sides agreed that consulting in a team was not right for him, and they created a role in which Graham forms a bridge between BCG and healthcare clients. He plays a key role in introducing, making proposals, and being the "glue" in client relationships, though it has taken a long time to reach this happy place. Changing business needs, even since his return, have made it necessary to shift the role. BCG has finally identified ways in which they can tap into Graham's skills and expertise, and now they can focus on this both in an expert role and beyond the BCG teams.

BCG has the luxury of being able to take the time that many other companies would not have the patience for: their whole model is strongly apprenticeship-based, so they have a high tolerance for learning and taking the necessary time, adding self-reflection and candor to the mix. They try to ensure that they regularly ask the question: "Is it working for the individual as well for the clients?" They aim to make the expert returners feel that they have a real home, instead of just using them transactionally, deal by deal.

Nick and James observed that the number of returners and experts is rising dramatically, and that a different approach for recruitment will be required as they move in this direction. Is BCG alone in encouraging boomerangs? They answer that all consulting firms are busy building capability and experimenting with different models of expertise.

Back to the ongoing relationship with Graham – it has taken effort, energy and trust on his part too… and they know he has sometimes wondered about whether it was right. He has found balance by being part-time, and it is genuinely a mutually satisfying relationship, which they categorize as long-lived and successful.

L'Oréal is another company that is keen on rehires. Indeed, they currently make 250 rehires per year as part of their deliberate strategy. Their SVP for Talent Development and Chief Diversity Officer, Jean-Claude Le Grand, told us that the current approach is a 180-degree turn from the past. The current CEO, Jean-Paul Agon, was responsible for this change in strategy, and now about 6 percent of all management hires are rehires!

The company is encouraging many rehires, of the most talented people who have been "away" with the competition, such as Céline Brucker, who left to join Chanel for three years, and recently returned to L'Oréal as General Manager, Consumer Division, France. This strategy sends a clear and intentional message to both individual talents and the competition, says Jean-Claude, "we show that talents can gain from other experiences outside L'Oréal and we are willing to take them back under the right circumstances". The war for talent in the luxury and cosmetics space is unrelentingly fierce, and L'Oréal has found a winning new approach.

How do they do it? Well, by managing the connections in the alumni network. There are hundreds of members, and much work is put into keeping in touch and making it clear that the door might be open for return. This leads to an environment in which both push and pull happen, with some alumni asking to return, and some being invited specially.

What's in it for companies? In a 2016 article, Dr. John Sullivan remarks: "Boomerang efforts have one of the highest ROIs in recruiting. When you take the time to examine the profile of new hires who produce the best on-the-job performance, invariably previous employees returning to the organization, or 'boomerangs', make the list."[47]

Overall, employers face far fewer uncertainties when making boomerang hires compared to choosing an individual without prior experience in the company. Hiring managers will have great clarity about the skills, aptitude and cultural fit of former employees, which can inform decisions about where the person will best fit within the organization.

The advantages of rehiring former employees fall into three main categories:

- **Reduced hiring and training costs:**
  There is evidence that the use of boomerang hires can be 50 percent less expensive than normal recruitment channels (e.g. head-hunters, formal job postings). The accounting firm Deloitte estimated that in one year it saved $3.8 million in search firm fees by hiring former employees.[48] Cost effectiveness also comes from the lower cost of onboarding or retraining such employees and building their organizational commitment.

- **Strategic use of new skills and talent:**
  The professional who has worked with other employers brings new skills, talent, knowledge and experience acquired elsewhere. These can be used as a strategic advantage over competitors. The case of rehiring Gorsky as CEO of J&J brilliantly illustrates this point. Commenting on his selection process, the Wharton magazine wrote: "They had chosen him because of many different factors – including all the different businesses he had run… He had left the company and had come back with outside knowledge, and he had a chance to run the pharmaceutical business in Europe, the Middle East, Africa and Russia and learn how the geographic locations affected the different markets."[49] Similarly, Olivier's own sense of value remained intact when he re-entered Alcatel, as he realized that having seen other businesses, he had a fresh and useful perspective to bring. He describes it as an "external training" experience, which has allowed him to grow his value. Nardelli, too, saw that he gained extra benefits during his time away, not least the quality of

tolerance. He has since seen the opportunity to return the favor and brought back several talented individuals.

- **Inbuilt trustworthiness and a possible long-term relationship between employee and employer:**
  Both parties are well known to each other, so there is less need to worry about the trust between them. One can assume that this creates long lasting relationships with each other for the future – which we will discuss later in this chapter.

Tips for Rehiring Companies

- Make sure all exit interviews and processes make clear the possibility of a return, where this is something you might like.

- Ensure your people keep an open dialogue with you about their satisfactions and frustrations, to avoid departures that might be otherwise dealt with.

- Accept that a "breakup" may only be temporary, and stay civilized.

- Communicate regularly and positively with each segment of your "alumni" group, and facilitate their helping you with marketing, recruitment, project work and more.

- See the boomerangs as a source of renewed energy, expertise, and vision. Treat them kindly as they return, and encourage them to take a good look around before re-engaging.

How can companies use boomerangs strategically? This has been a much-discussed question for quite some time. As is often the case, the consultancies have led the way, and organizations such as McKinsey, Deloitte, EY and Microsoft are all pioneering corporate alumni programs to track good employees who have left and may want to come back. SAP, Nielsen and the Gates Foundation use online platforms to stay in closer touch with potential boomerangs, and rare is the larger company these days that does not, at the least, have an alumni group on LinkedIn. Booz Allen Hamilton has gone further, and created a dedicated team called the "Comeback Kids", which encourages increased boomerang action.

At A.P. Møller, an extremely traditional family business model was turned upside down, and the unthinkable done. As Jasper Madsen says, "I think we have grown out of the family-oriented type of business culture into a more performance-driven culture where it's not really about engaging into that marriage type of relationship with a company, but it's about making a contract where you agree that as an employer, we would like to get you in. And as an employee, I would like to get in, and offer my services for a period of time, and perhaps some time down the road, I want to try something else, but if I've been a good performer, I can certainly come back. So I think that the rationale behind that change should be seen as a change – or at least a modification – of our DNA."[50] If the centuries-old companies are able to shift their attitudes and actions, then any organization should, at least theoretically, be able to take advantage of this approach.

How to Make the Transition Happen

What advice do we have for the boomerangs? Louise and BCG recommend taking time. Both agree that this is a crucial investment, but it is a long-term strategy that not all may be comfortable with. Can was clear on the importance of friendly dialogue, and Nardelli underlines this, stating that extreme sensitivity is needed, as you never know which doors will be open and which not. Greg also "gets" the need for time, and a fresh view. This looks increasingly like one of the few guarantees of success in making a boomerang work effectively.

It is crucial to join employer groups on Facebook and LinkedIn, as well as to keep an eye on active job postings. The loops boomerangs may make are not necessarily predictable, as we have seen, but everyone can make themselves ready for it in this way. Nardelli closes by saying that it is important to ensure that you leave for the right reasons, and money and title "are not among them. Look for an opportunity that will allow you to grow, both personally and professionally. Hopefully, your companies' leaders will not hold such a decision against you, so long as you continue to share their vision, purpose and culture."

Tips for Boomerangs

- Keep dialogue light but clear and honest, and leave doors open on all exits.

- Understand a big element of your decision is based on humans, and remember humans are fallible and not in control of all aspects of destiny.

- Breaking up with your "family" is hard to do, but you can manage it.

- Do not expect to find your old company unchanged when you return – seek the opportunity to step back and renew your acquaintance.

- See every move to a new place as an opportunity to extend your expertise; then, whether you go back or not, you will be more highly valued.

When we asked ourselves if the boomerangs are still happy and if they have stayed, the answer is overall mixed. Three years on, of our six subjects: Can, Olivier, Jonatan and Bill are still with their companies, and Louise and David have moved on again. Of those who have stayed: Olivier is still in the same position, but his company has been acquired by Nokia, so it remains to be seen if he will stay long-term. Jonatan is in the same company, and more relaxed, settling into a happy personal life once again, and conscious of the privileges. Greg will likely stay until retirement, as he stated at the time. And Can will likely stay, as this new role is the one in which he found his maturity and his "place".

Of those who left: Louise seems to be pragmatic and opportunistic, having moved on to a CMO role in a smaller biotech company. This apparently contradicts her earlier conviction that "if you have a good boss and great colleagues... you can make it work". David, who showed signs he would move on for both growth and expatriation, is now with Apple Retail as EMEIA Employee/Labor Relations Director.

Should I Stay or Should I Go?

So, do boomerangs stay for good? And does it really matter? We hypothesize that the propensity to stay in the rehiring company is not high. It may be like the failure rate of second and third marriages: past statistics have shown that in the U.S., 50 percent of first marriages, 67 percent of second and 73 percent of third marriages end in divorce. In the end, the right question might be: does it really matter? For the professional, as long he or she is coming back for the right reasons and at the right time, and his or her overall career benefits... why not? For the company, they know exactly why they are rehiring someone, and are probably realistic about whether the person will stay.

High Profile Boomerangs

Name	Boomerang Company	Top Positions (Inside or Outside Boomerang Company)
Steve Jobs	Apple Inc.	Co-founder, Chairman, and CEO of Apple Inc.
A.J. Lafley	Procter & Gamble	CEO, Executive Chairman of P&G
Howard Schultz	Starbucks	Chairman and CEO of Starbucks
Michael Dell	Dell Technologies	Founder, Chairman and CEO of Dell Technologies
Alex Goski	Johnson & Johnson	CEO of Johnson & Johnson COO, Novartis Pharmaceuticals Corporation
Guillaume Faury	Airbus Helicopters	CEO of Airbus Helicopters and member of the Airbus Group Executive Committee Executive Vice-President R&D of Peugeot SA
Pierre Laubies	Mars Incorporated	CEO, Jacobs Douwe Egberts Global Petcare President, Mars Incorporated
Marie-Anne Aymerich	Unilever	Senior Vice President, Oral Care, Unilever Brand Managing Director, Parfums Christian Dior

Summing it Up

We can see that this sort of return transition creates a huge opportunity to build on the past and to create a new future. This future presents certain risks, but far fewer than those involved in a brand new recruit. We see some of the pitfalls in these stories, but far more possibilities for both sides that the exercise creates. The number of companies actively seeking to exploit this fruitful talent pool is growing, and this upward trend is likely to continue for many years to come. For both individual and corporation, this is something that can be positively managed from today onward.

Though we see the "diminishing returns" effect even more strikingly now that we are two years on from our research, and some of our boomerangs have moved on again, we still emphatically recommend this approach to all at some stage of the career or recruitment cycle. Even if the "stay" on return is typically shorter than the first time, it does seem pretty clear that the marginal benefits far outweigh the "troubles".

Further Reading and Information

▌ ARTICLES AND BLOGS

"Leaving Is Painful. Coming Back Is Amazing", by Bob Nardelli, LinkedIn blog post, 9 September 2016

"Companies Tap Alumni for New Business and New Workers", by Lindsay Gellman, The Wall Street Journal, February 21, 2016

"Welcome Back: Boomerang Employees Are On The Rise", by Kerry Hannon, Forbes, 7 September 2015

"Boomerang CEOs: 10 Top Executives Who Came Back to Rescue Their Companies", by Millie Dent, The Fiscal Times, October 5, 2015

"Boomerang bosses", Schumpeter, The Economist, June 1, 2013

▌ WEBSITES

BCG Alumni "Once a BCGer, Always a BCGer"
www.bcg.com/people/alumni/default.aspx

Booz Allen "Comeback kids"
www.boozallen.com/careers/find-your-job/former-booz-allen-employees

L'Oreal Alumni Association "A Beautiful Network" www.lorealalumni.com

Chapter 8

Back After a Long Break

Navigating Your Way Back In

It is 2017, and it has been more than fifty years since women defiantly burnt their bras in the struggle for equality. Yet 95 percent of executives who take a career break for child-raising or family caring are still women. This galling fact was presented to us by Julianne Miles, co-founder of a revolutionary firm called Women Returners, which, as its name suggests, exists to reduce the risks for both the individual and the organization in orchestrating a return to the workplace after a prolonged break.

Even more saddening is the fact that return to work is typically extremely difficult, for a variety of reasons which we explore in this chapter. The stories we tell range from dismal to inspirational, and should serve to stimulate us all to greater and better action in this tough, but common navigation.

Barbara

We start with Barbara, who has recently undertaken what she calls her "fourth transition", confidently having become an expert over the years in reflecting on what changes of context are appropriate for her at any given moment. Having dropped out of university with literally no idea of what she wanted to do, she entered the advertising industry via the secretarial route, and fought hard to climb up. She worked for a few years in a variety of independent agencies, progressing in a series of account management roles, and then decided to pursue an MBA. During a lecture on intangible assets, she had an "Aha!" moment, concluding that the next big business issue would be people, so she signed up for the HR route.

Having returned to the advertising industry and moved effectively up the HR ladder, she then slipped out of the fast lane while taking a calculated break to raise her two growing children. She had returned each time after giving birth, and juggled a mix of full-time and part-time roles, refusing to step down a level in compromise, but was finding this increasingly difficult. When the children reached ages 6 and 8, she felt they needed more support from at least one of their parents, so she took a total break from her role. The plan was to take five years off, until they were both in secondary school, while doing constructive things around her parenting, like local volunteer work and a doctorate. But after the break, she found that she did not really want to go back to the corporate world. This carefully considered choice was facilitated by financial comfort and stability, as her husband was the major bread-winner.

While Barbara was clear about what she did not want to do (big corporates or HR for SMEs), it took her about a year to identify what she did want to spend the rest of her working life doing. Her passion for people and HR had not disappeared, but her slightly "north of fifty" age did not help, and she did not wish to play the old corporate games any longer.

Having established that setting up on her own was the best option, Barbara, whose thinking was facilitated by Women Returners, finally identified a clear niche business opportunity in the home decoration area, despite not having, as she puts it, "a craft bone in my body". The Doubleknot Company, which hand makes blankets, has been in existence for over a year, with promising repeat and multiple purchases giving Barbara a sense she has made the right decision. Though, as she says, "I am old enough, nevertheless, to know that there will be bobbing and weaving involved to maintain the success and the growth".

Though she did grieve her old corporate life for some time, especially the companionship, the brain-storming, the resources and the professional identity, that mourning is over, as she relishes the freedom and flexibility. She recognizes that family support, both mentally and financially, have been crucial in this transition. When asked what advice she would give, she refers to a need for comfort with ambiguity and a flexible attitude. "Use those flexibility skills in combination with a plan", she recommends.

She believes that resilience and tenacity are key to surviving the juggling act of working parents, and that young people should be encouraged to acquire resilience early, whether through sport or other activities that require sustained effort and commitment. The pressure to manage transition comes quickly in most careers these days. Barbara adapted successfully multiple times, demonstrating to us all that even the most apparently challenging transitions are possible with a large dose of resilience.

Jenna

Jenna's story is less encouraging, though she is far from unhappy. The transitions she has made in and out of the law profession are actually impressive, and her story is possibly more one of a missed calling elsewhere, combined with exceptionally tough non-controllable events.

A brilliant scholar at Cambridge, Jenna graduated in Natural Sciences. She possessed a passion for numbers and analysis, but she ended up prepared for a career in law. After training, she worked in structured finance in an investment bank and did extremely well, being lucky to be in the boom of the early '90s. But when her first daughter was born, she had just changed companies, and had no rights accrued to maternity leave or a proper return. This started a pattern of what might be called "odds stacked against her".

As a result of these constraints, Jenna returned to work rapidly after giving birth, though this situation was shortly to be interrupted by her tax lawyer husband's move to partnership, which meant that they moved house, thus causing her to leave the job to which she had only just returned.

A brief period spent in her husband's firm helped get her CV current again after the two-year break she had experienced, and this allowed her to move to another firm where the hours were unbearably long. At the same time, her husband's job was under threat, and his health was at risk, with the possibility of a brain tumor. In the end, it was Jenna's own health that posed even more of a problem, and she suffered a heart attack, aged less than forty.

While convalescing and taking stock, she did some more teaching and then wanted to return to the legal world, which proved to be a far greater challenge than she had expected. The recession had dug in, and she had built up a significant amount of time away from her high-flier role. She was now perceived by the headhunters as out of date and redundant. She was looking for a part-time role, and they told her that this was impossible.

Having given up on help from headhunters, Jenna injected some common sense into the situation and began contacting the law firms closest to her home. To her amazement, she found that the very first one she asked was happy to talk. They worked out a comfortable arrangement with her that meant she worked four days per week, in school term time only.

However, despite the wonderful return to ideal circumstances, Jenna's bliss was not to last long. Her second daughter fell ill, and needed to have proper care from her mother. At this point, Jenna left the law firm. She has never returned to formal employment. She does manage a real estate portfolio and has been on non-executive boards of various kinds, so her brain is not idle; this time she too believes she has become unemployable.

She dreams of returning to academia and of doing a Maths PhD, and one senses that she is really more cut out for that approach to work than the city rat-race. Having total financial security, she points out that she lives on a road of multi-million dollar houses occupied by highly educated, highly competent women who no longer work. Jenna still finds fulfillment in teaching a local boy who has dropped out of school and in supporting others in her community, but her ennui and search for the next part of the "continuum" she describes are palpable. Did her earlier juggling and remarkable instinct for survival kill the instinct to continue? She herself says "I have never made 'head' of anything, indeed, I sometimes wonder if I am just a quitter". And yet, is it really Jenna who has a lack of grit? Or is it the system that makes it so hard to effect a comfortable return?

Argyro

Argyro is someone who has known work for a long time. Family constraints forced her to begin her career at the age of 17. She paid her way through university and found her first job in a French retail company thanks to her early experience in the tourism business in her native Greece. After an initial stint in customer services, she moved into sales and purchasing, finishing up as European Purchasing Coordinator in Geneva. During this time, she saved hard to do an MBA, and on graduation from INSEAD, "ended up more or less by accident" at McKinsey in their London office. At the same time as this, she met her future husband, a Greek entrepreneur.

While she loved the challenging assignments at McKinsey, Argyro decided to return to her home country and found a role organizing the retail division of the Athens International Airport in the build-up to the Olympic Games. From this came an invitation to help one of the airport "tenants" to build stores and brands, so she entered the world of luxury as General Manager of their Greek subsidiary, which she thoroughly enjoyed.

As she discovered she was pregnant with her first child, Argyro started to see strong signals that her company was going to be acquired. Her reluctance to be a part of the post-merger structure, as well as a recognition that she did not want to sacrifice time with her baby led her to part ways amicably with her company, but she was not planning a long break.

However, another pregnancy prolonged the gap, and this was the first time since she was seventeen that Argyro was able to take stock and ask herself a few "serious questions". She wondered if she had the opportunity for a "second career". Should it be about joy? Passion? Expertise? Sustainable for a later stage of life? This reflection showed her that what she most enjoyed was people: "creating beautiful teams of talented people and helping them grow". So she went to do a second degree, this time in Strategy and HR Management, while still pregnant with the second child.

After a failed attempt to return to work after baby number two, Argyro managed to get back after number three, once she had realized that she needed to use her experience as a consultant as the lever. Although she was aiming for a line HR role, it was now obvious that being an HR consultant first was the route to take. This she got, and spent one year happily developing her abilities, after which she was called by a London-based multinational spirits and beverage company to work as HR Director, Greece. From this role, she developed fast to Europe-wide roles of increasing seniority, and finally left when it was no longer possible to add strategic value from Athens when the roles she was suited to were in London.

Argyro now occupies a key strategic and global role in one of the largest companies in Greece, and has apparently got things well figured out. She talks of the importance of knowing her own limits, and working constructively with them. She also mentions that she "chooses" to work with nice people: "We all have families, so it is engrained that we all encourage a healthy balance". She and her colleagues measure her performance by what she accomplishes and not by how she organizes her day to accommodate work and family commitments. She points to an increase in maturity of attitude in this regard, at least in her environment.

Reflecting on her career and life journey, Argyro tells us how clear it was to her that her husband's support had been crucial. She describes him as a generous supporter who welcomes her growth and is proud of it. He is a participative parent, and things are equitable between them. They work as a partnership, and balance and development are a priority for both of them.

Tim

Tim also made a choice to value parenting over corporate life, though in a different way and order than that used by Argyro. After a classic, successful and travel-heavy start in FMCG marketing, moving from single brand/single country to increasingly senior roles mostly across Europe, his situation was comfortable, with a wife and young family in tow. He was often away on business and worked late in the evening, but this was nothing unusual at P&G. His wife was also carving out a career in the same company, but they somehow juggled as best they could all the different travel itineraries, deadlines, and the raising of their two children.

Questions had started arising in Tim's mind about whether the balance was quite right, but the house of cards was not tumbling down yet, so he persisted. One evening, he came home from a long business trip to Africa to find a note on his bed from his nine-year-old daughter, asking that he attend a "meeting" with her ASAP. The next day, she explained: "Daddy, how can I love you if I never see you?". Tim resigned only ten days after this bombshell, fortunately in the knowledge that his wife had been offered an opportunity to take a role in the European HQ of P&G. As he and his wife worked through the aftermath, they recognized many other shocking aspects, such as the fact that their younger daughter's language was increasingly dominated by Tagalog – the language of their wonderful Filipina nanny!

Tim says he does not judge those who do not hear or heed such wake-up calls, but he also does not pretend that the change was easy. Moving to Geneva in itself was not a big challenge, but his new role as full-time father took more getting used to. He missed a familiar list of routine and having plans, and experienced a certain amount of emptiness and guilt, both at what he had caused and what he had given up.

Unlike other "stay at home fathers", Tim threw himself actively into a variety of tasks, including doing the school run morning and afternoon, socializing and building constructive relationships with other school parents – almost exclusively mothers. There was no problem whatever in his being accepted into the group, despite his obvious difference. And when, after a year, he found himself able to say "my name is Tim and I am a stay-at-home dad", he knew he had "made it".

While Tim was occupied with several other projects at the time, such as a role in a small start-up and designing and building a house, he describes his role of father as a 90 percent occupation of his time. As his daughters grew, his involvement with the school grew too and Tim's question became: "Can I mix the important parts of being a dad with the world of work?".

When, by serendipity, he was contacted by a consultancy firm, he took on a project, which led to another, and now he is helping them to develop their business. This is facilitated by an actively present grandmother, who willingly supports and helps out.

On the subject of the future, Tim is open and relaxed. For now, he sees the win-win of combining all the good parts of work with the emotional parts of being a father. He remains open to reverting to father at work/mother at home, if that ever feels appropriate again. He is actively modeling his approach in his workplace, repeating often that "he does not want this to get in the way of his being a dad". As he puts it, "this role has become a necessary part of 'being me', though I find a way to ensure the client always comes first". This is achieved by his being in the office early and working creatively from home and office to get things done appropriately.

When quizzed on how this works out for the couple, he is unequivocal: it only works if the two are perfectly aligned, and it helps tremendously if there is capital already saved so as to avoid a drastic drop in lifestyle. As he says "nobody is deprived, but we do control our spending in a way we would not have done a few years ago". He recognizes that the feelings of guilt and discomfort at the outset were inevitable and the reflection of a substantial change, but that they have been more than compensated for by the positive change in the family as a result.

The final big advantage as a result of his choices is that of having become a better decision-maker. Tim says he is much better at identifying and setting priorities and bringing the right mix of emotion and practicality to any choice he faces these days.

Tim and his family should be admired for making this brave choice, but we should recognize that it is "exceptional" only because he is a man. The kinds of challenges he describes are no different to those undergone by countless mothers, apart from the fact that he is a man, not a woman – to which we will return later in this chapter.

Mui Gek

A Singaporean national, Mui Gek fell into the shopping center business by accident. She spent a few early years as a civil engineer before being referred by a friend to a leasing role in the years that Raffles City shopping center was being renovated and repositioned. She excelled in this role, becoming adept at development, analysis and tough negotiation, and was soon snapped up by the giant Hong Kong Land when they were entering the local market with a new mall. Her reputation and her quick learning came into play, and her success was once again resounding.

When the mall was open, she was given responsibility for marketing and tenant relationship management.

In the meantime, Mui Gek had married a Frenchman, and they decided to move "back" to France, landing in a provincial city just after 9/11. She aimed to use her experience to enter the French luxury goods industry, and so started out by studying the language and doing an MBA in a local business school. From here on, the story becomes one of grit and determination, as it was a Herculean task for Mui Gek to find a job in a tough market as a visibly and audibly foreign person in a provincial French city.

She created an extensive network from scratch out of her immediate friends, MBA teachers and family. The networking exercise landed her first job, working in a family business, with a large project to go and explore the Chinese market for shopping centers. On her return, with the news that it was not yet ripe for the offer, her employers encouraged her to stay on a while longer. Mui Gek wasted no time in learning new skills. The breadth of ability she was developing was to serve her soon in another, more challenging search.

While pregnant with her first child, Mui Gek and her husband decided that she would take a break to have the baby and to figure out her next move. However, less than two years later, they found themselves with a toddler and newborn twins. While handling the 600+ diapers per month, Mui Gek was happy to become a mother, and was well supported by her husband, though she admits she had not instinctively been a maternal type. But when the twins were approaching two years old, she started to feel it could be interesting to return to work.

Yet again, networking skills came to the fore, and she worked her little black book harder than ever before. This time, it led to an introduction to none other than Antoine, one of the authors of this book, who was at the time recently appointed as head of talent at LVMH. Mui Gek's mix of skills was unusual, to say the least, and not one that neatly fit any particular vacant job in the luxury group. Her difference was that, beyond her obvious real estate and retail experience, she had doggedly stayed up to date on workplace issues, fashion, luxury and more.

Her conversations with LVMH were pleasant, but not fruitful. In the meantime, her husband's work was moving geography and they were planning a move to Brussels. But shortly before the move, she received a call from LVMH offering her a perfect job that required all of her skills. The couple realized it was an opportunity not to be refused. As her husband Olivier said: "If you don't take this, you will never work again".

Her demonstration of consistent learning was the clincher. This new role was created especially for her. LVMH felt they needed this mix, given that their real estate strategy was inharmonious, and an expert hand with negotiation and diplomacy skills could be a great asset. She was, as she says, "the right person at the right time".

Career Transition Navigator

EXPAND

Mui Gek disproved the naysayers, getting past her language and accent problems, networking furiously to make friends and allies all over, and using her unique blend of knowledge, passion and persuasion to bring them on board. As a result, not only has she created a hitherto unheard-of collaboration between previously hostile, competitive brands, but she has also been offered increasingly interesting and developmental roles, which she handles with confidence, disarming more than one senior executive, and somehow charming them with her frank, different style. Mui Gek hopes to continue to create options for herself and the company while keeping balance at home.

What's Going On? The Tortuous Route Back to Work

Our stories in this chapter are perhaps more similar than in other chapters, and this may well be significant. While we have attempted to show a range, we have nevertheless not related any total shipwrecks; of these there are many. We know that the subjects we interviewed in this case are all naturally endowed with sufficient self-confidence to have beaten the odds.

However, even in their case, it is clear that there was a feeling of losing touch with the business world, as well as loss of practice in the self-promotion that is such an important part of survival in daily life in a corporation. It follows that numerous rejections, as a person attempts to return, will do little to restore confidence, and indeed lead potentially to a sense of uselessness and social pressure that could easily end up in failure to return. Only those who are built of stern stuff, or those who are helped and supported, will get past this significant and constant obstacle of questioning.

A recent high-profile case of a top executive stepping down in order to assume a caring role is that of Christi Shaw, CEO of drug giant Novartis's U.S. business.[51] She tendered her resignation in order to care full-time for her sister, who is fighting cancer and is involved in a demanding and critical clinical trial. This has caused much surprise both from inside Novartis and from the business world, though Christi sees this as a necessary risk – one worth taking whatever the odds: "Am I taking myself off the career track? Have I leveraged the skills I have to become a CEO? That's still a question. But I have to say, I'm okay if I derail myself", says Shaw.

The external perception of an individual who is trying to return to the workplace plays a major role. Most headhunters and recruitment departments are unwilling to get past their view that the individual has lost his or her skills, and that they have thus become inherently "risky". The situation is further exacerbated by those recruiters' inability to see the value of what the returner has been doing during the break. If the competencies derived from organizing the priorities and managing a family of five, or from analyzing and researching the market for appropriate schools are not clear, then it is important to ensure that this changes. It is easy to talk glibly about "transferable competencies" but perhaps harder to put the idea into action.

Another extremely important factor is that the desire or need to return to work typically coincides with a broader series of changes and questionings that include such aspects as growing family, spouse changing job or status, relocation or expatriation and so on. This means that the return is only one small piece in a complex jigsaw puzzle, making it even more difficult to tackle. Jenna really is the best example of this, as she pushed past all kinds of other challenges on her route to find the right way to return. It can be overwhelming to start the search, and there may be a real or sensed lack of time to devote to it, especially if there is no family or external support. We know from our own experience how difficult it can be to carve out time for a job search when you are attending to domestic responsibilities, and this becomes an ongoing issue for many.

The stretching of time that comes about in this protracted break period tends to lead to an opportunity to redefine oneself or one's career, and many, like Argyro or Barbara, end up making a much bigger change to their status than they might have initially planned. They not only return; they transform. A 2005 study done at the Wharton School showed that only 39 percent of returners take the same kind of job they were doing when they left, and this fact, while liberating on the one hand, makes focus on "just getting back" even more difficult.[52] A reader of our original article, published in INSEAD Knowledge, commented, "I also think there is something positive about being thrown out of your career. You need to focus, set priorities and think hard about what you want in life. And that is a unique opportunity a lot of people who never leave their hamster wheel don't have."

We see in our accounts individuals who have been supported by family and comfortable finances, however difficult this balancing act may have been. The constant and unerring support and friendly ear of a partner, or the willingness to switch roles at home, make it easier to envisage big change elsewhere. There are also countless individuals who are not so lucky with their family situation. The balance is a lot less easy to find if you are on your own and there is no friendly grandma down the road – a reality faced by millions.

Finances can affect the situation in both directions, as exemplified by some of our interviewees. If the situation is economically comfortable, there can be a lack of incentive to return, as with Jenna; though others might respond with the sense of freedom to choose and redefine themselves without constraint. However, if there is not enough money, then the pressure to return, whatever the circumstances, can lead to stress and compromises that create later challenges. This is probably one area in which we cannot lay the blame in any way at the feet of the corporations...

In Tim's story, we commented on how his choices would have been relatively unexceptional had he been a woman. This is in no way to detract from the courageous path that he and his wife have taken, but it is, unfortunately, a reflection of a grim reality. The impact of a gap and subsequent return, and the way these are perceived, is different in men and women. A 2005 study by Reitman and Schneer found that early career employment gaps had negative effects for as long as 25 years after they occurred, and that such interruptions also had a negative impact on career satisfaction for men, but not for women. Men probably get the tougher end of the deal if they make the choice to take a break, as demonstrated in a 2007 article by Eve Tahmincioglu: "Men have the added problem of trying to return to work in a society that just doesn't get why they made the decision to leave a budding career in the first place. Even though women face similar discrimination, experts say, society is more accepting of moms making such a choice. Men, on the other hand, are thought of as 'unmanly', when they decide to become the nurturer and take time away from the traditional hunter role".[53]

It is worth recognizing that, according to U.S. government data, the mother is a full-time stay-at-home mother in over 31 percent of all married couples with children. Stay-at-home fathers make up less than 5 percent. This balance may well be influenced by the national strategy of each government with regard to issues such as parenting leave, costs and availability of childcare and so on. But the difference is significant.

While we see some signs of change, even our "success" stories show that most companies are insufficiently equipped for and lack the flexibility required to facilitate re-entry. There are still limited part-time opportunities or flexible arrangements available compared to the needs of those contemplating a return. Though this varies by country, there is much to be done even in those with the best situations currently. Thankfully, there are emerging initiatives, which we shall cover later in this chapter, and these need substantial encouragement if we are to create hope.

The Voice of Companies: A Bridge Back to Work for Talent

Given the distance that needs to be covered before conditions for return after a break are optimal, there were not so many company directors willing to speak to us about their record and their (not so) proactive attitudes. However, we were able to talk at length with the founder of Tim's employer, Will Hogg. It is clear from his comments that Kinetic Consulting is friendly indeed to returners of all kinds.

He started by explaining that for him and his board, when they were considering whether to offer a role to Tim, the fact that he came with "strings attached" was simply not a big deal. Indeed, it was abundantly clear to them that this was his situation, and that it was up to them to accept it, embrace it or reject it. Tim told his story on first introduction to them (as he continues to do) and part of the attraction was that they were already specifically set up to accommodate situations like his.

Indeed, this is the "norm" at Kinetic, as the network is ready to work with different life stages, work stages and lifestyles, with this adding to the value of the work they do for their clients, given the breadth and diversity of perspective and experience it implies compared to traditional models. They have people on reduced schedules for a broad variety of situations, with some on job share and others who have taken a career break for personal reasons. They have always offered full flexibility so long as the principle is mutual benefit for the employee and the company. Indeed, one of the significant advantages perceived by Will and his colleagues is that the company's engagement, and therefore retention rate is extremely high, given that changing needs can be catered for, and everyone feels included in a genuine way, instead of the lip service that so many companies pay to the diversity and inclusion question.

He adds that one theoretical disadvantage is complexity in terms of managing different arrangements, but this is seen as "nothing, compared to the advantages". This attitude brings hope to the picture, and indicates some of the key behaviors, attitudes and actions required of a company that aspires to make a return easy, rewarding and satisfying for all parties.

Emerging initiatives from corporations to help professionals return to work also give a ray of hope. Financial institutions and professional services firms have woken up to the attractive qualities of a pool of talent that they have overlooked. In an effort to access scarce skills, a growing number of these organizations have introduced "returnship programs" to provide a bridge back to work for high caliber men and women who want to return to corporate life and find the path blocked by a gap on their CV. Goldman Sachs first coined the phrase "returnship" in 2008 to describe its 10-week paid program to reintegrate people – usually mothers – after extended career breaks. This innovative route back to work reached the UK in 2014, and many other international financial institutions followed, including Morgan Stanley, Credit Suisse, RBS, JP Morgan and Lloyds Bank.

Is there any evidence of the success of these returnship programs? Longer term data from Goldman Sachs indicates the bank has consistently taken on half of their returnship participants into permanent positions. More recent data on UK returnship programs suggests that retention rates may be even higher. Interestingly, those who have found permanent jobs have subsequently sparked discussions with their employers about more flexible forms of working. This has prompted banks to think about their returners before they have even left. According to research by the consultancy Women Returners, the overall number of programs in the UK has tripled, from three in 2014 (all in banking) to nine in 2015 (five in banking). Evidently, these schemes are proving popular and transformational and are spreading rapidly across countries and industries, with banks, professional services firms, universities and government agencies most prominent at this stage.

There are an increasing number of consultancies and coaches who specialize in supporting individuals of both sexes during their re-entry attempts, though the majority of these are geared towards women. These include prominent companies like iRelaunch, She's Back and Women Returners (interviewed by us for their expertise in this area), and multiple smaller firms and individuals, like Talking Talent.

Not everyone will want or be able to seek professional help to facilitate a return to work, but there are alternatives. A number of articles and blogs exist on the subject, and a list of these can be found at the end of this chapter.

Those individuals who wish to return need to deal with the realities of their situation. This includes recognizing that more than half of workers returning from career breaks sign on with companies smaller than those they left, and that smaller employers tend to be less hung up on conventional career ladders. This fact makes checking out such firms even more important in a challenging economic market. A degree of persistence and grit will be required to battle the odds, and this may be something that needs further development in this challenging phase.

Corporations could undoubtedly make these returns easier, and the returners themselves, who battle history, tradition and practical reality with courage every single day will need to continue to bring out their steeliest nerves in order to make these transitions productive and rewarding. A study shared on the She's Back website showed that "failure to re-engage with mums who have left the workforce" cost $3m per year.[54] We look forward to a time when all corporations genuinely do something about this in order to create benefit, value and comfort for all.

How to Make It Happen?

Whether helped by coaches and consultants or not, the returners must be clear about what they want before they chase it, and must be strong and creative in their search to find it. The fight for the right treatment will not be easy. By the same token, the "receiving" companies will do best if they properly understand the predicament their returners are in, and make room for that to become a strength rather than an obstacle. Below are eight key tips we have gleaned for the returners.

- **Clarify your future career goals** – Take stock and use your time to know yourself better, define what you want to do and plot where you want to be in ten years time.

- **Update your skills and knowledge** – Stay current with your fields of expertise, upgrade your credentials, invest in relevant training and do volunteer work to learn or hone skills.

- **Use creative job search strategies** – Classic job search tactics will not work; headhunters will ignore you. Mine neighborhood or local job opportunities and investigate "returnship" programs.

- **Network in depth** – Reactivate and broaden your professional and personal networks for feedback, support, advice and leads.

- **Seek family support** – Secure financial, mental and emotional support from your partner, agree how you will rebalance or switch times and roles and look for help from participative parents.

- **Boost your confidence** – Be clear and confident about your strengths and emphasize the value you can bring to an employer rather than your time away.

- **Be prepared to compromise** – Get ready to adjust your standards of living; be open to taking a step down in pay and status; and consider part-time, interim or freelance work.

- **Build resilience early on** – Be prepared to navigate through multiple career breaks and non-controllable events, and develop a flexible attitude and a resilient mindset.

Final Thoughts

Of all the battles our subjects have had to go through, this one looks, on the surface, like one of the hardest to handle. However, we can see much evidence for the speedy implementation of many more returnships, as they are rapidly demonstrating their value in such a tangible way.

Despite the challenges for each individual, we see that when it is well-handled by the company, the net result is simple to achieve – and not necessarily even all that costly. The returner knows how to do the job, even if some skills need to be sharpened, and so the adjustments necessary are more about common sense than anything else.

Frequently, when the barriers to good change are only low, as here, the change is easily tackled and quickly becomes a norm. We can only hope that this will be the case across the board, and soon. We will also do all we can, as professional coaches and consultants, to see to it that organizations fully play their part.

Further Reading and Information

❙ BOOKS AND STUDIES

"Back on the Career Track: A Guide for Stay-at-Home Moms Who Want to Return to Work", by Carol Fishman Cohen and Vivian Steir Rabin, CreateSpace Independent Publishing Platform, August 2008

❙ ARTICLES AND BLOGS

"How to return to work after a long career break", by Julianne Miles and Katerina Gould, The Telegraph, August 29, 2014

"Helping Women Get Back in the Game", by Jennifer Preston,

The New York Times, March 17, 2014

"7 Keys To Rejoining The Workforce After A Long Break", by Susan Adams, Forbes, November 18, 2013

"Getting From At-Home to On-the-Job, Even Now", by Sue Shellenbarger, The Wall Street Journal, July 29, 2009

▌ WEBSITES

"How to get back to work after a career break", Carol Fishman Cohen, TEDxBeaconStreet, November 2015

iRelaunch – The Return-To-Work Experts
www.irelaunch.com

Women Returners – A coaching, consulting and network organization which specializes in enabling the return to work of professional women
womenreturners.com

Goldman Sachs Returnship Program.
www.goldmansachs.com/careers/experienced-professionals/returnship/

Chapter 9

Diaspora Returns

Handling the Landing Back "Home"

The tide of brain drain from developing to developed nations has turned, as a growing number of highly skilled Indians, Chinese, Brazilians and Nigerians are flooding their home countries after a long time away. They originally left either as children with their emigrant parents, or for study or early career opportunities. They return in search of identity, in search of bigger opportunities, to look after aging parents, to seek their roots or a combination of these. The countries they leave are increasingly the losers in this transaction as these are typically the brightest and best.

In this chapter, we wanted to see what happens when these individuals hit the ground "back home". What are the challenges? What are the chances of success and of staying in this new "home"? Has the period away been of value in making them successful on home terrain? Is it worth the upheaval? Our subjects have experienced a variety of situations and reactions, displaying a great complexity of context. Through their stories, we hope to find some wisdom and advice for those contemplating this sort of journey towards repatriation, and for anyone who is considering employing a repat.

Marta

Perhaps our most classic case is that of Marta, who is the founder and CEO of Wasi Organics, in Peru. She left her home country for study in Spain as a high school graduate, and went on to increasingly senior marketing roles in consumer-driven companies, including L'Oréal, American Express and Burger King, across Europe and the USA. She took a year in the middle of this 20-year expatriate stint to do an MBA at INSEAD, which further broadened her already global outlook. Having initially left Peru because of the glass ceiling, Marta ironically found herself working for a couple of years in Saudi Arabia, where she had to conform to local customs and dress and behave as was expected of a woman in that environment. While she enjoyed the challenge, she realized that she did not fit. As she did increasing amounts of travel and found herself married with two small babies, her tolerance for the busy executive lifestyle dwindled.

EXPLORE

Career Transition Navigator

The trigger for Marta contemplating a return to Peru was when a headhunter in London invited her to lunch, offering her the chance to take a CEO position. While she was tempted by this particular opportunity, she was intrigued that she was now perceived as a potential CEO, and she started to think hard about what she really wanted to do. It was not long until she concluded that she wanted to start her own business and to give back in some way to her own country. Sometime during Marta's twentieth year in Europe – eight years ago now – she returned home.

She had expected the transition to be difficult, but she did not expect being "completely lost". For three years she decided to go with the flow and not attempt big professional activities, as getting used to being back was "just too much". The three biggest challenges, as she describes them, were "getting a satisfying job" (never happened), "engaging the kids and settling them" (achieved, but easier for one than the other) and "getting a social life" (not as easy as expected). It took a while, but eventually Marta was able to put the pieces of the jigsaw puzzle together and create her own "not just for profit" company. Her giving back consists of working with small farmers to create excellent organic food products, taking advantage of the huge biodiversity and purity of the environment in Peru.

She realized that despite 20 years experience, a startup is not so easy to make work in her home country. She had to fine-tune her skills to a level she could not have imagined, and coming from abroad, it was a big stretch culturally. She hints at the bureaucracy and highlights the difficulty of dealing with people who say yes but do not deliver. Another huge struggle has been the perception that her employees and collaborators have of her direct, no-nonsense and demanding personality. While this worked wonders in her former companies, she believes it is only because she has a much "softer" business partner that they are still in business. Marta adapted her style somewhat once she realized the problem, and has found ways to soften her approach without compromising her grit and resilience.

While she is currently focusing on meeting milestones with her investors, Marta is open to more social entrepreneur opportunities and plans to seek a lifestyle traveling between Peru and Europe. Her children's study and future life is more likely to be in the latter, so she plans to build her professional life to straddle the geography.

Her advice to those contemplating a return to Peru is to practice yoga and meditation! She recommends enjoying the best things in life and seeing the glass as half-full. She emphasizes that trying to change everything does not work, and there is a huge grey area between imposing and giving up.

Ferdi

In a different part of the world, in the Philippines, lives another type of repat. Ferdinand is of Filipino ethnicity, but was actually born and raised in the U.S., his parents having immigrated there during the 1950s. His big difference is that he was raised as an American, with his parents even refusing to teach him Tagalog due to fears of racism and discrimination.

Ferdi's study and experience led him into increasingly senior roles in training and offshoring in large corporations. He became known as the Philippines expert, as his ability to empathize and understand the Filipinos is high. Despite appearances, though, he is still a foreigner. When dealing with Western clients or colleagues, he struggles to convince them that things are so different and difficult on this island nation, where most people speak disarmingly fluent English despite having attitudes and behaviors that are profoundly Asian.

The main struggle comes from the fact that Ferdi looks like a Filipino, but he is not treated as one by his employees. He has now been in the country for several years building an ambitious company, Doctourz, which aims to offer greater choice in medical services. Despite his role as a beneficent employer and as a talented connector of people and opportunities, he is stuck with staff who will not treat him with the disproportionate "on a pedestal" respect afforded to white expats but also refuse to communicate with him as a fellow countryman. He solves this by persevering in his work and surrounding himself with a small faithful "tribe" of like-minded repats and others. They can rejoice and commiserate on their lives as "bananas", as they are affectionately known (yellow on the outside, but white on the inside).

Ferdi believes that working in the Philippines is definitely still an opportunity, both financially and operationally, but admits it is a daily struggle. However, he says, while it is difficult, it is something he knows how to manage and this makes it all "worth it".

Does he see a future in the Philippines? Next year he is marrying his Filipino sweetheart, and this may attach him further to the country. He is also aware that most Filipinos, and he seems to count himself among them, have a deep attachment to their homeland, and that means many of them return for the latter part of their lives, even if they have spent decades away working overseas. With his own company growing and his status as CEO established, his struggle is diminishing and the fruits of his labor are ripening. He is gradually being eased up onto the pedestal, and things are getting easier daily. This looks like a successful integration, though it has been neither swift nor simple.

Bambina

While Ferdi has been back in the Philippines for almost 10 years, our next subject, Bambina, has only been back there for a few months. This Filipina-Spanish mestiza had spent a total of 30 years away from the Philippines, in many locations across Asia, Europe, the Middle East and Africa. Much of this time was spent pursuing a career in the luxury goods industry and public relations. Her studies of journalism and art history served her well, as did her remarkably international childhood, full of visits to her home from diplomats, journalists and other dignitaries from all over the world.

Although she had not travelled overseas much as a child, her first choice for university was the U.S., where she gained places in prestigious colleges and universities. However, conservatively, her parents refused to let her take these up, as she was only sixteen years old at the time, and they felt it was too far for her to go alone. Unperturbed, Bambina chose to go to study in Paris after her bachelor's degree, and thus started a period of several years in Europe and then Hong Kong. She worked mostly in the luxury goods industry, and most notably as head of business development of the jewelry business of Chanel Hong Kong.

For the many years she "followed" her expatriate (now ex-) husband, Bambina used her resourcefulness as well as her talent to garner all kinds of interesting writing and project work. After a protracted divorce, Bambina found herself stranded in South Africa with no official right to work, but needing to support her children and her new solo lifestyle. This was a challenge she rose to, ensuring a constant flow of freelance journalistic and media consulting projects.

As her girls grew up, she began to consider where her next move should be. While she might have been happy to go and live and work in Spain, she decided that the economy in Europe was not buoyant enough, and chose to return to her home country. Despite appearances, this has not been an easy transition. Bambina states that she is grateful for the fact that the Philippines is one of the rare cultures that rewards and values resilience and grit, and that seems to work strongly in her favor.

Slipping back into comfortable childhood friendships has been superficially easy, but it has been harder to feel "aligned" with those same people, however welcoming they are. Little by little she is finding the right level socially, feeling thankful that she comes from a certain class that allows her to move fluidly among all kinds of influential and interesting people.

While there was a significant professional project from the beginning of her return to the Philippines, Bambina has juggled freelance work with more long-term work, and spent a brief but professionally significant and happy period working as the head of communications for the APEC Business Advisory Council during the Philippines' chairmanship of APEC. She also held the role of lifestyle editor of one of the Philippines' major newspapers until recently, leaving due to professional differences. This break is no doubt emblematic of the tensions of a return, the culture clashes inevitably rearing up, and a sign that Bambina will not have an easy path to professional security. It is heartening to see her fighting to build a life that is in line with local conditions, but on her own terms. This is surely the challenge of any returner.

Yang

Another recent returner is Yang, who has only been back in his native China since the spring of this year. He is still in the "honeymoon" period of his return, wide-eyed at the noisy market in his street, where he can "buy breakfast of any kind whenever he wants", and disoriented in the perpetually changing mega-city that is Shanghai.

Nothing indicated that Yang would have a taste for travel and exploration. His parents were both in the Chinese military and forbidden to travel abroad; thus it was surprising that he chose to study English at university – less so when one discovers that he simply chose the subject he found most difficult, as a special challenge to himself.

During university, he did an internship in a significant Chinese consulting firm and noticed that "everyone in the glass offices around me had either a pretty decent education or else 20 years' experience in the industry". He decided to fund his own further education. On completing his undergraduate degree, his father gave him a gift of $30,000. Despite the lure of Beijing real estate, he decided to spend it on a British master's degree.

Yang was welcomed in St. Andrews, but struggled with all kinds of cultural challenges. He went to the pub for the first time, and, not knowing how or what to order, he copied his friend and ordered a gin and tonic. Through sheer inexperience and lack of confidence, he continued to order the same thing for months. Stumbling from one cultural gap to another, Yang made huge progress and performed well academically, even embarking on a PhD.

Early years of work were in companies that were able to exploit his foreign status. He grabbed every opportunity possible and finally started being able to approach headhunters, which coincided with a trend for offering "*diverse*"candidates. Finally, Yang's "foreignness" was a plus. This led him to an opportune graduate role at Thomson Reuters. From here on, his upward mobility was unstoppable.

As the only Chinese in Thomson Reuters Europe, Yang started to specialize in Renminbi, exploring ways of supporting banks in facilitating cross-border deals. His high intellect and curiosity, coupled with his abilities in networking, meeting and questioning the right people, allowed him to advance, even collaborating and signing agreements with significant ministers and decision-makers in both China and Europe. His proudest moment was being quoted by Bloomberg while he worked at Thomson Reuters.

Yang could have endlessly pursued his roles in the UK as a rainmaker, a star at Thomson Reuters and advisor to a prestigious Cambridge foundation. But a few months ago, some Chinese friends asked him to join them back in Shanghai, and Yang became a partner in Yaozhi Asset Management, an investment fund. Novelty and unfamiliarity surround him, but Yang's thirst for learning and knowledge is helping him once again. He even asked his new partners for an assistant to help him navigate both physically and practically around his new city. He talks more like a new expat than a native of this country.

Not content with changing sector, status and country, Yang began studying the cello. He does not know yet whether he will stay in China definitively, but he does understand that, for now, he is going to need to work incredibly hard in order to fit into the Chinese working culture. A few weeks back, he suggested that he might take a break in order to go deliver some lectures at the Cambridge foundation, and was told that it would not be appropriate for him to take a break at this point. Yang accepted this contrasting attitude, despite its clash.

What would he recommend to those considering a return to a home country – especially to China? He answers that people should ask themselves the following questions: Am I motivated? Am I flexible enough to readapt to this extraordinary culture? Do I have friends who are aligned with my thoughts, feelings and experiences? If your answers are yes, then go ahead and live a great adventure. Yang is still in the early stages of his adventure, but it would seem that he is going to make a success of his repatriation, however hard that might be.

Ike

Finally, we look at Ike, a serial entrepreneur and seller of highly successful businesses. He was born in Nigeria into a diplomatic family, and spent his nomadic childhood building his first companies – selling popcorn to his friends at movie nights in Zimbabwe and cold drinks to the inhabitants of his residential towers in Nigeria. This beginning predisposed him to a lifestyle of travel beyond the national borders and with entrepreneurship strongly featured. Of our five subjects, Ike has been back home for the longest time. He seems the most settled and, on reflection, enthusiastic about his return.

Having ended up in the U.S. for his studies, almost by coincidence, he found that he really enjoyed the contrast afforded by different approaches, and the chance to make close friends and connections in both his cultures. Ike states repeatedly that he believes he was dealt "an incredibly lucky set of cards in life", with a Silicon Valley education, an engineering qualification and a taste for business. This was the magic combination for success in a series of start-ups. Having navigated several national cultures before, it was easy for him to manage the two worlds of engineering and business to his advantage. When quizzed on what drove him to create, Ike talks about a lack of fear. With mostly a laugh, he said that "If you have been put alone on a plane from Harare to London, aged nine, and had to get yourself from Heathrow into central London, and then onto a train to South Devon, finally hailing a taxi to a new boarding school, you can probably find the courage to start your own new company!".

Having sold his first company, and attempting but rejecting retirement, Ike decided to go to business school at Wharton. What he loved were the conversations that never mentioned "too ambitious", but were rather always full of possibility and aspiration.

It was about the time that Ike and his wife were expecting their second child that they started to contemplate a return to Nigeria. The couple felt that it was important for the children to have a strong identity of who they were and of their roots. They observed fellow expatriates in the U.S. allowing their children to grow up with a muddled sense of identity, and did not wish this for their own children.

The first attempt to return was cut short at the last moment by the last big financial crisis. Frustrated but not deterred, Ike set up another company. He reflects on the benefits of career "spaces" as opportunities to reflect and to open up to other possibilities. In this case, through advice from Nigerian friends, he began to look for a job through a private equity fund in Nigeria on the basis that "everything takes twice as long there, and that can burn a lot of money".

For the past two years, Ike has been back in Nigeria working with eTranzact, an exciting company in the payments area of finance. He went ahead alone, his wife and children following quickly, as they preferred to be together. Indeed, the first "benefit" that Ike cites when talking about the transition is the close family life, and no need to worry about incidents while far away.

Settling has been slow for all, although it certainly helps to understand the stages of adjustment that all of them go through. Ike feels confident he has chosen to work in a promising sector, and he is far from ready for retirement. He never once mentioned the inconveniences of his new life in Africa, but focused more on the development of new talents and new businesses in his home country.

When quizzed on the advice he would give to people returning, he suggests that they "find out why" by undergoing a solid introspection and eliminating rosy childhood memories, which tend to be wrong. By reducing the stress and planning well, as he did by avoiding another start-up, you have more chance of enjoying the process, however frustrating it might be in some ways. He strongly encourages those who have the inclination to take the step once they have gone through this thinking process. While Ike does not project beyond the time when his children will go to university, one senses that he really is happy in his home country and more than motivated to continue to develop talent and ideas in this extraordinary place.

What's Going On? Gone Are the Rose-Colored Glasses

A 2011 study revealed that there are now over 215 million people living in a country other than the one in which they were born, and that this number has doubled in the last 25 years. This represents three percent of the world's population.

Of this huge group, a significant and apparently growing number decide to "go back home", though this phrase can confound many. Most commonly used are "repatriates" or "returnees" to describe diaspora who move back home. However, to most people in the Western world, the notion of "returnees" is a foreign concept, as a person who studies abroad would almost always expect to return "home". Some countries have their own nicknames: in India, it is NRIs (for Non-Resident Indians); in Vietnam, they are called Viet Kieu, meaning "overseas Vietnamese". In China, they are "sea turtles", or "Hai Gui Pai", although some jealous, more land-bound compatriots dub these new arrivals "Hai Dai", or "seaweed". Some examples of this sort of migration include a three percent rise in returns to China in 2015, or nearly 400,000 people; and the fact that more Chinese people live outside mainland China than French people live in France. Some 22 million ethnic Indians are scattered across every continent, and according to the Financial Times, India's corporate sector is expected to hire about 35,000 returnees this year alone. This return tide started with the tech bust in 2000, when many Indians working in California lost their jobs; the joke then was that B2B meant not "business-to-business" but "back to Bangalore." The trend grew as U.S. companies began sending data processing and call center work to cheaper labor markets in Asia and India. An estimated 11-17 million Nigerians still live abroad, and it is estimated that almost half a million South Africans have returned "home" from abroad in the past five years.

With an economic slowdown in the "developed" world, and thanks to Nigeria's economic performance in the last decade, Lagos is now welcoming thousands of new returnees. A growing middle-class lifestyle and improving democracy in Nigeria makes it easier for the diaspora to contemplate moving back.

Although there are these obvious macro-level drivers that explain the growing trend of returning diaspora, we want to examine the individual aspects of the transition. What are the specific circumstances? Why does someone decide to move back home? How do they experience the transition back to their home country?

In most cases we looked at, even though there were other broad reasons, the family environment provoked the move abroad. In the case of Ferdi, his parents moved to the U.S. before he was born. For Ike, the diplomatic family background and nomadic childhood gave him a taste for traveling and discovering other cultures. It was a similar case for Bambina. Once again, we are confronted with an excellent example of more nurture than nature. What is more, Ferdi's parents' fear of racism forced him to assimilate more than many, and therefore he was actually deprived of many aspects of his own culture and language. Ike's early diplomatic travels set him off on his journey, and Bambina's life of socializing with diplomats no doubt also played a motivating role.

But for others, the decision to leave their home country is a more personal, deliberate one, triggered by the expectation of doing something "different" or "better" abroad. Yang's total lack of exposure to the idea or the realities of travel certainly did not indicate he would be motivated by a departure, and Marta left mainly because she could see a glass ceiling in her future.

While the transition for most of our subjects happened during their teenage or young adult years through studies abroad, in some cases the subjects are refugees who fled their country due to war or conflict: Vietnam, Nigeria and South Africa all spring to mind as common examples, and there are hundreds more. While this may be traumatic in the short term, and leaves long-term traces, it can also be a door opened to greater opportunity, and thus critical in catalyzing development for the individual.

All of our subjects enjoyed a rich, multicultural life and career experience different from that of the average local person. They were able to build on their "foreignness" and hone in on distinctive skills or expertise: Marta and Bambina did this by taking roles in a variety of countries at the behest of one or more companies. Yang and Ike used education as a springboard to increase their reach and potential, and Ferdi focused on one location, becoming the go-to expert on that place.

While the initial move to the country may have brought some early challenges of cultural adaptation, like Yang's gin and tonic habit, most were able to adapt quickly and actually exploited and expanded their multicultural nature as a core strength. Ike and his incredible multiple adaptations is probably the best example of the extent to which it is possible to develop and grow.

We can assume our subjects always kept the idea of returning at least in the back of their minds. For most of them, the idea of going back was driven by a mix of professional and personal circumstances: Marta's tolerance for the stresses of child-raising with too much travel pushed her over the edge; Bambina was faced with several less attractive choices, and so took the "obvious" option of returning "home". On the other hand, the external market of professional opportunities also played a significant role, as for Yang, when friends asked him to join their business, or Marta, seeing her potential as a CEO when approached by a headhunter.

In many other cases, the decision to move back home is driven by a sense of belonging and a desire to "do the right thing" for themselves, their families or even the broader community/country/society: Ike and his family were seeking stronger roots, and Marta felt a desire to give back. These examples are echoed by Adabara Abdullahi, a London-educated banker, who established "Move Back to Nigeria", an online community for returnees. He believes the motivation of thousands of returnees runs deep and beyond pure economics: "... the number one reason people return to Nigeria is the sense of belonging and purpose. Most returnees feel that they can do better things in their societies. People who understand both Nigeria and other countries can make a big difference."[55]

For most, however, it seems the transition is a difficult one. They go through a wide range of feelings: surprise, pain and happiness, as for Yang; confusion, as we saw with Marta feeling "lost"; frustration, as we observed with Ferdi, who like others suffers due to daily practical struggles. But assuming they were "locals", they were not prepared for this re-entry shock, and it is surprising to see Marta being overwhelmed. Yang behaves more like a new expat, asking for advice and support from his office. Marta took her biggest career break yet, unable to take any more change. And Ike admits that the settling in has been slow for the whole family.

At a deeper level, they experience the challenge of "finding their place" and reconstructing a new identity which ideally would combine both cultural experiences. An especially tough challenge is to realize their limited ability to re-apply some of their professional skills or practice in their new work environment, because what they learned abroad does not fit with the local way of doing things. This is particularly the case for Ferdi, who is stuck between the two, and not necessarily reaping the benefit of either. Marta too had to make a huge shift in her behavior and reactions, while at the same time reconciling somewhat, accepting that some of her "toughness" is a good foil for her business partner's softer approach.

An aid worker who moved back to Uganda describes beautifully the identity challenge: "The hardest part about reentry is that people seemingly do not care how my life had been transformed, and reconciling that with the people and things that had remained the same at home."[56] Akshay Rathod, a returning Indian consultant, mirrors Ferdi's dilemma of identity: "At times, I feel more split and divided – Indian when I'm around Americans and American when I'm around Indians", he says. "I've become constantly aware of these differences".[57]

One of the other key challenges for returnees is the loss – or non-existence – of social contacts and/or a professional network. They are coming back to their country with significant work experience and at a career stage when a network should be their primary source of job or business opportunities. This point is well illustrated with the case of Chinese entrepreneur returnees, as cited in a 2015 article in China Daily: "The top concern of those returning from overseas who want to start their own business in China is difficulty in dealing with local governments... Many returnees who have spent several years abroad also face challenges posed by having lost social contacts."[58]

All of our subjects experienced what is called "reverse culture shock", which is the process of readjusting, re-acculturating, and re-assimilating into one's own home culture after living in a different culture for a significant period of time. This can be experienced in different ways, ranging from few, if any, effects of reentry to problems that last a few months to a year or longer.

Peter Adler's definition of culture shock is psychologically descriptive and explanatory: "Culture shock is primarily a set of emotional reactions to the loss of perceptual reinforcements from one's own culture, to new cultural stimuli which have little or no meaning, and to the misunderstanding of new and diverse experiences. It may encompass feelings of helplessness, irritability, and fears of being cheated, contaminated, injured or disregarded."[59] Adler's definition also highlights the chaotic and fatiguing nature of culture shock when he defines the construct as "… the frustration and confusion that result from being bombarded by unpredictable cues".

The above definitions are representative of many. In one pilot study, the results showed that the overseas Chinese returnees experienced more than reverse cultural shock. It is the Chinese social environment and their double identity that gives them a hard time in communication. In other words, it is not the cultural identity alone that is hindering their communication in China; rather, it is a combination of their social, cultural, personal, and psychological identities that makes them fail in communication with their Chinese community. Their experience abroad definitely changed their world outlook to some extent, and they have a double identity now. That is why these overseas Chinese returnees feel uncomfortable when coming back to their motherland.

It may be too easy to hang problems encountered around a return on the "repatriation". Some of them may in fact be due to other factors, including personal style and development. While culture and context shift are an enormous burden, as all our stories and research show, all of us would do well to consider looking at improving our behavior as far as we can in trying times such as these, in the hope that this may ease the challenge.

4 Key Challenges to Expect When Landing Back Home

1. **Underestimating the Need to Readjust**
   Don't assume "I'm just going back and I already know the ropes here". It will not necessarily be a swift and smooth reintegration. Novelty and unfamiliarity will be all around, and you may initially feel like a stranger in a strange land.

2. **Experiencing Frustrations in Daily Life**
   Lack of predictability in daily life events is omnipresent. Things can take longer than you expect and cost more than you budget for. Depending on where you are landing, you may experience heavy traffic, bureaucracy or even power cuts.

3. **Getting a Social Life**
   Building a network will not be as easy as expected. Reconnecting with your childhood friends can be superficially simple, but it will be harder to feel fully aligned with those same people who may not relate to your other life.

4. **Gaining Professional Acceptance**
   The knowledge, skills and style you have acquired overseas will not automatically apply or be effective in your new work environment. In Asia, staff and co-workers may label you as a "banana" (yellow on the outside, white on the inside) and refuse to treat you as a fellow countryman/woman.

The Voice of Companies: Spotlight on Africa

In the past few years, there has been an increasing wish to localize leadership positions in many companies and regions. This is due to several factors, as reported by our contacts in several companies that are active in both Asia and Africa. Jérôme Petit, CEO Africa for Bolloré Logistics, a French logistics company, states his main reasons for this trend as being the high cost of expat packages, a need for business continuity and sustainable client relationships. This is all the more needed in countries that are relatively unstable or otherwise dangerous, where expats would traditionally stay for only short periods, as the upheaval on change of leadership would be considerable in all these respects. In addition, education systems have evolved considerably over the past ten to fifteen years in some countries. In Senegal, for example, there is a larger supply of well and locally educated managers with experience in multinational companies who can amply fill the management positions that might once have been occupied by serial expats.

The diaspora fall between the two traditional – expat/local – categories, and this can be a point of tension, as many of them, while wishing to return "home", hope to be offered packages comparable to those of an expat, which is less and less likely to happen.

Do companies target diaspora? All companies we spoke to were clear that there was a need for "non-Caucasian" leaders in their organizations, so whatever the local conditions, more and more of those native to the country are being hired, whether educated locally or overseas. This is particularly the case once success stories have been established and the company starts to feel comfortable that these leaders can generally bring value without too much trouble.

Eric Legrand, HR Director of Eurapharma, a leading distributor of pharmaceutical products and services in Africa and the French overseas territories, tells us that for the last six or so years, his company has been hiring both diaspora and locally educated managers, with mostly great outcomes. The number of "non-French" expatriates is now up to almost a third of the total and growing. This success is also attributed to the use of a culturally appropriate HR management approach, which is facilitating the Africanization of the company there. At the same time, there is a system in many companies of internal recommendations, so the African general managers pass on the CVs of their network, most of whom are still working in France or Canada, and the process begins again. Another method of recruitment is to use specialized agencies or networks, such as that run by Tomiwa Igun, the "Young African MBAs" (YAM).

Are diaspora the main recruitment target? Where it was once not possible to recruit locally all the different types of senior management necessary for a large multinational company, the educational and social changes mentioned above are coming more and more into play, according to the executives we spoke to at Bolloré, and there is less necessity to look solely to diaspora. The line of demand seems to be switching direction, or at the least splitting, so that now it is as much about the diaspora, such as Ike and his family, who are actively looking for opportunities to return "home", rather than being merely seduced by fat packages. Indeed, with the current wave of nationalistic politics in the West, work permits are becoming harder and harder to obtain or maintain, and thus a pool of willing returnees is forming.

What advantages are these diasporas perceived to have? Regardless of their line of referral, the obvious first aspect is education. Tomiwa sees the biggest demand in the middle management area, and the most often expressed requirements are those of having experience abroad and possessing a strong knowledge of the local "lay of the land". Whether the manager comes direct from abroad, or is more home-bred, the main value according to Tomiwa is that he or she can leverage global best practices and develop local game-changing strategies.

All the companies we spoke to perceive a major advantage of a "returnee" to be the capacity to "see" both sides. Jérôme Petit, CEO Africa of Bolloré Logistics, says that those who return to Africa are open-minded and flexible, with a sensitivity and understanding of the culture of the HQ, as well as of the local situation. This is commonly agreed to be crucial, and the few failures mentioned by each company we spoke to are largely seen to have been caused by an imbalance here.

So what can go wrong? Or what can be challenging along the way? Salary and employment package are issues with most of the diaspora hires that were described to us, though these pale in significance compared to the stress of finding that a diaspora hire is not able to straddle the differences properly and finds him/herself negatively perceived for trying to "play" both systems. While these cases are rare, they are to be avoided where possible, and common consensus was that fit needs to be ascertained early on in the recruitment process.

Just as Ike mentioned the need to be absolutely sure of one's motivations, the companies all talked about the need to dig deep into this area during the recruitment process. Some even suggested that it should be obligatory to make a "reconnaissance trip" in order to test motivations and reality. Bringing a family along can be particularly challenging in a significant expatriation, as can the "certainty" of one's motivations. Does the candidate truly want to "return", or is it just a temporary thing? "This all needs teasing out as far as possible at interview", asserts Paul Marques, the HR Director for West Africa at Bolloré Logistics.

Another significant challenge is that of the societal pressure that faces some of the returnees. Once back in their home country and context, they are faced with constant demands to provide jobs to friends and family, while this is neither the culture they have been using while overseas, nor that of the company hiring them. One solution to this, mentioned by both Bolloré and Eurapharma, is that of moving the person around his or her own continent, thus using their cultural abilities while removing the pressure of friends and family.

Lack of cultural humility can also be a huge problem. The idea of bringing back a highly educated leader sounds good in theory, but sometimes local conditions are not so much about huge intellectual challenges. Sometimes the solution to a business problem in a developing country is simple and does not need a big brain or education, and that can be hard to take. Tomiwa suggests that this contrast must be explored with the diaspora candidates, as some could struggle to realize their long hiatus away from "home" may require as much business landscape learning on their part as is expected of some of their expat counterparts.

Daily life can be a big shock to many diaspora, however well they think they know their "own" country. It may be a while since they left and things can change − or the "rose-tinted glasses" can be pretty powerful − leading to shock and intolerance of poor conditions, including power outages, traffic jams and generally poor logistics and infrastructure.

Finally, there is another issue of importance raised by several of our companies: the woman's perspective. Work and social conditions are often extremely different from those they have become used to in the West, so the return to a different environment in this respect can be shocking. Not all women will be willing or able to work through that, so much candid discussion is needed to manage the gap.

Some solutions suggested by the companies we talked to are interesting and useful. The problems caused by more rootless and out-of-touch older hires, can be avoided by recruiting more recent graduates. Bolloré does this, as does HSBC, which has a "China Returns Program" for fresh Chinese graduates in the UK. The graduates spend two years working in

UK-based functions before returning to populate and contribute to the bank's fast-growing network in China. This would seem to be the best of both worlds for organization and individual.

One final caveat, from Eric Legrand of Eurapharma: He stipulates that he certainly does not wish to move towards a quota situation, as in the United Arab Emirates, where hiring a certain percentage of nationals is now mandatory, for example. He just wants the best people in the right places.

Many companies are now working with local education systems to raise the in-country level of education and experience. Morocco has declared its intention to become the leader in African education, and similar ambitions are being expressed across the developing world. The more the companies already in situ can sponsor, advise, and generally commit to making this work, the greater the chances of successful outcomes for all. Once this succeeds, there may be less need to look outside in such a consistent way for high-performing managers, and thus the diaspora hires will become less critical as a process, making way for more clarity and likelihood of success and integration.

And, Out of Africa...

In the end, beyond the cases of companies like Bolloré or Eurapharma, we need to ask what is in it for companies. Is it worth it for them? Research on the topic suggests that international returnees help companies in emerging markets capture and utilize the knowledge they have gained overseas. Other "benefits" include diaspora leveraging their international network: Ramana Nanda and Tarun Khanna, in a 2009 study found evidence that cross-border social networks play an important role in helping entrepreneurs circumvent the barriers arising from imperfect domestic institutions in developing countries.[60] In some countries, such as India, where the needs are vast, governments are even trying to lure diaspora and their wallets back to the homeland. They are reminded that the primary example of the homecoming Indian is Mahatma Gandhi, who quit his legal practice in South Africa to lead his country's independence movement.[61]

Hiring diaspora in local organizations may not always be a good strategy, as Jack Ma, CEO of Alibaba found when he finally ended up firing 95 percent of the returnee executives he had hired upon obtaining funding from Goldman Sachs. He likened his mistake to installing aircraft engines in tractors. Overall – at least in China – the jury is out when it comes to the impact of returnees. In a 2015 paper, Tinghua Duan and Wenxuan Hou found returnee CEOs guilty of causing many regulatory clashes and inciting inferior performance.[62] On the other hand, where international expertise is in demand, there can be a positive effect. Indeed, where IPOs were completed with returnee CEOs aboard, these outperformed those with local CEOs, and the difference was even more pronounced where such firms were backed by venture capital.

How to Make the Transition Happen

All of our subjects worked hard to adjust and adapt their style. The whole process of adjustment takes a long time. Yang understands the lengthy task ahead of him, and Marta continues to bite her tongue. Even now, Bambina is still struggling to find a role where she really fits.

An important way of adapting is to remember why they came back, and thus to keep their sense of purpose. This tends to put things in greater perspective: Ike's determination probably demonstrates this the best, with a solid focus on looking forward positively at all the opportunities, rather than being trapped or frustrated by the challenges.

We heard their tips within their stories, but it is useful to summarize. Universally there is a feeling that it is important to think hard before acting. Marta's advice about meditation was not made lightly – any more than Yang's caution to ask a specific set of questions. Yang's and Ike's lists are not dissimilar; the question of "Why?" comes up in both, and that of flexibility and adaptability. But in the end, there is also that aspect of "just doing it". Once the thinking process is over, there is a hurdle to tackle, but it is possible to tackle it. All of our subjects just took the plunge, finally.

There is also the notion of going back to chase a passion. This is equally observed by a Chinese former McKinsey consultant, Lan Kang, who said in a 2007 paper: "Many times, the opportunities presented to us are to become the pioneers, to develop something from scratch, to make a significant impact, to leave your mark on a company, an industry sector, or sometimes even on society as a whole." He also points out, however, that there are always tradeoffs, such as good home food versus pollution. Cheap home help versus clean food and water. His final advice is to talk to other returnees and involve family in the discussion, to do your homework and negotiate a package, which ensures that you return with a good starting point and without assuming that life will be easy and simple. But he does assert that it will definitely be exciting.

7 Tips for Those Considering Moving Back Home

1. **Answer the Why Question**
   Find out, or clarify, what your reason is for returning. Ask yourself "How motivated am I?", "What is my vision?" and "Am I flexible enough to adapt to the culture?". This may require going through a solid introspection and eliminating rosy childhood memories.

2. **Have a Plan, but Keep an Open Mind**
   You need to come back with a plan while setting realistic targets. Your expectations may not be met and you will have to adjust your goals or your timing. Keeping an open mind, being creative and embracing change will play a huge part in your success. A view towards the impact that this move will have on a longer-term plan can be very useful too.

3. **Be Patient and Stay Optimistic**
   Anticipate you will go through numerous frustrations and emotional highs and lows. Understand the stages of adjustment that all returnees go through. Exercise your patience muscle, persevere and keep an optimistic mind. Above all, do not expect to find what you left behind.

4. **Fine-Tune Your Skills**
   Be prepared for a cultural stretch. Your new working environment will not understand or embrace your ways of doing coming from abroad. Fine-tune your skills and adapt your style with a view toward gaining acceptance while not losing your competitive edge.

5. **Seek Support**
    If you repatriate to a country where you have family ties or prior experience, reconnecting with past contacts can provide nuanced insights into the local context and curtail the process of acting and thinking like a foreigner. Ask your new friends or colleagues to help you navigate both practically and socially around the local culture.

6. **Actively Network**
    Many major cities have vibrant communities of returnees who provide a familiar reminder of the experience of living abroad. Network with other returning business people who can give you valuable advice. Establish relationships with individuals who can serve as professional mentors, business partners, and a social support system.

7. **Take It Easy and Enjoy**
    Trying to change everything will not work, so it will help if you can maintain a balance between persistence and giving up. Follow Marta's advice to practice yoga and meditation. Enjoy the best things that your new context brings.

Are diaspora back to their home country forever? What are their plans for the future? It's definitely unclear if all our subjects will stay. We can predict that those who have found a new balance – both personally and professionally – will do so, as seems to be the case with Ferdi and Ike. Ferdi has a marriage to a local woman to hold him, and Ike's wife and he are more motivated than ever to make Nigeria a long-term home.

For the others, options for the future seem open: Marta is already strategizing her next move, driven by her children's study and work future, as well as her opportunities to build her business more broadly. It may be too early to tell for Yang and Bambina, as their return is so recent, but there is no clear evidence either way.

Final Thoughts

Our five subjects, from four continents, lived their repatriation in different ways. While all of them are making progress, it would seem that this is slow and challenging, whatever the attitude of the individual, though it surely helps to be optimistic and flexible.

Recognizing the need to change is a fundamental of good leadership, and not unique to those who choose to return. In almost all of our stories, we encountered individuals who had experienced and embraced change when they were young. So it might be reasonable to ask the "chicken or egg" question here: Did they courageously tackle their return precisely because they were born with that courage? Did they make it work because they have learned to reflect openly and from different perspectives? Does that perspective come thanks to the international moves? We may never know, but we find that an increasingly common theme in our research is one's destiny being set in early childhood. Do the values and experiences our parents pass on give us a clear path through life, or do we really blaze a trail ourselves? Yang's story would seem to reflect the possibility that you can get past your predefined destiny, but maybe his parents transmitted a certain sense of openness to change which we don't know.

It is easy to see the value that comes from these departures and returns, but not so easy to see that the value translates in situ on homecoming. Fewer than half of our subjects are in prominent corporate jobs in their home countries, though this does not appear to be for any reason other than lifestyle choice and perhaps a desire to be in control of an uncontrollable environment. Do they fare better at "home" because of their experience elsewhere? Probably the empathy they have derived from experiencing so many world-views is helping them, but the sum of positives and negatives does not seem to be really so clearly defined. Their experiences reflect the inconclusive studies we have found in our research too.

However, there may yet be a "middle way". Perhaps diaspora can also help their home country, without moving back home; thanks to technology, easy transport and communications, they can be "both here and there", not only committed to the country they live in, but also closely connected to their country of origin. Key members of the diaspora can play a great role in their home economies without having to make a permanent return. Brain drain can become brain gain and brain exchange. This idea, posited in the Global Diaspora Strategies Toolkit in

2011, is certainly being lived out by several of our contacts and subjects and will no doubt engender a future article of interest.

Further Reading and Information

▍ ARTICLES AND BLOGS

"Returning expatriates : South Africans return from abroad", by Claire Bisseker, Financial Mail, January 2014

"The rigours of India's 'repatriates'", by James Lamont and Neil Munshi, Financial Times, April 25, 2012

"Back to India" and "Revisiting Vietnam", by Robyn Meredith, Forbes, July 2007

▍ WEBSITES

MBTN (Move Back To Nigeria)
www.movebacktonigeria.com

HSBC China Returns Programme
www.hsbc.com/careers/students-and-graduates/programmes/
china-returns-programme

The Homecoming Revolution – A pan-African recruitment firm for global African professionals
homecomingrevolution.com

Options Executive Search (India) – A firm helping companies find the best local talent globally and supporting the hiring of returning Indians for CXO roles
www.optionsindia.com

Chapter 10

Second Acts

Making an Impact Post-Retirement

The average life expectancy is growing apace across the globe. It was clocked at over 71 in the years 2010-2013, and this figure includes war- and HIV-ravaged countries in Africa, where it can be as low as just under 50. With this seismic change continuing, most of us face the prospect of working in some shape or form until we are far past the traditional retirement age of sixty. This may be partly due to increasing obligations to work until the age deemed appropriate by our governments, and thus our employers.

However, there is also the possibility of using the years at or towards the end of our more traditional employment obligations for other activities. Instead of reaching immediately for the golf clubs or the gentle walking groups, we increasingly choose to do "more". The resultant "encore careers", or "second acts", as they have become known, make for a fulfilling time, regardless of the route taken to reach them. In this chapter, we look at five baby boomers from around the world enjoying a satisfying finale. We discovered that some of them do not even regard this round as the finale at all.

Steve

Steve looks very much like the classic case of an encore actor. He had spent his entire career in the advertising industry, mostly in New York, where he eventually led media departments. He lapped up the glamour, the rush and the pressure of his industry. However, when he and his wife decided to seek out a calmer place in which to raise a family, he took a role as account director in a large Chicago firm. Three firms and hectic roles later, when their twins were born, Steve decided to go part-time in order to help out on the home front. He was, as he admits, starting to feel burnout anyway. It was clear to him that spending more time with family was a greater priority than selling more advertising.

His next move was to head the marketing department at the Frank Lloyd Wright Home and Studio. In this role, Steve came to love cause marketing. The feeling that he was working with a purpose made the huge drop in pay insignificant. However, in a reorganization, his entire department was laid off and he was faced with making an unexpected choice about the next step. This was the ideal opportunity for him to further develop his increasing appetite for making a difference, and he took a huge step.

Career Transition Navigator

EXPLORE

Steve had long been on the board of his children's school, and had also taken on a role in another local non-profit organization – so he was already turned firmly towards public service. As he says, "The time I had after being laid off gave the idea of making a difference time to take a hold". He felt that teaching might be the solution. He was friendly with another "dad" who had recently switched careers to teach, and was able to obtain first-hand feedback about the process. This was enough to encourage him to go back to school in 2013 and start teaching in a first-grade classroom.

Steve now says he wishes he had made the move ten years ago. He states that he "absolutely loves" his work, with a sense that he is on stage all day every day, and that the performing is what he enjoys. He also thrives in the community of teaching colleagues, and sees that there are a number of transferable skills he brought from his corporate experience. He likens the communication with the students to that of dealing with multiple constituencies in the business world, and suggests that planning a teaching day is similar to gearing up to a big presentation each day.

The advice that Steve has to offer those considering this kind of move is mainly based around getting information and ideas. "Get in a classroom", he suggests, "or wherever you want to be, and try it out". But he is quick to add that it's different to a corporate job. "You feel like you are a kind of performer who is 'on' all day and you really have to have a lot of patience and be able to multitask. There are some days when I have to get into the groove of dealing with young kids which can be stressful but the upside is that the kids are so much fun and you really feel like you are doing an important job and making a difference in their lives."

The other unexpected benefit that Steve notes is that in his community, teachers are held in high regard. He is proud to be working in a profession that is admired, whereas despite his lofty role he was previously perceived as "just a salesman".

Gayle

Gayle started her career in IT sales. Her mother was a lifetime IBM-er, and Gayle grew up intending to avoid the same fate. However after studying mathematics and computer science at UCSB in California, she accepted a job with the upstart computer organization at HP. She moved her way rapidly up the company, becoming a manager at 25 and joining the pioneering consulting arm of the company shortly thereafter. Global responsibilities came along, and she was extremely happy with her progress. However, the well-known transformation of the HP organization picked up speed, and she became more and more frustrated by the culture shifts and other developments.

So when Gayle was offered a "phased" retirement at the age of 56, she was sorely tempted. Her husband is a little older than her and the couple figured that this could be a real opportunity for them. Having done some careful calculations to fully understand the implications, Gayle accepted the offer. In her mind, though, her career was most definitely not over.

She met a representative from the Encore Fellowships Network, a program of Encore.org which works in collaboration with corporations to offer "fellowships" to retirees, allowing them to bring their skills to non-profit organizations while earning a stipend. Gayle liked the idea, and while she saw it as something to do "later on", they called her with an ideal offer. She felt compelled to accept the role she was offered at Second Harvest, a large and highly regarded food bank in the San Francisco Bay area, not least because they had an excellent reputation for "value per donation" and because they were looking for a program-creator like her. She is now helping them evaluate and develop a program to increase donor engagement and commitment, focusing presently on donors with children.

The recruitment process surprised Gayle by its thoroughness, as she was put through many interviews. She took a frank and honest approach throughout, telling them as much as she could about all that she did not know about the non-profit world. At the end of the process, while she felt it was early, since she had only had six months off with her husband, she took the offer. This was a chance to do something using her skills beyond consulting, which she had already decided she did not want to do. The couple was delighted that she would be doing something fulfilling, and even bringing in a modest salary besides. As she says, "You cannot play for forty hours per week".

The discovery of this new environment has been full of pleasant surprises for Gayle. She is thrilled to encounter people who are not ridden with politics, and tells the story of how she was suggesting that perhaps donor families would be motivated to give more if they could engage with children in need. Instead of the resistance to change that would have been the likely initial reaction in a corporate setting, she saw eyes lighting up and heard many ask what they could do to make this happen.

An important part of becoming oriented to Second Harvest has consisted of going out in the field to get to know the different services. Her encounter with an 89-year-old volunteer left her thoughtful and inspired, especially as the fit lady in question explained that she could only volunteer for a few hours in the early morning; after that, she needed to go to her day job running a 70-unit condominium. Another aspect of great satisfaction is that Gayle feels included. This is best exemplified by the fact that she has been given access to quarterly strategy meetings and to all the senior members of the organization.

Gayle has a lot of advice to offer to aspiring encore career candidates. She firstly says that if at all possible, it is better to do this kind of volunteering through fellowships or other similar arrangements. In this way, you are likely to be given greater responsibilities, as well as 10-15 percent of your former salary. Her other big piece of advice is of critical importance: "If you like to be recognized for your past achievements and career expertise, then do consulting; if you are willing to learn new things, then Encore programs are really rewarding. If you are humble and willing to learn, then the non-profits will be appreciative indeed." She speaks of feeling that she has found once again the pleasure of "just loving" what she does, and may well find it hard to ease out once her statutory year is over.

John

John, another Encore program fellow, has already finished the projects he did within the program. His vision is slightly less enamored than Gayle's. His long career, spent exclusively in the product and R&D functions at Procter & Gamble, had taken him from engineering-driven roles in Florida to global roles in Germany; from pulp to paper; and from junior to expert. He felt he had more or less "seen it all". The excitement and challenge of his role in Germany, as global head of R&D for a baby product, were difficult to replace, and John also realized that he was less interested in running large teams than he was in organizational capability and how he could contribute to that. In that vein, he spent several years in the U.S., on return from Europe, trying to find a role that suited him. His efforts were to no avail.

At that point, the first of several rounds of early retirement was announced, and John decided to take advantage. Like Gayle, he did not see his career as being over, and he started to look for other opportunities. P&G offered him the standard exit package, which included a time of consulting and advice from an outsourcing company, which he describes as "not particularly effective" for him, although he does admit that the process allowed him to take the time and effort to reflect and to look for more.

In his thinking about what was important, John remembered that he had a love for the environment and the outdoors, and this started to shape his search for the next challenge. He hit on the sector of renewable and clean energy, and began to look for roles within this area. However, this was not to be, despite making a few applications. At that point, a lunch meeting with a friend revealed an opportunity he had not been expecting.

The friend introduced him to another "encore" organization, this time "YourEncore", and he agreed to remain open to offers that might come in. The first role that John undertook was not a good fit with his skills and experience. But shortly afterwards, he was given the chance to undertake a project to audit some manufacturing locations belonging to P&G, and he leapt at the chance to get back "out in the field". The travel involved in this audit suited him perfectly. Being out and about was what he loved, and this was a great reminder. The project lasted some time, as there was a great deal of inspection to be done, and it involved John delving into some more current training and best practice work so as to deliver the project optimally.

Now that the project is over, John is not entirely sure he would take any offers of other work. He sees that YourEncore is an organization that does "great work", but which also has its drawbacks. He has neither interest in nor talent for developing their business for them, and would not take on "just any" project coming in. What he is most proud of is the flexibility he has created in his life. He can do what he wants according to mood and circumstance, and he is unlikely to give this up soon.

The advice from John? "Network like crazy!" This is something he admits he failed to do younger, and that is now the most critical part of the process. He started networking much too late, and found it difficult to create his own opportunities. He also advocates "living below your means". In this way, he says, you can make decisions about what is important, rather than making decisions based on fear and ignorance. Ultimately, he believes we should all find out what brings us joy, and work towards that, adding that it is never too late – or early – to start.

Daniel

Daniel is a natural connector, leveraging his contacts, knowledge and the power of the network to great effect. From a modest background, he was encouraged by his mother to break out of the humdrum. He showed early signs of commitment to society and its causes, as he was involved in Scouting and Abbé Pierre's charity from his teenage years onwards. He believes that any life lived without commitment is a life half-lived.

Having travelled across the world as a young man, Daniel continued to make trips now and then during his lifelong career at Kaufman & Broad, the real estate developer. He requested a sabbatical year at forty-five, which caused much consternation on the part of the CEO. Eventually he was able to explore different parts of the world, as well as to discover other opportunities to give back to humanity. He travelled a great deal with his wife, whose painted murals now decorate orphanages and homes in Vietnam, Mexico and more. He also tried volunteering for the "Restos du Coeur", one of the largest homeless charities in France, but found that frustratingly bureaucratic and inefficient. His true path was not yet clear.

Daniel returned to work and settled down. His absence and the awareness of his motivations afforded him a special sort of "aura", as he describes it, which allowed him to broaden his professional and social circle considerably. At the age of 58, a few years shy of the normal retirement age, Daniel decided to end his professional career, sensing that it was time to get ready for the next stage of his life's path The exact timing was influenced by the fact that his company, previously a large, paternalistic family business, had been bought by a venture capital fund, and the atmosphere was no longer as attractive to him. He set out his plan, which was to give himself and the company a couple of years to manage the transition, to ensure a successor was in place, and for him to make plans for exactly what to do.

His departure just before Christmas was celebrated with champagne, but he found himself alone by the time the holidays were over. The satisfaction of identifying the first few charitable projects to which to contribute more than made up for this. It was fortunate that Daniel's stock options were worth a small fortune, and that he had passed them on to the foundation which he set up, thus allowing choices to be made easily about which projects to sponsor. Daniel travelled to a project in

Togo and Benin which had attracted his attention, and thus the first money from the foundation was allocated. More projects followed, and Daniel tries to give his choices a sense: a personal link of some kind.

An incidental aspect of Daniel's activity is that of advisor to religious bodies which have real estate questions to tackle. Daniel's expertise as a trusted consultant is sought in order to ensure the transactions go in the best way possible, and he in his turn makes sure that 30 percent of his fees are sent straight to the foundation. He constantly finds new challenges, and seems never to tire of bringing his experience to the benefit of others.

Although it is a constant juggling act, Daniel does make time to visit all projects he sponsors, and makes sure that he can report transparently and positively to the donors. As he moves forward, he aims to continue to motivate more people to donate, and has made plans with his children to continue the work and management of the foundation when he is no longer able to do so himself. He even has plans for other "retirement type" activities, once he turns 70. He plans to learn Spanish, to travel more and to continue to visit projects, even if he is no longer managing the foundation directly himself.

The advice Daniel has for others is simple: "Plan and get passionate". He cites the CEO of his former company, who has just retired with no visible plan or idea of what to do. "Life is a one-way trip." He recommends making sure to prepare for a long and satisfying time, and to ask a few hard questions of oneself: How can I be useful? What is my place in society? What do I know how to do? What can I usefully learn? What are my constraints and limitations? Daniel sees much time wasted on ventures that do not suit, and tries to reach out to and advise maturing executives before they make rash decisions.

Finally, he believes it is our duty as human beings to keep ourselves not only active after retirement, but also in good physical shape, and looking good through making an effort to dress well. He has seen too many retirees lonely at home in their sweatpants, lost to themselves and to the world. He begs us all to do better than that, for our own sakes, and for humanity. Giving our lives a sense is crucial, according to Daniel, and he seems to embody the verve and bounty that he recommends seeking out.

Arup

Arup comes from a family of philanthropists, his uncle having worked alongside Mahatma Gandhi, so it was no surprise to find him volunteering with Mother Teresa as a high school student in his native Calcutta. His energy and commitment to bettering the world are on par with Daniel's, and his career is actually hard to divide into "before" and "second act" stages at all, as he has constantly been involved in the fight to improve the lot of those in need.

While he worked with "Mother", as he calls her, his strength of character and resolve emerged. He raised the idea of schooling the children, in addition to just feeding them. She actually resisted strongly before agreeing to let Arup set up a system to get children into local public schools, despite their "untouchable" status. From this initiative, the Tomorrow's Foundation was instigated, though Arup was not involved in day-to-day operations.

Arup qualified as a chartered accountant, then obtained a job with PricewaterhouseCoopers. After earning a master's degree, he was all set to head off to the U.S. to do a PhD. It was only on failing to be granted the necessary visa that he realized that he wanted to travel anyway, and a curious series of serendipitous events followed whereby he was given financing by someone who died shortly after, and was invited by friends in Europe, who initiated him into the basics of the textile and garment industry. He was introduced to the CEOs of Pronuptia, Galeries Lafayette and Christian Lacroix, who found him sufficiently convincing to place some initial orders.

Far from experts in the industry, Arup and his twin brother set up a company to deal with all these orders. The Indian economy was opening up, which was a plus, but on the negative side was a great deal of abuse of workers in this "low-cost" manufacturing destination. Arup vowed to be different, and set up a social enterprise. He engaged thousands of workers in villages to make the items his European clients had ordered, providing good work conditions, training and education. In no time, his company had reached $4 million turnover, while he still described himself as a lucky amateur. However, an over-ambitious initiative with a venture capital company a few years ago meant Arup decided to close down.

At the same time as this unhappy ending, the executive director position came open in the Tomorrow's Foundation, and Arup decided to take the plunge. The twenty-fifth anniversary of the company was fast approaching, and it was a great opportunity to take stock and assure the future. Arup also explains that he is not particularly enamored of fashion, and that he was extremely happy and relieved to be able to get back to "giving back".

Another benefit of the return to the Foundation was that Arup learned to impose increasing humility on himself, and he enjoyed the accountability that was required, both to the Board and to himself. However, by his own admission, Arup is not an "operations man", but more focused on vision and strategy, so he does not see himself in the position for much longer. He has done his job in refocusing the Foundation and readying it for the future. Now he is at another crossroads, once again asking himself "What's next?"

Still in post at the Foundation, Arup has created the Human Initiative, a consultancy focused on CSR initiatives and strategies. He wishes to offer a unique package of expertise to the world at large, particularly in the textile and garment industries, helping them to improve the way they leave their footprints, in every sense. He explains this approach and motivation in the following way: "In India, we don't see things as separate parts, but as a whole: the material, spiritual and so on are all in the picture together, and what we seek is a balance". This applies to his motivations as much as it does in the setting up of the Human Initiative, and he adds that "it is obvious that you have to help, when you see the reality in front of you every day".

His reflections on why and how he has chosen this path are best summarized like this: "I am lucky to have something to share, and I think about the problems of others all the time. How can I best share it?" Now is a great time to be taking this sort of approach, as the Indian government has introduced an obligatory two percent spend on CSR for all corporations, so there will be many takers in the home country as well as from overseas. However, what is even more exciting to Arup is the opportunity to reverse engineer things. For too long, the models have come from the West; now is the time to show the rest of the world what India can do.

What's Going On? The Persistence of Purpose

Marci Alboher is an expert on late-stage careers. She wrote: "Research shows that roughly 9 million people are already in encore careers and another 31 million are keen to move in the same direction. Although they come from different places, large numbers of people in their encore years are looking for the same thing – making a living while making a difference."[63]

When looking at our subjects' earlier careers, we see some commonalities and differences. With the exception of Arup, every single one of them had had a classic, consistent career in either one company or at most one industry. None of them actually had a strong vision of their career, but rather fell into good jobs, having worked hard at school. Classic, "successful" baby boomers. However, despite the linearity regarding company or industry, what is clear is that all of them were rapid climbers who regularly and successfully changed roles to reach a management level quickly, like Gayle and Daniel; and to find value geographically, like John and Arup.

Useful Definitions

A **Second Act Career** is full or part-time work, usually for pay, after retirement. Often second acts involve a transition to a completely new career, such as college teaching or creating and running a business.

An **Encore Career** is an emerging sub-category of second act careers that involves work (paid or volunteer) that tackles social challenges, such as health care, poverty, or education. Seeking to give back to their communities or to worthwhile causes is a major goal of many retirees, and 4 in 10 currently work for a non-profit. Nearly 75 percent of those in encore careers receive some remuneration for their work, and many encore workers had previously volunteered in a related field.

But what made them consider this shift? We can see that all of them accumulated some frustration with their jobs. Steve was tired of the hectic environment, while Gayle and Daniel found it less easy to enjoy their changing company cultures. And Arup welcomed the opportunity to move on from facile fashion. Equally, over time they became more aware of their professional likes and dislikes – which then led to questioning how they would want to continue their work. The idea of doing something useful to society was present early on for Arup, but not so much for the others. Steve was inspired by cause marketing, and for Gayle and John, it was a part of their transitioning out of corporate life. For all of them, there was definitely a stage in their career where they challenged their sense of purpose and fulfillment in their business careers, and this prepared them to make the jump.

Research suggests that sense of purpose is indeed one main reason; and that this is usually combined with the need for providing (some) income. Marci Alboher remarks that: "The desire to have a positive impact in the world seems to grow stronger with age, as if it were programmed into our midlife DNA". In his book "The Pause Principle", Kevin Cashman explains this psychological process well: "The classic midlife crisis is the gut-wrenching realization that well-earned achievement and competence in the absence of meaningful contribution is not enough. It is the anxiety-provoking realization that our strengths have not been in service of something bigger."[64] By this time in life, as psychologist Eric Erickson adds, "people have identified plenty of things that need fixing, and they've also figured out that helping others is one of the easiest ways to get a happiness boost".

In all cases, it would seem that there was a clear trigger point: while the seeds of a more purposeful career were already planted in their mind – and for some of them, it had already blossomed – all subjects made the jump following a clear-cut separation from their employers. Steve was laid off following a reorganization; Gayle, John and Daniel took early retirement packages. In Arup's case, he made the decision to close down the company he had set up with partners. All of them saw their separation as an opportunity to start a new chapter in their business career – one in which they could make a difference.

But how did they get started? How did they make the leap from seeing the opportunity to actually getting on with it? The stories of our five subjects illustrate the many ways one can begin a second act, with varying speed and efficiency. For Arup, it was a quick decision to return to the foundation he had helped to create years before, and his move feels straightforward, almost predestined. Daniel followed a similar, organic path. He had invested the money from his stock options in a foundation, and unsurprisingly became interested in investing his own time in managing or overseeing the projects he sponsored. Steve was not completely new to the world of non-profit, and was determined to make a difference.

In contrast, Gayle and John were not totally clear about what to do next, apart from having a vague ambition of making a more purposeful contribution, and a certain view of the areas where they wished to contribute. John's love of the outdoors led him to target the renewable and clean energy sector, for example, and both did a proper job search and received some assistance from dedicated "Encore" organizations. It is worthy of note that this formal process is relatively easy and widespread in North America, where this system is fairly well established, but almost nonexistent in Europe and Asia at the time of writing.

We can see the benefits of using these organizations which act as intermediaries between a pool of available, experienced talent and multiple non-profit organizations who are in short supply of these skills. They facilitate the matching process and provide the opportunity for encore talent to try out different roles in different organizations via projects. It is thus to be hoped that such encore organizations will spread geographically and proliferate.

With almost all of our subjects, the transition to the second act involved more use of formerly acquired skills and experience than it did retraining. Steve logically enough was required to do a teacher training course, but the others used their existing skills to great effect in the new context.

Surprisingly, we did not hear once of any age discrimination. This may or may not be typical, but it is certainly heartening. Naturally, all of the new roles contain some elements of frustration, but these are experienced as being tiny, compared to the satisfactions. The relative freedom to contribute at levels outside the normal scope of a traditional job is a common and positive theme too.

With the exception of John, who carried out projects in his area of expertise to help other companies, all of our subjects went into the non-profit world through NGOs or education.

This seems to be representative of the trends observed. In his article "3 Great Opportunities for Encore Careers", Mark Feffer sees three main fields to consider for those in the U.S. who want to leverage the professional experience gained during their first career to help others during their "next stage": non-profits, healthcare and coaching. The world of non-profit, as seen by several of our subjects, has a lot to offer. Feffer tells us: "There are some 1.4 million non-profits in the U.S., ranging in size from single-person volunteer organizations to national groups with hundreds of employees. The attractions of working at a non-profit are obvious. You'd be on the front lines addressing social problems and would likely be able to see the impact of your work first-hand. Chances are you'll be able to find a group that focuses on causes near and dear to your heart, so you can combine a job with a passion."[65]

The other two areas, healthcare and coaching, also provide a range of opportunities. They represent, respectively, a pressing and growing need for professionals who can help older people locate necessary medical services, manage their treatment and prepare for their own next stage of life, and a chance to help people in their professional or personal lives. The coaching business is immense and growing, and is now worth more than $1 billion a year, according to the Harvard Business Review.[66]

How are they actually experiencing their transition? In Gayle's case, it has been full of pleasant surprises, with a complete break from politics and negativity with regard to change. For Arup, the chance to guide his own non-profit to its next stage has been a blessing. Daniel has found the purpose he has been toying with all his life, and Steve is a new man in his role as a teacher. The only one we feel less convinced about is John, who did his projects with some satisfaction but does not seem particularly keen to continue.

The Voice of Companies: New and Attractive Transition Pathways

Sadly, companies seem to be generally lagging behind the times, still operating under a traditional employment paradigm – working until age 60 or 65 – and have not integrated the "longevity revolution". Also, they have negative perceptions of older employees, especially in terms of their salary and indeed even viability as contributors. In an article in the FT

Magazine in 2015, Emma Jacobs comments: "The longevity revolution is often discussed in terms of the burden of social care and pensions, but it is also having a profound effect on working lives. People today are expected to work longer than they did a generation ago, in step with their elongated lifespans and as stretching out retirement savings becomes more difficult. Today's fifty and sixty-somethings are at the vanguard, configuring careers they hope will last longer than their parents'."[67] How to sustain a career until 70 will become a pressing issue. Yet, it is not straightforward. Some employers characterize workers even in their fifties, let alone their sixties, as expensive, inflexible, out of touch, technologically illiterate and coasting to retirement. Men may feel vulnerable, having historically been prone to defining themselves by their work, but women do too. The Commission on Older Women found that this is a group that may feel doubly discriminated against on age and gender grounds, described as "older earlier".

Overall, we can see that companies have not done much historically to support second act careers. However, in the past few years, there have thankfully been a lot of good initiatives.

What are companies doing to support second acts? Many companies, including IBM, HP, Intel, P&G and PwC, have set up systems to encourage and manage second act careers. Some of these are run internally, and some join together to facilitate the process. The programs range from IBM's Transition to Teaching program to PwC's Project Belize, focused on education and development.

An example of how these programs are promoted comes from Intel's website:

- **Encore Career Fellowship Program**
  Intel has worked to improve the experience of Intel employees as they prepare for retirement by sponsoring retirees interested in the Encore Fellowship program. Current U.S. employees who are eligible to retire have the option of being Encore Fellows as they transition into retirement. Making 1000-hour commitments, Fellows provide experienced talent to non-profit organizations; they receive modest stipends; and they join a group of peers making this transition to learn about social purpose organizations. Similar to the Tuition for Teaching program, this is an alternative

for employees to consider as they prepare for the transition into retirement.

- **And further, we can see the rationale and results of this program, as explained by Intel:**
Both internal and external research revealed a strong desire among individuals considering retirement to transition into new opportunities, including personally meaningful paid or unpaid community work, rather than forge a traditional retirement. The company also conducted an analysis of historical retirement trends at Intel and projections for how those are likely to change in the future, including financial readiness, retirement ages, and demand for workforce skills and experience.

New and attractive transition pathways for those completing mid-life careers at Intel include UCLA online education courses for re-skilling, entrepreneurship seminars, flexible part-time work schedules, and an Encore Fellows Program for those wanting work with a non-profit. The goal was to show retirement-eligible employees alternative retirement paths and career options once they left the company. Early success of a local pilot spurred a gradual expansion to a national program, and feedback along the way was used to adapt the model as the program grew. Reflecting Intel's egalitarian culture, the program was intentionally designed to offer a broad array of fellowship opportunities accessible by everyone in the company: manufacturing and administrative staff, executives, managers and field and technical staff.

Today the Intel Encore Fellows Program is available to any regular, active Intel employee who is retirement-eligible throughout the United States. Participation in the program is completely voluntary. The employee is matched before the retirement date and the fellowship starts up to six months after they have formally separated.

To date, 200 retiring Intel employees have taken advantage of the Encore Fellowship Program, exceeding the original expectations of employee participation. Evaluations have shown an extremely high level of satisfaction among the participating non-profits and Encore Fellows. The program has grown rapidly, and employees have participated extensively across geographies, grade levels, and functions.

Intel highlighted several factors critical to their success:

- Eliciting feedback directly from employees about their perceptions to better shape new offerings and structure the program;
- Determining how to provide participants time flexibility and choices;
- Making the program voluntary;
- Focusing communication on the employee experience through personal stories;
- Using word of mouth to drive awareness; and
- Reducing administration by working with a third-party vendor.

When we observe this sort of resounding success, we find it surprising and a shame that there is little initiative on the part of non-profits themselves to instigate such programs. In a 2013 Forbes article on Encore careers, Richard Eisenberg observes that "you might think non-profits would jump at the chance to hire part-time or full-time people passionate about helping them fulfill their missions. Turns out, not so much."[68] Others cite a lack of awareness as the reason for this gap, while yet others think the lack of initiative may be due to lack of funds available to pay those who would wish to do an encore stint with them.

Another unsolved puzzle is that of why the only examples we can find are American. We have not heard of similar programs outside the U.S., and so are perplexed, but hopeful that it is only a question of time.

How to Make the Transition Happen

Are most of our subjects happy and satisfied with this new stage in their career? Are they meeting their expectations, and what trade-offs are they required to make?

As observed earlier, they seem to be overwhelmingly fulfilled – especially those who discovered a new environment, like Gayle and Steve. Gayle's inspiring encounter with the sprightly almost ninety-year-old was a hit, as was her inclusion in the strategy sessions. Steve is categorical that not only does he love his work, but also that he should have made the move earlier. He is particularly struck by his rising social status and the pride he feels at his contribution. Daniel and Arup also highly engaged in their current acts (and they've been passionate about their "cause" for many years). Even John, who is a bit less enthusiastic about his Encore assignments, enjoys the flexibility he has created in his life.

What about the question of remuneration? In most cases, our subjects are receiving their pension payments. Their bonus is what comes from the second activity. Gayle is happy enough to bring in even a modest salary, and sees a direct link between that and her contribution at the food bank. John, in accordance with his recommendation to always live below your means, appreciates the benefits of some extra, previously unexpected income.

What is the future likely to bring for our not-yet-retired friends? We can speculate that Steve and Gayle will continue to enjoy their second acts for some time yet. John may take on more projects, but he will be more cautious and selective in choosing them.

Daniel's and Arup's second acts will likely continue with the same passion, and these two may well create third, fourth or fifth acts. They seem full of endless ideas... and for them there appears to be no such thing as a retirement in the classic sense.

What advice do our subjects have for people who are considering a Second Act? Below is a summary of the advice gathered from our subjects and other sources.

7 tips to consider
before you leap into your next career chapter

1. **Reflect, Prepare and Plan**
   Do not make rash decisions. Think about the key strengths and skills that made you successful and where you think they could be applied. Clarify what is important to you, where your passions lie, what your place is in society and how you can be useful. Take enough time to prepare and create a plan with realistic goals.

2. **Be Ready to Earn Less Money**
   A large majority of those in encore careers experience gaps in their income when they transition, so be prepared to "live below

your means". Change your lifestyle, trim your expenses, and learn to value the intangibles. There is no direct correlation between your salary and your worth to society.

3. **Gather Information and Experiment**
Once you have chosen an area to pursue, immerse yourself in industry news, look up organizations that appeal to you and talk to people who work there. When possible, pursue these opportunities while still working as a full-time professional. Try different things. You can begin as a volunteer, fundraiser, event worker, or member of a non-profit board.

4. **Take Advantage of Programs and Resources Available**
Find out if your employer provides early retirement or similar support packages. Check what is available: encore fellowships, grants or scholarships for training and education. If you are in the U.S., go to websites dedicated to encore careers: www.encore.org, www.bridgespan.org, www.idealist.org, and www.volunteermatch.org.

5. **Network and Seek Support**
Actively network with both older and new connections relevant to your project. Join professional groups online and offline via LinkedIn Groups or others to join in conversations and attend networking events. Coaching might also offer the chance to help you with your search or entire transition.

6. **Adapt to Your New Environment**
Be aware of the differences which might be a surprise. If you work for a non-profit, the culture probably will be different from what you are used to. You will not get the same budgets or support you had if you have worked for a Fortune 100 company. And since non-profits focus on getting things done, you will be expected to juggle a number of responsibilities.

7. **Express Your Energy and Passion – and Enjoy**
Do your best to promote the active, passionate part of your personality during networking activities and in interviews. Think about your wardrobe, appearance, energy level and the topics you bring up during conversations. Enjoy the journey and the feeling that you have found something you care about and love to do, and which has a positive impact on people's lives.

Additional advice may include a need to choose one's sector carefully, and to prepare and anticipate for a while before making the move. The eminent management writer Charles Handy explains that preparation is key to elongated careers; people need to change and start the second curve of their career before their first curve peaks. Handy says: "You must have some energy and resources to retrain. And that's difficult, because you're reaching the peak of the first curve when you're quite successful. You want to go on. If (you are too) late you're already downhill and it's very difficult to get up again. If you want a successful third age, you need a third act. You need to plan for it."[69]

And finally, Marci Alboher tells us that, for many, even though it was not the case for our subjects, the process may take some time: "Contrary to the ubiquitous magazine profile of the lawyer-turned-teacher, moving into new kinds of work is not quick or easy. Usually, the transition is a slow metamorphosis involving baby steps, detours, persistence, creativity, and a do-it-yourself spirit. Some find their encores through a subtle tweaking of what came before, but many find the need or desire for a wholesale reinvention. This is complicated at any age, and all the more so when your friends and family worry that you've lost your mind, and when the workplace seems dominated by young people not exactly warm to working alongside people who look like their parents."

Final Thoughts

Every one of our subjects is to be admired in one way or another. Each one has taken the steps necessary to give back in their own way. We sense that for all of them, the story is not over yet. There may be many more iterations before any of them picks up the golf clubs or buys the condo at the beach. Is this the new model? Will everyone, sooner or later, view his or her latter years in working life as an opportunity to give? Certainly this group inspires us to believe so, but the road is long, and the key will be to make more noise about this kind of opportunity. There are certainly more reasons in the early 21st century to be continuing to work past the age of sixty, and not all of them are necessarily that pretty.

On the corporate side, HR departments and the C-suite could and should be doing more to help employees who may want to consider a second act career. The U.S. examples of HP, Intel and IBM show how companies can actively work with partnering organizations to support retiree transitions to their second act. Indeed, in the U.S., the "encore" idea is spreading and highly organized, whereas all the Europeans to whom we talked about this topic struggled to understand the concept, as it is far from widespread here. Perhaps this will come soon; perhaps we, as talent experts, can contribute to that happening. Maybe it will even end up being part of our own career swan songs.

Evidently, as we have seen even in previous chapters, many of those lucky enough to be on the wealthy side of the big divide feel moved to build some mechanism to give back, to support those less well-off. From this fact alone, we see some hope that the movement will grow, and become an automatic part of all professional careers, imbuing them with true meaning and positive social impact.

Further Reading and Information

❙ BOOKS AND STUDIES

"Second-Act Careers: 50+ Ways to Profit from Your Passions During Semi-Retirement", by Nancy Collamer, Ten Speed Press, 2013

"Life Reimagined: Discovering Your New Life Possibilities", by Richard J. Leider and Alan M. Webber, Berrett-Koehler, 2013

"The Encore Career Handbook: How to Make a Living and a Difference in the Second Half of Life", by Marci Alboher, Workman Publishing Company, 2012

❙ ARTICLES AND BLOGS

"Why Baby Boomers Refuse To Retire", by George Lorenzo, Fast Company, 11 February 2016

"The Encore Career Movement Grows Up", by Richard Eisenberg, Forbes, February 2016

"Working Older", by Emma Jacobs, FT Magazine, 3 July 2015

"3 Great Opportunities For Encore Careers", by Mark Feffer, Forbes, December 2014

"As One Career Wraps Up, Finding That Next Role", by Kerry Hannon, The New York Times, 26 September 2014

▌ WEBSITES

Encore.org – A U.S. non-profit advancing second acts for the greater good
www.encore.org

NextAvenue.org – PBS' (public media) journalism service for America's booming older population
www.nextavenue.org/

Chapter 11

How to Navigate Your Career Transitions and Thrive

As we have seen in our subjects' stories, each case of career transition is different, and each of our protagonists has experienced his or her journey differently. Leaving the military or a sports career, for example, represents a major shift – not only a radical change of one's professional environment and role, but also a challenge to the person's sense of identity. Other transitions appear to be less extreme: consultant to business leader, for example, or boomerang. But we learned that, despite the apparent limited extent of the change, these two transitions could not be "taken for granted". The consultant moving to corporations still has to learn, adapt and shift his mindset; the rehired employee still needs to reacquaint herself with the organization she once worked in.

The Nature of Transitions

Before introducing our transition navigator, it is important to appreciate the characteristics of career transitions. As in climbing a mountain, the paths we use might be more or less winding, more or less steep or have different lengths. Maybe we take a particular path willingly, or maybe we are forced to take it. It is possible we do not know how long we will be on that path until we reach its end. And possibly, there will be no way back. Blake Ashforth, who researched the topic extensively, provides valuable insights on the attributes of role transitions. According to him, "The attributes of a role transition affect the difficulty of making the transition and the valence (attractiveness) of the transition. A role transition will generally be easier thus more positively valent if it is of low magnitude and long duration and is socially desirable, voluntary, predictable (…), and reversible."[70] The table below summarizes key findings from Ashforth and other academic research.

The Nature of Transitions – Continuum of Attributes

Attribute	Description
Low Magnitude.............High Magnitude	Extent of the change, degree of role contrast
Socially Desirable..........Socially Undesirable	How positively, prestigiously the role is regarded by others: colleagues, society, etc.
Voluntary...........................Involuntary	Degree of choice you are able to exercise in exiting or entering a role
Predictable.......................Unpredictable	Ability to anticipate the timing of role exit, the onset and duration of role entry period
Long Duration.................Short Duration	Length of time between when you think about exiting a role and when you are "up to speed" in the subsequent role
Reversible...........................Irreversible	Extent to which you can exit a role and go back to your previous role or initial career

Source: Adapted from Ashforth and Taylor (1990), Ashforth (2001), Ebaugh (1988).

It is interesting to review how these transition attributes affected the professionals we interviewed.

Low Magnitude vs. High Magnitude – According to Ashforth, "the magnitude of the transition will strongly influence the experience of the remaining attributes. Under a low-magnitude transition, where continuity is by definition high, the other attributes become far less consequential." One illustration of this is Louise, the boomerang executive whose return to a pharmaceutical company seemed almost non-eventful. But while magnitude is likely among the most critical attributes which affect the difficulty of making a transition, there remains a question about how to measure it. No one will argue that the day-to-day activities of a professional athlete are far different from those of a manager in a large multinational company. Yet transitions, and therefore their magnitude, can be experienced differently by different individuals. Kavitha's move from big league tennis tournaments to Coke's consumer marketing environment appears to be much smoother than John's tough move from Olympic-level rowing to policy advisory for business and government.

Socially Desirable vs. Socially Undesirable – In general, the more socially desirable, the easier the transition. This appears to apply in most cases. A classic example is professional sports people (in a socially desirable activity for most) shifting to more "regular" jobs, say in business (less socially desirable), and finding this transition challenging. Other transitions appear more neutral from the perspective of social desirability: first job abroad, diaspora return or boomerang. But there again, social desirability cannot be treated as an absolute feature. It can be relative, depending on the individual and the environment that matters to them. For example, moving from a for-profit company to an NGO will likely be seen by the incumbent as the "right thing to do" (i.e., doing good for society), and thus a socially desirable move. However, it can be perceived differently by that same individual's social environment. Maybe their spouse, children and friends will not value this transition the same way, as they might be concerned by the loss of status or the lesser salary that results from the transition.

Voluntary vs. Involuntary – The degree of choice you are able to exercise in exiting or entering a role no doubt has an impact on the ease or difficulty of your career transition. Wounded soldiers and injured athletes forced into retirement typically experience their transition as more difficult and have a harder time finding a new role. The same applies to business professionals forced out of their job through layoff or redundancy. The "Back After a Long Break" transition is interesting to examine from this perspective. Barbara, Jenna, Tim and Argyro voluntarily left their jobs – handing in their resignation – to spend more time with their family. Yet this voluntary, straightforward exit found its opposite circumstance months or years later when they tried to return to employment. All found themselves involuntarily excluded from jobs they were qualified for. This very aspect of their transition is probably what made it the most difficult to deal with.

Predictable vs. Unpredictable – Our subjects' transitions present a broad range of predictability. While none of the moves were totally predictable, many were the result of the individual's decision, who had some control especially over the timing of their role exit. Our military men and women planned or prepared their move, our athletes took a conscious decision to leave in view of their performance or other reasons, and our second career professionals deliberately took advantage of the pre-retirement packages offered by their company. The entry into a new role was, however, less predictable for some. For example, those who had a long break were surprised by the time it took them to re-enter the workforce. Unpredictability creates uncertainty, which then may turn into frustration and anxiety; all of these making the transition more problematic.

Long Duration vs. Short Duration – Ashforth suggests that the longer the time between when you think about exiting a role and when you are "up to speed" in the subsequent role, the better. The relationship between this time attribute and the ease of transition may not be so linear. The swift, dramatic entrance into the corporate environment that Ton experienced after leaving the military seems to have been well-managed and non-traumatic for him. So, short does not always mean difficult. Conversely, those who struggled to re-enter the workforce after a long break found the time went too slowly and did not enjoy it.

Reversible vs. Irreversible — With the notable exception of exits from sports, military service and second acts, it looks as if most transitions have some degree of reversibility. Boomerangs are a case in point, and it is interesting that the subjects involved were not considering returning to their employer at the time they left. In general, however, it is fair to acknowledge that irreversibility affects career transitions in a significant way. If you leave a role or profession knowing your move is irreversible, you will naturally feel some pressure and anguish knowing that there will not be a way back in case your next move fails.

There is one other attribute to add, which academics have not isolated as such: the degree to which an occupation influences an individual's sense of identity. This is especially true for careers in the military, sports or performing arts. These literally shape people. Think about the army, sports leagues or ballet companies, for example. These professions create a strong sense of belonging and their members live in a closed community, isolated in some manner from the "normal" world. Leaving these occupations is like leaving a family or a community, and makes the transition more difficult. This results in having to redefine your identity without an "umbilical cord" to your previous nurturing environment. And the longer you have spent in this environment, the more difficult it is to leave it and do something different.

We have been discussing the transition attributes one at a time, but as Ashforth rightly points out, they are usually experienced jointly. The voluntariness of role entry is likely associated with its social desirability. And conversely, involuntariness may strongly bias how the individual interprets and experiences the subsequent transition process. In general, based on the nine transition scenarios we examined in this book, we suggest that magnitude and "voluntariness" may be the two most critical attributes. We should keep in mind, again, that each of the transition attributes ultimately exists in the eye of the beholder.

Understanding the key characteristics of a particular career transition is a good place to start. But what do you do next? How do you actually navigate a transition? Let's assume that you have enjoyed a good career so far as marketing manager in a large global life science company. You have made steady progress, taken on increasing responsibilities, even enjoyed an international assignment in Asia. But somehow you do not feel as engaged as you were before. Something is missing in your career, and you are not sure what it is. Since you are back in the headquarters, you now wonder "Do I really belong here?". The work atmosphere is stuffy, the pace is slow, there is a lot of politics. You simply cannot imagine yourself in 10-15 years as one of those grey-suited, grey-haired senior executives that you meet in the elevator or at big meetings. And you're still a tad bitter about that promotion to general manager that you and your boss discussed last year, which – as you learned recently – was eventually offered to someone else (ironically a good colleague and alumnus of your B-school).

As you reflect on these developments, you also realize that over the last few months, you have met quite a few people who are entrepreneurs or joined small start-up companies. Is this a coincidence? You think about the dinner you had last night and the intense, fascinating conversation you had with this guy who was telling you about his first profitable quarter in the start-up he created with three friends last year.

Your Career Transition Navigator

1. What's Your Starting Point? Your Self and Your Environment

Before launching yourself into the dynamics of transition, which we will describe in the coming pages, it is important to gain a deep and thorough understanding of who you are and of your environment. To do this, you need to pause and take a step back. Kevin Cashman, Senior Partner with Korn Ferry and CEO advisor, introduced the *Pause Principle* as "the conscious, intentional process of stepping back, within ourselves and outside of ourselves, to lead forward with greater authenticity, purpose and contribution". So take a deep breath, slow down, and begin this powerful purpose-filled journey with us.

My Self

The Swiss psychiatrist Carl Jung said, "Your visions will become clear only when you can look into your own heart. He who looks outside, dreams; he who looks inside, awakes." We are defined by a multitude of personal characteristics, all of which had and will continue to have a massive impact on our career. The challenge therefore for us is to "awaken" and invest time and effort to get to know who we are. We ourselves know, from our experience as coaches and advisors to thousands of professionals, that self-awareness is a difficult undertaking and one which tends to happen rather late in most lives and careers. Our basic education usually does not encourage us to explore our inner personality, our values or interests. As young graduates, we tend to rely and focus heavily on our knowledge, technical skills and other cognitive abilities. Even MBA students who are largely in their late 20s, as both authors have experienced, do not naturally pay much attention to their softer side. Only over time do we get to open up and appreciate the importance of looking inside ourselves and trying to make sense of who we are and what really drives us.

Our practical advice, consequently, is to spend quality time taking stock of where you stand. A lot of this simply starts with being aware and accepting of your factual biographical data: your age, gender, education, health, financial situation, place of living, family situation and so on. Age, for example, can be an important driver of career decision, as Herminia Ibarra reminds us:[71]

> A long tradition of adult development research suggests that mid-career change is often motivated by age-related concerns. (…) It appears that approaching mid-life has a least two effects that may motivate change: 1. The feeling that time is running out, and 2. Greater self-knowledge combined with a reduced tendency to make choices based on social or family approval. While reaching a certain age like forty or fifty may not have any distinct objective effect, for many people it serves as a symbolic marker that the time is ripe to make a change.

Whatever your age might be, you now want to build a clear and consistent picture of your career to date: your experiences and the skills and competencies you have built over time. At this point, this sounds pretty much like revisiting your resume and should be a fairly easy first step. The more challenging part starts with defining in more depth your actual self: what are your personality traits or preferences, your values and interests, your passions and aspirations? Answering those "what" questions is a crucial step which requires personal reflection, input from trusted people around you and many iterations. A simple and effective framework we recommend you to complete is shown in the following chart.

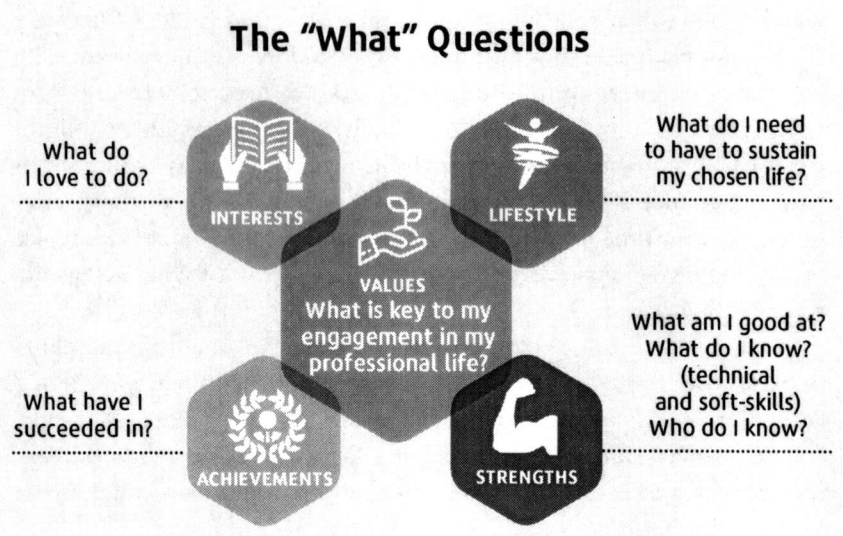

The "What" Questions

What do I love to do?

INTERESTS

What do I need to have to sustain my chosen life?

LIFESTYLE

VALUES
What is key to my engagement in my professional life?

What have I succeeded in?

ACHIEVEMENTS

What am I good at? What do I know? (technical and soft-skills) Who do I know?

STRENGTHS

To summarize this first step, here are our main tips:

1. Self-assessment is key
2. Reflection takes time, so plan in advance
3. Get help from loved ones, close friends, alumni, career professionals, etc.
4. Do not reinvent your wheel: retrieve earlier reflection and assessments (MBTI, 360° feedback, etc.)
5. Write. Write down plans and thoughts. Carry a dedicated notebook
6. Regularly repeat this process, even when you are in a stable role

My Environment

Many of us believe in our capacity to influence our own thoughts and behavior, and have faith in our ability to "control our life". This is what psychologists call our "sense of agency". By no means, however, should the "My Self" exploration we just described become a selfish exercise. It must be complemented by an equally rigorous consideration of our environment: our family and friends, the communities we belong to and our professional network.

Here we would like to emphasize how family influences our careers much more than we might think. Many of the stories shared by our subjects, and a review of some of the key research literature, reveal that individuals are susceptible to influence from their families of origin with regard to occupational choice and prioritizing work over family, or vice versa:

- **Impact of family of origin on career choice** – Think about Eric and Kavitha, who practiced horse riding and tennis, then turned these activities into career starters. Take Devendra and Priya, both surrounded by "olive green" while they were growing up, who "naturally" enrolled in the military. Most of us are influenced by values, interests, or occupations from our family of origin. In some cases, occupational choices are entirely made by parents: "Our older son will be a doctor, our daughter will be an architect...". This predestination pattern takes its ultimate embodiment with family businesses, where dynasties become a substitute for rational succession planning. Familial heritage sometimes plays a role in occupational choice in more subtle ways. According to psychoanalytic theory, individuals will tend to choose an occupation that enables them to satisfy needs that were unfulfilled in their childhood, and realize dreams passed on to them by their family.

- **Impact of work-family values or expectations on career choice** – The desire for a balanced lifestyle between work and family also affects decisions to change jobs or accept a geographical transfer. It can help shape employees' intentions to depart an organization or an entire career. Examples of this abound in our subjects' stories as well as our own. Rupert was tired of travel and corporate values, Mui Gek was bound to her husband's job moves, and one of your two authors has shaped her career to fit around the need to raise four young children alone. As we have seen, career opportunities, in the form of prospects for advancement within an organization or more generally in one's chosen field, are impacted by family commitments and the use of (or lack of) flexible working practices designed to help employees balance their work and home responsibilities.

We note from the stories of our subjects the significance of family and work-life issues in career-related decision making. To our regret, we also observe the persistence of gendered parenting roles and their negative effects on women's careers. The influence of family and work-life balance will continue to grow with the younger generations. According to a 2016 study by Deloitte, Millennials value work-life balance higher than all other job characteristics – which includes job progression, use of technology, and sense of meaning at work.[72] This means as a result that organizations need to pay increasing attention to family-friendliness for recruitment and retention, a topic we will discuss later.

You may also find that once you have started your "grown-up" career life, you start to gravitate towards those with similar ambitions and wishes as you. This may be unconscious at first, but will become more obvious as the years go by. If you are an investment banker with a stay-at-home spouse, it is more likely that your social circle is similarly composed, and thus you will find it easy to continue to "validate" your choices. Breaking out is painful, as it means severing the ties, or at least reshaping them. Conversely, it is often the case that a community of friends and colleagues will encourage you in a new direction, if that is what they are also thinking about. The bonds that tie us are strong.

Now that you have spent some time building a complete picture of your starting point, answering questions such as who you are (so far) and what your current environment is, let's progress to the first step of your change journey.

Career Transition Navigator

CHANGE TRIGGERS
- Life event
- Professional event
- Serendipity
- Epiphany / Aha moment

MY SELF
- Age, gender
- Education
- Health and lifestyle
- Financial needs
- Personality
- Values and interests
- Career capital
- Skills and competencies
- Career anchors and aspirations

CHANGE OUTCOMES
- Speed and ease of transition
- Satisfaction in new role
- Career success
- Financial success
- Overall life satisfaction

1. EXPLORE
2. EXPERIMENT
3. ENGAGE
4. EXPAND

REFLECT LEARN MONITOR

MY ENVIRONMENT
- Family
- Social
- Professional network

SUCCESS FACTORS
- Commitment
- Control
- Curiosity
- Change agility
- Connections
- Confidence

2. Navigating Your Transition Through the 4E Pathway

To guide you in navigating your career transition, we are suggesting the following four-step approach: Explore, Experiment, Engage and Expand. We will go through each of these steps in the following pages.

Step 1 – Explore

What is this?
- Reflect on who you are
- Think about why and what you want to change
- Consider your career options

So now, while you are more aware of yourself and your environment, you have in mind the idea that you no longer want to continue working as a marketing manager in a large life science corporation. You have some ideas about what you would like to do next, but it is all still vague and confused. You need to answer the "Where to?" question.

This stage is the forward-looking process of searching for or deciding about the right next position. It's about examining the future, identifying opportunities and recognizing the "pull" of the next step or position. Our key advice here: it is urgent not to hurry.

Instead, take time to dream first. Jenny Blake, author of "Pivot", former career coach at Google and co-founder of the company's career development mentorship program, recently shared how people can transition into the careers they want.[73] "When you're looking for the perfect job, there's one thing you should avoid: taking action based on fear or 'shoulds'. When people are guided by fear or what they think they should do, it keeps them stuck in unfulfilling jobs", she says.[74]

The "shoulds" that Jenny Blake refers to are particularly insidious. As we have seen previously, our social environment – family, friends, professional networks – plays a big influence on our career decisions. Each person you care about will have their own views, their best piece of advice (sometimes contradictory) and some will apply pressure on you without you necessarily realizing it. Our recommendation then is to allow yourself to put all the external noise aside and start to "dream it."

Dreaming is something you typically do on your own, and to quote Carl Jung one more time, "He who looks outside, dreams." That is exactly what the exploration stage aims to do.

What Next?

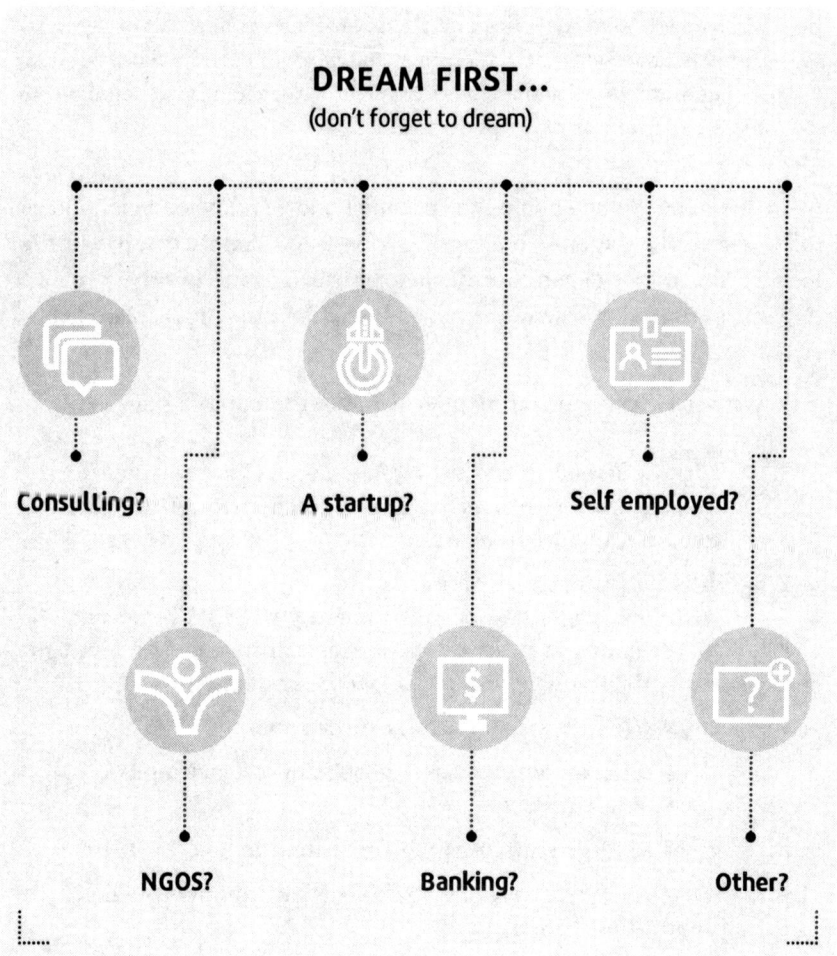

The verb "to explore" suggests examination and the investigation of unknown regions. So be ready for this. As Jelena Zikic and Douglas T. Hall highlighted in their paper "Toward a More Complex View of Career Exploration":[75]

> It may be more realistic to consider career exploration processes as a bit more chaotic and unpredictable than previously assumed. For many individuals, career exploration will be the result of both planning and chance events (…). In practice, this means we need to be open to frequent and unexpected changes and work to become more open to, and ready for these unpredictable career influences that sometimes may turn careful planning upside down.

So do not be too hung up on the planning, and be ready for an emotional roller coaster. In the table on page 237, we have identified some of the feelings you might experience during this stage. Some positive: excited, hopeful, optimistic. Some negative: confused, doubtful, stuck, scared…

Below are some questions to ponder while in the Explore stage:

1. What do I want to do? What is my target career or role? (e.g., from advertising manager to school teacher, from marketing executive to entrepreneur…)

2. Why do I want to transition?
   - How long have I been considering it? (e.g. I've been dreaming of it since I was a kid, I met a teacher a year ago and felt totally inspired by what she does…)
   - What are my main drivers, motivations?
   - Do I really want a career change or just a change of environment?

3. What will I give up or gain if I transition to a new career?

4. What positive drivers (e.g. myself, my environment) will support the change?

5. What adverse drivers (e.g. myself, my environment) will make it difficult?

6.   What skills and competencies will I need to be successful
     in my next role?
     ▪ How big is the skills gap? How can I compensate for it?

     ▪ What are my strengths, and how can I apply them
       in the new career or role? Which of my current
       skills are transferable?

7.   Who do I need to check in with ahead of this change?

8.   How long might it take me to make the change?
     How much am I willing to invest (e.g. time,
     resources, education, etc.)?

Step 2 – Experiment

What is this?
▪   Try out new things in small steps
▪   Build new connections
▪   Reframe and zero in your search

While a good deal of exploration is needed, meticulous planning may
be neither possible nor desirable. We saw from our subjects' stories that
successful career transformation does not follow a linear and predictable
path. The truth is, making a big career change is a messy trial-and-error
process of learning by doing. This is one of the key ideas in Herminia
Ibarra's book "Working Identity: Unconventional Strategies for
Reinventing Your Career".[76] "To make a big change", she says, "reverse
the conventional 'think before doing' logic. Resist the temptation to
analyze or plan a new career, then start off with a big decision that
dramatically alters your situation." Almost no one gets it right in one big
step. Instead, test reality through small steps in directions that attract you.
Small steps gradually lead to big change.

In her book "Pivot", Jenny Blake explains how launching little
experiments can help people transition into a role they love. These small
pivots could be taking on a different project at work, pitching a new idea
to a client or starting a blog. "Even the pivots that didn't seem to pan out
from the outside taught people valuable information for their next move
after that."

Ron Ashkenas, in his 2016 HBR article "Navigating the Emotional Side of a Career Transition", provides a good example of what this testing approach can look like, using his own transition as an example:[77]

> Before jumping to your next thing, consider what else you can do to prepare for a career transition – what might possibly make the transition as smooth as possible? In my case, when I began to think about doing something other than being a full-time consultant, I spent several months as an "executive in residence" at a business school as a way of testing what it would be like to do something else. The point is that a career transition is not necessarily a "leap" – it can be a considered series of steps during which you deal with not only the practical issues but also the emotional ones.

This process can take time, and it's a good idea to keep a day job while experimenting. In his book "Originals", Wharton professor Adam Grant describes how many influential creative minds have stayed in full-time employment even after earning income from major projects:[78]

> Selma director Ava DuVernay made her first three films while working in her day job as a publicist, only pursuing filmmaking full time after working at it for four years and winning multiple awards. Brian May was in the middle of doctoral studies in astrophysics when he started playing guitar in a new band, but he didn't drop out until several years later to go all in with Queen. Soon thereafter he wrote "We Will Rock You." Grammy winner John Legend released his first album in 2000 but kept working as a management consultant until 2002, preparing PowerPoint presentations by day while performing at night. Thriller master Stephen King worked as a teacher, janitor, and gas station attendant for seven years after writing his first story, only quitting a year after his first novel, Carrie, was published. Dilbert author Scott Adams worked at Pacific Bell for seven years after his first comic strip hit newspapers.

This habit of keeping one's day job is not limited to celebrities. In the stories we shared in the previous chapters, you may recall Daniel, the real estate general manager, who tried volunteering for the French homeless charity "Restos du Coeur" before setting up his own children's foundation. Ramon and the other founders of Emzingo took a similar approach to the startup phase of their social enterprise, each one holding on to his previous role and salary for some time.

So, the "doing" advice from Herminia Ibarra does not mean quitting your job abruptly and running around like a headless chicken. It is about testing with intent, or at least with some hypothesis in mind. And while our navigator model presents Exploration and Experimentation as two separate activities, these actually overlap and it is perfectly fine to go back and forth between the two. It is an iterative process which can go like this: Try something new, evaluate how well it really fits with your needs and preferences, take another step, probe new possibilities, experiment again, and so on – until you feel ready to move on to your next role or career.

Bear in mind, however, that the experimentation inevitably takes time. Remember, career transformation is difficult and slow: two to five years is common for a transition to happen and to consolidate.

Building new connections plays a big part in successfully progressing through this experimentation stage. Herminia Ibarra observed that the networks we rely on in a stable work situation are rarely the ones that lead us to something new and different. She advises career-changers to pursue new contacts as far away as possible from their daily routines, and to see their plans as an escape from the status quo, often referred to as "getting out of the building" by the great entrepreneurship educator Steve Blank.[79] So how do you begin networking effectively for your new desired role? This particular step probably will not be as dramatic as you might imagine. Much of the networking you will be doing will be the same, with just a few exceptions. Below are some tips we suggest.

- **Let People Know** – Even though many of the people in your immediate network will not be in your target industry, you never know who might be in their networks. So let people know you are thinking about making a change, and see if they know anyone you can connect with.

- **Do Your Research** – Does your university give you access to an alumni database? Have you searched on LinkedIn for people in your target role to check out their career paths? What are the professional organizations that are active in your targeted area? This mapping exercise is important to lay the foundation for your future networking efforts.

- **Find Others Who Have Done It** – While reaching out to people who have an extensive tenure in the industry can be helpful to learn more about the trade, the most useful people for you to connect with will be those who have already made the career change you would like to make. LinkedIn can be particularly useful here, since you can view people's career paths on their profiles.

- **Seek Advice** – Meeting and talking to people at a networking event is hard work, but surprisingly it can be easier when you are new to an industry. Think about it this way: networking is all about telling your story, asking questions, and getting advice. As a career changer, your story is going to be more interesting than most, and being "new", you will naturally have questions and require advice. Use this to your advantage.

- **Go to Industry Events** – Professional organizations frequently have both social and professional development events that you can benefit from. These will help you learn more about your target industry and you might end up meeting the person who will be key in helping you break into the field.

Obviously, one additional way to penetrate a new field and community while preparing for your transition is through continuous education or training. One of the advantages of training is to deepen your exploration and experimentation while possibly staying in your current role. And it's even better if your employer can support it financially. Examples of using training to facilitate career change abound in our subjects' stories. Upon leaving the military police, Ton signed up for university, studying organization and labor psychology, which helped him get a job as head of change in a construction company. Quite a number of our subjects also went the popular MBA route, like Devendra, who was conscious of the need to strengthen his business skills to support his move out of the military. For a few others – such as Richard, Mui Gek, Andrew and Kavitha – the MBA was not necessarily a compulsory entrance ticket, but rather an accelerator that boosted their longer-term career in the new field.

The *Experiment* stage might take a while to get through. But remember, it's actually not a bad thing to take your time, while recognizing that you might feel some confusion or impatience during this critical period of your change journey. In the end, through this ongoing, iterative process of experimentation, meeting new people, testing ideas and further reflecting, you will be able to reframe and zero-in your search with greater clarity and commitment.

Career Transition Navigator

Your 4E Pathway

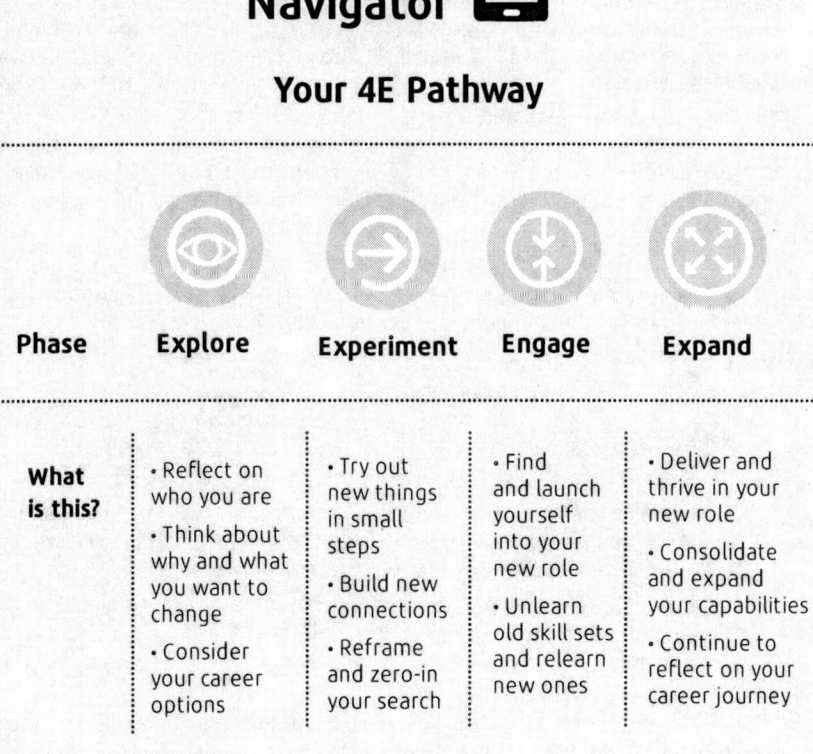

Phase	Explore	Experiment	Engage	Expand
What is this?	• Reflect on who you are • Think about why and what you want to change • Consider your career options	• Try out new things in small steps • Build new connections • Reframe and zero-in your search	• Find and launch yourself into your new role • Unlearn old skill sets and relearn new ones	• Deliver and thrive in your new role • Consolidate and expand your capabilities • Continue to reflect on your career journey

Phase	Explore	Experiment
Who went through this?	*Almost all of our subjects went through this phase, with a varying degree of assiduity. Everyone had a moment of discontent or frustration or some sort of trigger that set them thinking. Some examples include:*	*Many of our subjects missed out on this phase, and there is no doubt some correlation between that omission and the later struggles. Those that did experience it gained useful perspective and vision. Examples here are:*
	Marta was intrigued that she was now perceived as a potential CEO, and she started to think hard about what she really wanted to do. It was not long until she concluded that she wanted her own business and to give back to her own country.	**Steve** had long been on the board of his children's school, and had also taken on a role in another local non-profit organization – so he was already turned firmly towards public service.
	Diana went back to school in Oxford and literally shut herself away for a year, hoping to figure out her new destiny.	**Daniel** travelled a great deal and tried volunteering for the "Restos du Coeur", one of the largest homeless charities in France.
	Rupert had become disenfranchised and bored with consulting, and felt motivated by the possibility of controlling his own destiny while creating value.	**Ton** signed up for university, studying Organization and Labor Psychology. He also started volunteering with a crisis hotline, similar to the Samaritans, learning non-judgmental listening.
	Thinking about what was important, **John** remembered he had a love for the environment and the outdoors. This started to shape his search for the next challenge.	With advice from his father, **Andrew** mapped out a five-year plan, bearing in mind that he wanted a serious job in business.
How might I feel?	*Positive* ❏ Excited ❏ Hopeful ❏ Enthusiastic ❏ Optimistic *Negative* ❏ In doubt ❏ Confused ❏ Stuck or pigeonholed ❏ Seeing greener grass on the other side ❏ Sense of guilt ❏ Scared	❏ Energized ❏ Enthusiastic ❏ Encouraged by progress ❏ Skeptical ❏ Disappointed ❏ Confused ❏ Impatient ❏ Sad about the past ❏ Depressed ❏ Inept
What should I do?	❏ Make sense of the past, current and future of my career ❏ Explore my career future options ❏ Design alternative scenarios ❏ Reconnect with the contacts I have made over my career ❏ Experience new people and new ideas to uncover new possibilities ❏ Share my thoughts and feelings with my family, friends and trusted ones	❏ Test and experiment new activities ❏ Build new networks, find new role models and communities ❏ Attend significant events in my targeted area ❏ Reflect, reframe, refine, confirm my goals ❏ Create a plan to land in my new role ❏ Identify what transferable skills will help me in the target role and where my skills gaps are

Engage

This stage is one of excitement, and is often enjoyed. It can be a disquieting, frantic time, but one in which the rewards start to appear. Some of our stories included:

On joining McKinsey, **Andrew** was excited by the speed, the challenge, and the strong team spirit. He felt it was like "pressing the reset button" and recognized the vast amount he had to learn.

Marta realized that despite 20 years experience, a startup is not so easy to make work in Peru. She had to fine-tune her skills to a level she could not have imagined.

Returning to her previous company, **Louise** found many familiar faces, but decided to spend time getting to know people once again and finding out "how things are done round here".

Yang asked his partners for help to navigate around his new city, seeing himself more like a new expat than a native of his own country.

- ❏ Thrilled ❏ Excited
- ❏ Nervous ❏ Surprised

- ❏ Apprehensive ❏ Careful
- ❏ Awkward ❏ Unsettled
- ❏ Disoriented ❏ Confused identity
- ❏ Frustrated

- ❏ Draw from previous meaningful experience to deal with transition
- ❏ Carefully plan and manage my transition plan
- ❏ Clarify expectations
- ❏ Build relationships in my new environment
- ❏ Make sense of my new work environment
- ❏ Reduce any person-role misfit
- ❏ Let go of old patterns and habits
- ❏ Adjust my personal identity

Expand

This is the stage where the going gets fun. All that time spent experiencing, exploring and engaging now comes to fruition. Enjoy and don't forget to spend time reflecting on future possibilities:

Consulting helped **Rupert** in his "modeling up" of the coffee industry. He has used sophisticated techniques to become a big player and to approach clients and suppliers with increased confidence and credibility.

Kavitha has been at Coca-Cola in various roles for the subsequent years, putting her top three sports-transferable skills into action: discipline, composure and globally aware adaptability.

In her new role, **Mui Gek** got past her language problems, networked, and used her blend of knowledge, passion and persuasion to bring all stakeholders on board. As a result, she created an unheard-of collaboration between previously competitive brands, and was subsequently offered increasingly interesting and developmental roles.

Ike believes in the benefits of creating career "spaces" as opportunities to reflect on and open up to other possibilities.

- ❏ Fulfilled ❏ Satisfied
- ❏ Energized ❏ Buoyant

- ❏ Disillusioned or disenchanted
- ❏ Self-critical ❏ Insatiable

- ❏ Enjoy
- ❏ Leverage my skills and experience to deliver outstanding performance
- ❏ Strengthen my edge
- ❏ Consolidate and further build my brand
- ❏ Avoid complacency
- ❏ Continuously learn and update my skills
- ❏ Reflect and think about possible new opportunities

Change Triggers

In her working paper "Career Transition and Change", Herminia Ibarra discusses the influence of trigger events on careers:

> A diverse set of studies and theoretical perspectives have converged on the key role of trigger events in stimulating change. Triggers may be positive or negative; momentous or small. They range from major job, organizational and personal life changes or shocks to jolts produced by more mundane interactions. Scholars concur that critical events do not directly produce change; rather they trigger personal explorations and trial experimentations with new forms of social interaction, which may lead later to career changes.

As we analyzed the stories of our forty-four subjects, we identified various trigger patterns which we illustrate below. Bear in mind that these triggers are not necessarily unique. Often, a combination of triggers will work together to stimulate the change.

Trigger	Example
Life event	• Pharma executive Christi Shaw tendered her resignation in order to care full-time for her sister, who was fighting cancer and involved in a demanding clinical trial.
	• As her girls grew up, Bambina began to consider where should be the next move. She decided that the economy in Europe was not buoyant enough, and chose to return to her home country.
Professional event	• The changes in the HP organization took on speed, and Gayle became more and more frustrated by the culture changes and other developments. So when she was offered a "phased" retirement at the age of 56, she was tempted and eventually accepted the offer.
	• Argyro started to see strong signals that her company was going to be acquired. Her reluctance to be in the post-merger structure, as well as a recognition that she did not want to sacrifice time with her baby led her to part ways amicably with her company.

Serendipity	• Yang could have endlessly pursued his role in the UK as a rainmaker and a star at Reuters. But a few months ago, some Chinese friends asked him to join them back in Shanghai, and Yang became a partner in Yaozhi Asset Management Co., an investment fund.
	• Influenced by the frequent calls of headhunters, Thomas decided to take up the challenge offered to him by one of his clients whose CEO offered him the position of VP for Europe of the company.
	• When Tim was contacted by a consultancy firm, he took on a single project, which led to another, and now he is helping them develop their business.
Epiphany (or Aha moment)	• After working for a few years in a variety of agencies, Barbara decided to pursue an MBA degree. During a lecture on intangible assets, she had an "aha" moment, concluding that the next big business issue would be people, so she signed up for the HR route.
	• When Graham returned from a trip and his pregnant wife told him that she still felt tired from the weekend, he realized what an absurd feat he had just accomplished and seriously questioned his sanity. He realized that he wanted a "proper" job again, with a more reasonable lifestyle, and also budgets, staff and implementation.

Step 3 – Engage

What is this?
- Find and launch yourself into your new role
- Unlearn old skill sets and relearn new ones

Once you have confirmed what you want to do next and have defined a plan to reach your next position, a significant part of your time and energy will be spent on identifying opportunities through your network or job boards or any other sources. We will not go into the specifics of job search tactics, CV building or interview techniques, as these topics are well-covered by numerous easily accessible books and resources. It is useful, however, to highlight some of the unique characteristics of searching a role for which one does not have previous experience.

Draw from Previous Meaningful Experience to Deal with the Transition

A consistent learning from studying our nine uncharted transition cases is the importance of appreciating the skills you have gained in your previous career and understanding how you might put them to use in your new working environment. Doing this requires some reflection, critical analysis, and the ability to communicate to future employers a compelling value proposition around your transferable skills. Athletes might not have an in-depth understanding of business, but they can showcase some of the great attributes they have gained for competitive sports: self-motivation, speed, focus, discipline, high resistance to pressure, and flexibility, to name a few. Likewise, former military men and women should not be shy to bring forward their strength of character, fearlessness, cool headedness and caring personal traits – all useful attributes that will serve a business. The flip side of this is to become fully aware of the core skills or capabilities that you do not yet have which will be required for your new job – and to create a development plan to quickly fill these gaps.

At some point, whether your search was quick and easy or whether you went through a longer process involving multiple tests and interviews, you will receive an offer to join an organization in the new role that you have coveted. You are now about to jump into your new job, likely in an environment that you know little about. How do you approach this stage?

Plan and Manage Your Onboarding

The topic of onboarding has been well studied by a number of academics and practitioners. One of the best experts in the field is business school professor Michael Watkins, who authored the famous

"The First 90 Days: Critical Success Strategies for New Leaders at All Levels".[80] Watkins provides a framework for transition that helps leaders diagnose their situation, craft winning transition strategies, and take charge quickly. The following are a couple of areas of focus taken from Watkins' work that can help you plan and successfully implement your first 90 days.

- **Understanding the context and situation you are entering** – Being respectful of the past and ensuring a full understanding of the dynamics of the organization culture, relationships, business strategies and goals is critical to being effective in your first 90 days. Without a full appreciation of the context you are entering, you may inadvertently misjudge the water conditions and wind up sinking your career in that role. Do not be careless – be curious. Ask thoughtful questions; find out what has been done before and what is missing now, so that you will be effective.

- **Building personal and leadership credibility and achieving quick wins** – Building credibility is a journey, not a destination. It continues throughout your role and career. One way to help build your credibility is through achieving quick wins and successes through small milestones of a bigger project. Engage in interviews with all key stakeholders – your board, boss, peers, team members, suppliers and clients – to discover the pain point in the organization that will lead you to the quick win and a contribution to problem solving in the organization.

- **Developing key relationships for your success** – Engaging, assessing and building your team to ensure that your goals and the goals of the team are aligned with the organization's goals is critical. Clarifying mutual expectations with your boss early on and frequently checking in and negotiating timelines and resources for your success will indicate that you have a well-thought-out plan to contribute in your role in the organization. Identify your key stakeholders, influencers, knowledge keepers, supporters and opponents and invest in building relationship capital with the people you need to help you become successful.

Being deliberate about what and how you are going to learn and implementing your first 90-day plan will be the difference between sinking and swimming in the challenging waters of a new role or organization. This advice goes to all career changers, whatever their starting and end points might be. Even if a transition may appear "easy-peasy" at face value, we learned from our subjects that the change can be fraught with surprises. Marta, for example, realized that despite her 20 years corporate experience, a startup was not so easy to make work in Peru. She had to fine-tune her skills to a level she could not have imagined. Louise, who returned to her previous pharmaceutical company, found many familiar faces but decided to spend time getting to know people once again and finding out "how things are done round here". And Yang, despite being Chinese, asked his new partners for help to navigate both physically and practically around his new city, Shanghai, seeing himself more like a new expat than a native of this country.

Managing Your Emotions and Balance

During this intense onboarding period, it is also key to manage your emotions and personal balance. The challenge here is huge: you are in your new role, but also experiencing a number of surprises, frustrations and disappointments. You sense you are not yet fitting in and feel confused about how to respond to your new environment.

Herminia Ibarra has some helpful observations here: that research on the outcomes of career transition focuses on the idea of mutual adaptation, as well as the ease and speed of the process. The adaptation approach assumes a clear and identifiable role into which we can step, and the question becomes the extent to which we will shape the role to fit our interests and strengths, or indeed whether we will simply conform to the role's requirements. It is commonly agreed that person and role evolve interactively, creating a new synthesis beyond a simple compromise. Recent research performed by Adam Grant with Google confirms this idea that letting people be the architects of their own job, customizing their tasks and relationships to better align with their interests, skills, and values leads to increased happiness and job performance.[81]

Nonetheless, the emotional challenge remains high for career changers, especially in adjusting their personal identity and sense of self. According to Gallup research, 55 percent of people in the U.S. define themselves by their job instead of considering work as simply what they do to earn a living. Both authors have also seen that many executives are vulnerable. They cannot separate who they are from what they do for their careers; their personal identity is shaped by their work. So if your job or career changes, you will likely need to adjust your self-image too. Whether you like it or not, you will be in the process of "becoming an ex", to quote Helen Rose Fuchs Ebaugh, who studied people who underwent extreme identity transitions such as leaving a religious order or undergoing sex-change surgery.[82] Your career change creates the need to decode your former self-identity and recode your next satisfactory identity. This process should be based not only on your individualized identity work but also within your social and societal environment.

Some organizations have clever ways to help individuals redefine their work identity by using "rites of passage". In U.S. Navy boot camps, for example, within an hour after arrival a new recruit is told to remove all his civilian clothes, his jewelry, religious items, etc. and place them, along with wallet, comb, key ring, and the like into a shipping box that is sent home. These rites of transition, or passage, are often complemented by rites of integration consisting of collective actions that function to actually incorporate newcomers into their role. While we do not expect every new host organization to use such elaborate devices, we do suppose that they may provide some programs to that effect. Our recommendation is to embrace and take full advantage of these. We would go even further by suggesting that you create your own "rites of passage" to facilitate or accelerate your own transition. It starts simply by being attentive to the new language, clothing and other expressive means within your new environment (think about a strategy consultant moving into an NGO) and deciding for yourself how much you will embrace the various physical codes, symbols, lingo and other manifestations.

During this intense period, getting the support of a professional coach can be an effective way to help you go through this identity transition, as well as manage your first 90 days.

Step 4 – Expand

What is this?
- Deliver and thrive in your new role
- Consolidate and expand your capabilities
- Continue to reflect on your career journey

Delivering and Thriving in Your New Role

Once you are settled in your new role and working environment, having gone through your first 90 days, the name of the game is to stabilize, display ability and competence, and deliver results. At this stage, you should have built some positive momentum by securing a couple of early wins, laying a foundation – for example defining and communicating your strategic priorities – and building credibility with your key stakeholders.

It would be an illusion, though, to believe that life becomes easy and routine after these magical 90 days, for there are still plenty of risks and challenges ahead. A Right Management Consultants 2005 report indicated that about 30 percent of new managers and executives fail at their new jobs and leave within 18 months.[83] Another study evaluated that on average, it takes new executives a minimum of six months to become fully productive in their role. So it is probably a healthy mindset to see yourself as being on something tantamount to a trial period for an extended period of time and continue to seek to learn and adjust. You need equally to be careful to avoid traps such as getting behind the learning curve, becoming isolated, coming in too quickly with the answer, or attempting to do too much. Beyond delivering "work" and results, you should view your onboarding as unfolding over time, and as such should continue to build quality relationships and gain support from key stakeholders.

Consolidating and Expanding Your Capabilities... and Advancing

As you take on responsibility and continue to perform in your role, you will build new skills, gradually reaching some stability in your position, and that should feel more comfortable. In the meantime, we would expect you to have progressed in the process of recoding your new identity. This, however, does not mean ignoring your past strengths and throwing them out with the bathwater. There is a subtle balance to be found between acquiring new skills and leveraging your older skills.

Kavitha illustrates this well. After her tennis career, she has been at Coca-Cola in various roles for several years, putting her top three sports-transferable skills into action: discipline, composure and globally aware adaptability. Over time, those distinctive strengths – if well nurtured – will help you build your own leadership brand and support your career progress. We see this well with Richard's story. What has set him apart from his peers and supported a brilliant career at FMC Technologies are his intercultural team management skills and his ability to straddle the bridge between different national cultures – all of which he gained in the early stages of his career abroad.

While you maintain and uphold performance in your not-so-new-anymore working environment, it is imperative to avoid any form of complacency and seek to continuously learn and update your skills. Ask yourself these questions:

- Am I staying up to date on new developments, technologies, or ways to do things better?
- Am I seeking to update my skills through continuing education and training?
- Do I innovate? Am I seeking new challenges?

As we have shared in the earlier chapters of this book, the world of work is changing at increasing speed, and lifelong learning has become both a mindset and a practical necessity. A number of initiatives are being launched toward that end. In 2017, the business school INSEAD introduced several new alumni benefits and services and launched a new online learning program for alumni members. The first course that was offered to alumni was "Strategy in the Age of Digital Disruption". In a continuation of its efforts, the school will be offering more programs soon.

Continuing to Reflect on Your Career Journey

By now, you probably get a sense of where this is going… A career is a never-ending story, and as our 4E chart suggests, the process of Exploring, Experimenting, Engaging and Expanding is drawn as a continuous wheel. Our advice, then is straightforward: even if you are fully happy in your new career, thriving, enjoying it, expanding and more, do not forget to allocate time to reflect and think about possible new opportunities. Start to explore once again. Our diaspora subject, Ike, could not illustrate this better when he talks about the benefits of career "spaces", as opportunities to reflect, and open up to other possibilities. This period of reflection led him to find a role in a private equity fund in Nigeria.

As we reach the fourth and final stage of our career transition navigator, it is a good time to summarize and highlight some key points which can help you make the most of this tool:

- Transitioning is characterized by four steps: Explore, Experiment, Engage and Expand.
- Each contain a set of activities and developmental tasks.
- Mastery of these tasks prepares you to move onto the next activity.
- Not everyone will progress through these activities at the same age, the same speed or in the same manner.
- Progression through these activities does not necessarily occur in a linear fashion.
- You may be engaged in more than one activity at the same time.
- It is possible, and even likely, for you to re-cycle through earlier activities, regardless of the activity you are currently engaged in.

Building on the last point, we strongly believe that under our new environment where we see careers made up of numerous jobs and occupations through a disruptive world of work and extended human life span (see Chapter 1), our 4E model will be used multiple times throughout any career, as a series of mini-cycle transitions between diverse positions.

3. Success Factors: The 6C's

The 4E process we present in this chapter will hopefully help you to organize your transition, whether you are addressing one particular role change or multiple shifts throughout your career. As mentioned above, the time spent on each step, the pace of moving from one to the other, and the entire duration of the process – from the moment you are considering a change to the time you are settled into a new role – will be different for each individual.

There are many reasons that explain these differences. First, the nature and magnitude of each transition have a large impact on the difficulty and length to completion of the change. Second, your personal circumstances and environment will bring their share of positive or negative forces. And third, there will be this element of luck or serendipity that no one really has any control over.

On top of these, there are a number of personal attributes, or resources, which can equally impact your ability to "perform" the change. Mark Savickas, who has researched extensively on career development, describes the ability to adapt as "a psychosocial construct that denotes an individual's resources for coping with current and anticipated developmental tasks, occupational transitions, and work traumas." Based on the work by Savickas and others, enriched by the stories of the forty-four subjects we met, we have identified six success factors, or abilities, which support us while going through career changes.[84] These are:

- Commitment
- Control
- Curiosity
- Change agility
- Connections
- Confidence

In the following table, we describe the characteristics of each of these success factors which we call "The 6 C's".

Success Factors | The 6 C's

Factor	What Is It?
Commitment 	Extent to which you are focused and engaged in the process of managing your career. **Ask yourself: Am I...** • Concerned about my career? • Thinking about my future? • Taking action to create change?
Control 	Extent to which you feel some control over your career and a responsibility for building it. **Ask yourself: Am I...** • Making decisions by myself? • Taking responsibility for my actions?
Curiosity	Extent to which you are exploring the world of work and seeking information about roles, careers and their requirements. **Ask yourself: Am I...** • Curious about new opportunities? • Probing deeply into my questions?
Change Agility 	Extent to which you like to experiment, explore new options and cope effectively with the discomfort of change. **Ask yourself: Am I...** • Tolerant of uncertainty? • Introducing new perspectives? • Handling change well?
Connections 	Extent to which you are building your network, and the efforts you are making to meet people and create connections. **Ask yourself: Am I...** • Valuing the idea of networking? • Clear about who to connect with? • Initiating and investing in relationships?
Confidence 	Extent to which you have faith in your ability to make and carry out wise career decisions and realistic choices. **Ask yourself: Do I...** • Believe in myself and my abilities? • Overcome obstacles and recover from setbacks?

Success Factors | The 6 C's

What Does It Mean?

- You must first become aware of the options and choices that you can make.
- Anticipating the decisions and the moves that you can make should prompt you to become involved in preparing to do so.
- You will make better choices and changes by anticipating and creating your own plans.

- You can build a better career by being decisive and conscientious rather than relying on chance or luck.
- Be proactive rather than reactive.
- Take a disciplined, deliberate, and organized approach in choosing goals and creating the conditions for achieving them.

- The information you have is the limit of your possibilities.
- Increasing information and experiences increases opportunities and alternatives.
- You can reduce confusion by exploring your own abilities and interests along with careers and opportunities that fit your personality and talent.

- Staying calm under pressure and uncertainty will help you resist the temptation of making hasty career decisions.
- Valuing new perspectives and viewing problems as opportunities will make you more creative, resourceful and confident.
- You will better evaluate your aspirations by exploring new options and taking some risk.

- The way to succeed at networking is to reach out broadly to people who can help.
- Viewing discussions as learning opportunities, not just job inquiries, will lead you to better position yourself and refine your target.
- Networking requires a disciplined process of identifying, initiating, inquiring, investing in and intensifying relationships over time.

- By working up to your ability and learning new skills, you will succeed in solving the problems and overcoming the challenges involved in career decisions and changes.
- You must trust in your ability to handle the complex challenges that you might face as you seek and enter a new job and develop your career.
- Stay optimistic about the future and be aware that resilience can be built over time.

Different people use different strengths to build their careers. No one is good at everything; each of us emphasizes some strengths more than others. So as you find out more about these six factors, we suggest you ask yourself:

- How strongly have I developed each of the factors or abilities?
- Which ones am I good at?
- Which ones do I need to focus on more, or improve?

Are there ways to improve our "transition ability"? Can these six factors be improved or developed? The 6 C's consist of a broad range of specific knowledge, values and mindsets, skills, abilities and other personal attributes. Some will be harder to grow than others. The areas based on a trait anchored by birth or by one's life course will be harder to force to evolve. However, a number of factors – such as change agility or connection – can indeed be improved. These translate into skills, demonstrated aptitudes and practice that can be developed over time, provided you have the desire to improve and the right resources for support.

In this chapter, we have proposed a framework that should be of practical help in navigating your transition. We hope you find it simple, but not simplistic.

Ultimately, the challenges of the work environment mean that you should build the capacity and the capability to navigate many transitions. If you do not do this, you will fall behind. And given the speed of change, you will fail to see that building career adaptability and agility have become required. We will talk more about this in our final chapter.

Evidently, the larger share of the responsibility is on us to manage our careers and successfully get through transitions. However, we are not alone in these actions. Unless you decide to take on a life as a self-employed entrepreneur, there is an important role to be played by your organization too. They should be there to help you make the change. In the next chapter, we explore what organizations do, can do and should do in order to tap "uncharted career talent" and to get the most possible out of it.

Chapter 12

How Organizations Can Use Disruptive Careers

"It takes two to tango" goes the well-known expression, which suggests something in which pairing is active and inextricable. Indeed, careers are managed by both the individual and the organization. While careers are the "property" of individuals, they will be planned and managed by the organization – for employed people at least. Which of the two has greater influence? The pendulum has swung over the years. For quite some time, the onus of career development was shifted from the individual to the organization. But by the end of the 2000s, individuals began to have to take care of their careers again.[85]

In this chapter, we begin by reporting the failure of many companies to attract talent and manage their careers well. Contrasting this with the stories of our forty-four talented subjects, and recalling that quite a number of them struggled to find a job following their transition given their "atypical profile", we naturally asked ourselves: Why don't companies take better advantage of talent with disruptive career trajectories? We follow by advocating the case for valuing career-shifters in hiring decisions, and we provide companies with recommendations to exploit this untapped source of talent while profoundly rethinking their approach to career management.

The Poor State of Career Management

In the past few years, we have witnessed a renewed focus on career management among companies. The reasons are quite simple. On the one hand, employees remind them that career development is a big driver of engagement and retention. On the other hand, organizations are not paying enough attention to careers and do not challenge themselves to change their approach to career management. Below are a few data points which illustrate this disheartening state of affairs:

- Career development is one of the most overlooked and underserved areas of human capital management. Yet well-executed career development strategy serves as the foundation for integrated talent management – linking various talent processes in a way that strengthens employee engagement, improves retention, and increases overall productivity. Despite these benefits, only 26 percent of organizations invest in career development.[86]

- Organizations that provide career development are six times more likely to engage their employees and four times less likely to lose workers.[87]

- 82 percent of employees say they would be more engaged with the work that they do if career discussions were more regular, and yet only 16 percent of them show that they have ongoing conversations with their managers about their careers.[88]

In a nutshell, career management is important for employees, but companies are not good at it. Why is this so? One reason could well be that companies spend more time on talent acquisition, but not enough on career conversations. A large number of companies are facing the issue of finding suitable talent to hire. Consider the following:

- 31 percent of employers worldwide said they are having trouble filling positions due to lack of suitable talent. This is because the global demand for highly skilled labor continues to grow, and the skills distribution of available workers does not match that demand.[89]

- In the U.S., demand is particularly high in roles such as marketing managers, computer systems analysts, software developers and industrial engineers, which are characterized by a reliance on expertise in new technologies or advanced data analytics. Incredibly, these roles, plus another 17 roles, account for 40 percent of all jobs posted by S&P 100 organizations in 2015.[90]

- Talent shortages are having a real business impact: median time to fill critical talent positions has increased by a staggering 32 business days between 2010 and 2015, from 49 business days in 2010 to 81 business days in 2015.[91]

Given the above, maybe we should be more indulgent with HR professionals who are investing all their time and energy creating employer branding strategies and trying to find talent to fill these critical gaps. But here is the irony: if you want your candidates to accept your job offer, you still need to focus on career growth. This revealing insight came from a 2016 LinkedIn survey which said that when they have to give their final answer on a job offer, the deciding factor for candidates is how the company would impact their career advancement – as important as how stimulating the job will be both financially and intellectually.[92] So career management is key; there is no way around this.

If we put everything together – the demographic, social and technological shifts we discussed in Chapter 1 and the current shortages that negatively impact businesses today – how can we fix the talent mismatch? One answer is: change your mindset! Employers must recalibrate their approach to consider candidates who may not perfectly meet all the job specifications, but whose adaptability is higher and whose capability gaps can be filled in a timely and cost-effective way. Organizations should better value major career shifters when they recruit. They should also rethink their approach to career management with the idea of providing their internal talent with a greater diversity of experiences.

7 Recommendations for Companies

Because the talent market has become more challenging and companies do not do a great job at managing careers, they need to find alternative talent acquisition and career management approaches. The following are our seven recommendations to any organization open to trying novel approaches as well as common sense. They are inspired by the companies we met as part of our research on disruptive careers and are complemented by additional case studies and examples.

1. Expand Your View of Your Talent Pool

In the movie "The Intern", a retired widower in his 70s, played by Robert De Niro, is hired as part of a senior intern program at a fashion start-up in New York. He soon finds himself in the middle of an open workspace filled with millennials, forced to get a grip on technology and learn the fast-paced work style of the 21st century. The film serves to highlight an important issue in today's workplace: Organizations are largely not valuing older workers, and there is still a lot of age-related bias in recruitment practices. The same is true about candidates who changed jobs frequently or made significant shifts in their careers. Hiring managers are wary of resumes loaded with several job stints. They think you are an unstable or disloyal employee. Job hopping has long been – and continues to be considered by many – career suicide. And then there is the insidious bias against professionals who took long career breaks, as some of our subjects in Chapter 8 shared with us, resulting in the dreaded resume gap. "Out of touch, too old and too expensive" seems to be the belief commonly held by hiring managers and recruitment consultants alike.

Changing our mindset starts with recognizing that things have changed. "By 2050, the number of people over 65 years old will triple worldwide and the number of those over 80 will quadruple", says Yvonne Sonsino, a partner at Mercer who published "Age-Friendly Employer Research" in 2015.[93] She adds: "Some countries will be more affected than others but this demographic change is inescapable and, combined with reduced birth rates, the result is severe skills shortages". So it is in organizations' best interests to hire older workers. Aside from the wealth of skills and experience they provide, we are living in an aging population globally.

Likewise, employers and recruiters are beginning to have a different outlook on job changes. Here again, empirical data helps. According to the Bureau of Labor Statistics, the average number of years that U.S. workers have been with their current employer is 4.6, while the tenure of young employees (ages 20 to 34) is only half that, at 2.3 years. In a 2015 LinkedIn survey, 1 in 3 people indicated they changed jobs or changed careers entirely (new company, different function).[94] These career changers say they are hungry for new challenges and curious to try out a new industry. Recruiters are starting to appreciate that job changes can be advantageous in certain environments. As Laurie Lopez, a partner and senior general manager in the IT Contracts division at Winter Wyman, says for those in technology, "It allows them the opportunity to gain valuable technical knowledge in different environments and cultures. (…) In order to keep their skills fresh, it is necessary for technologists to remain current in a highly competitive market. (…) With employers being more open to hiring job hoppers, we expect the trend to continue."[95]

Our message to employers is therefore: expand the labor market opportunity. Do not make it hard for yourself to compete in tight labor markets by rigidly following hiring managers' overly specific requirements. Be open to new, untapped sources of talent, value diversity of experience, and flex your search criteria.

2. Understand and Value Career Changers' Core Capabilities

Claudio Fernández-Aráoz, a senior adviser at the global executive search firm Egon Zehnder International and the author of "Great People Decisions", has a brilliant take on disruptive careers. When he looks at a resume, he is actually looking for career changes. As he explains in an HBR interview: "I usually worry when I don't see major shifts. Their absence could reflect untested competence to adapt to new challenges and environments, and a lack of aspiration to learn and grow."[96] Claudio further elaborates: "A few things have changed. The world of work is increasingly complex – uncertain and volatile, global and diverse – and information is easier to access. As a result, experience and knowledge are less relevant, whereas the capacities to learn and adapt, be resilient, and connect with others have become more crucial."

When we reflect on the forty-four exceptional talents who shared their career stories in this book, it's easy to connect with many of the attributes that Claudio Fernández-Aráoz talks about. Think about our former athletes, who bring to the world of business their energy, passion, focus, discipline and high resistance to pressure. Consider the distinctive traits learned by Devendra, Ton, Priya, Tom and George during their time in the military: fearlessness, resilience, character, self-discipline and caring for people.

Claudio Fernández-Aráoz even goes a step further. According to the headhunter, career changes often indicate strong leadership abilities. He adds: "Emotional intelligence-based competencies, such as flexibility, empathy, organizational awareness, and relationship management, tend to differentiate stars from average performers at the top. Moves can also reveal a lot about a candidate's growth potential, as they show curiosity, insight, inspiration, determination and motivation."

Nonetheless, even assuming that not all career shifters have leadership potential, we want to encourage employers to look beyond the perfect job specification-candidate profile fit, and consider more openly this vastly untapped pool of available talent. In their 2012 study "Optimizing the Talent Pool", Manpower offer some practical and valuable methods to optimally identify and hire the talent that is available:[97]

- Know what you need, but be flexible. Define what you need but be willing to broaden the scope of skills and talents you are looking for based on what is available. Consider redesigning jobs so they become more engaging for the people undertaking them.
- Identify individuals with transferable skills. Think about candidates with comparable skills from other industries

or expand your search by sourcing candidates in different
geographies.

- Hire for innate talents and be willing to invest in training. You
may find a candidate with the right attitude, experience and
problem-solving skills but who lacks a certain certification or
skill set. Once you have defined the skills and talents required
for a position, prioritize the characteristics most important to get
the job done and areas that can be successfully achieved through
training.

3. Proactively Tap into Neglected Sources of Talent and Infuse Your Employer Value Proposition with Messages that Appeal to Them

We are observing hopeful signs of employers evolving their mindsets to
become more open in their recruitment approaches. One example is with
the rehiring of former employees. A U.S. study on boomerangs shows
that three-fourths of HR professionals and 65 percent of managers are
more accepting of hiring boomerang employees than they used to be.[98]
In South Africa, boomerang rehires are expected to reach 15 percent of
all hires at major firms.[99] Some companies are now making rehiring
a strategic talent acquisition differentiator. The global cosmetic leader
L'Oréal currently makes 250 rehires per year – by no means a small number.

Without a doubt, more companies are looking to stay ahead of the
trends and adopt new ways of targeting talent. It is probably not by
coincidence that one of the "hot topics" of the 2016 Strategic Talent
Acquisition Conference in Boston was called "Strategies to attract
pockets of candidates". From the nine types of uncharted career
transitions we have discussed in this book, we have highlighted many
examples of companies that have created specific programs to attract
alternative sources of talent. To name just a few:

- Adecco (in partnership with The International Olympic
Committee), GE, SNCF, Allianz and EY have been supporting
athletes through their career transitions for many years.

- Johnson & Johnson, Starbucks, Amazon, Jaguar LandRover,
Procter & Gamble, The Home Depot and GE are all striving
to become more military-friendly as they realize the long-term
benefits of hiring and retaining veterans.

- L'Oréal, BCG, McKinsey, Booz Allen Hamilton, Deloitte, EY, Microsoft, SAP, Nielsen and A.P. Møller have pioneered corporate alumni programs to stay in closer touch with potential boomerangs, and all are encouraging former employees to come back.

- Goldman Sachs, Morgan Stanley, Credit Suisse, RBS, JP Morgan, Lloyds Bank, PayPal, GoDaddy, Johnson Controls and Booz Allen Hamilton have introduced returnship programs to provide a bridge back to work for high-caliber women and men.

Take a look at their dedicated career websites and communication. These organizations have infused their employer value proposition with a demonstration that they understand the unique skills and motivations of these "different" talents. They have crafted tailored messages that resonate with them.

If your company is interested in making a start in this direction, consider some of the recommendations offered by the research arm of LinkedIn, which analyzed the behaviors of seven million LinkedIn members who changed jobs in 2014.[100] Below are ways to appeal to people's strongest motivations for changing jobs:

- Do not dismiss career changers: a whopping 1 in 3 people LinkedIn surveyed changed careers. Be open to recruiting them. Assess how their transferable skills and accomplishments apply to your role.

- Appeal to the #1 motivation for changing jobs: career opportunity. Close candidates on career opportunity, not compensation. Describe the work and expected results, not the background requirements and personality traits to be checked off.

- Would women want to work at your organization? Make that answer a yes by engaging women through highlighting your organization's quality leadership, culture fit and work/life balance. After you recruit women, deliver on your promises.

And when it comes to choosing the most effective channel of recruitment, LinkedIn could not be more clear: invest in referrals. Referrals, they say, are the number one way people across the world first hear about their new job. The subjects we talk about in this book positively confirmed this; for most of them, networks played a much bigger part in landing their new roles than job ads or headhunters. So start every search assignment with the question: "Who knows my candidate?". Ask, "Who's the best person you know in (field)?". Develop a deep network by connecting with all candidates, regardless of the outcome.

4. Engage as a Career Coach, Personalize the Job, Provide Onboarding

The days when recruiters were checking for the perfect job-candidate match and then "selling" the job to candidates are gone. Even if this approach is still dominant in many companies, it will not work well with career changers. While recruiters still need to define what they are looking for, they need to look at candidates in a different way. Rather than looking for the exact match in terms of experience and skills requirements, they should be open to broadening their scope when assessing candidates. Does he show passion and energy? Does she have the right attitude (vs. the right skills)? Has he already had to adapt to challenging environments? Is she flexible? Is he demonstrating an ability and willingness to learn and grow?

The most effective recruiters reposition themselves as career coaches; rather than just trying to sell the job, they prompt prospects to think about their careers and help them consider their options. By doing so, they earn the right to engage more deeply with prospects about their own organization's job opportunities. This fundamental shift is well described in the 2016 CEB white paper "Competing for Critical Talent".[101] According to CEB, 79 percent of recruiters are sales reps and 10 percent are career coaches. So there is still room for progress. What do the "career coach" recruiters do?

- **Facilitate career changes:** They reduce the prospect's effort and concerns by making the application and hiring process as easy as possible.

- **Prompt career discussions:** They focus on long-term careers rather than job opportunities, and explain how a role contributes to career growth.

- **Adapt to career considerations:** They provide information that directly responds to the unique prospect's needs, help them evaluate the opportunity in context and overcome their specific concerns.

This is a big shift but has a direct pay-off. Companies that do this well approach their interaction with prospective candidates in unexpected, non-recruiting settings to better stand out – for example, by relying more on referrals or targeting industry conferences and events that prospective candidates might be attending. Their messages are deliberately thought-provoking, inviting prospects to think about whether they want to do work that is meaningful and make a difference. This allows recruiters to act in a more consultative way, serving as true career coaches rather than just trying to pitch an opportunity.

Companies should also consider redesigning jobs so they become more engaging for the people undertaking them. This recommendation is valid for career changers who will not immediately meet all the job requirements, but it can also benefit all employees. Wharton professor Adam Grant, who teaches the concept of "Job Crafting" in his management classes, has worked with Google's People Analytics team to help Googlers "customize" their jobs to make them more meaningful. He describes their experiment:[102]

> We partnered with Jennifer Kurkoski and Brian Welle, two innovators behind Google's people analytics work. We designed a workshop introducing hundreds of employees to the notion that jobs are not static sculptures, but flexible building blocks. We gave them examples of people becoming the architects of their own jobs, customizing their tasks and relationships to better align with their interests, skills, and values – like an artistic salesperson volunteering to design a new logo and an outgoing financial analyst communicating with clients using video chat instead of email. (…) They set out to create a new vision of their roles that was more ideal but still realistic.

According to Grant, the Googlers who participated in the exercises were rated as happier and more effective by their managers and coworkers just six weeks later. There is more. When Adam and the Google team added a feature to encourage employees to see both their skills and jobs as flexible, the gains lasted for at least six months. Instead of using only their existing talents, they took the initiative of developing new capabilities that enabled them to create an original, personalized job. As a result, they were 70 percent more likely than their peers to land a promotion or a transition to a coveted role.

Our advice to companies interested in hiring career changers is to use job crafting whenever possible. It will help your future employees align more clearly with their talents, interests and strengths, therefore making them more effective and helping their career in the long run.

The hiring process, however, should not stop when the candidate has signed their contract. As we highlighted in the previous chapter, companies should provide carefully designed onboarding for the newly hired talent. This is even more critical for career shifters, since they are making a more dramatic change when they start in a new role. As we have witnessed through the stories of our forty-four subjects, the degree of role contrast can be massive.

Think about the shock that Gabriel experienced when he started his job in an auto plant in China; recall John's tough move from Olympic-level rowing to policy advisory for business and government; remember how Marta had to adjust her skills when she moved from her 20-year corporate experience to a startup environment. Onboarding is more than orientation. It should include a process for providing a range of integrated, well-planned and highly tailored dimensions of support for the new hire. The goal is to ensure successful assimilation into the organization's culture, shorten the time to productivity, minimize the risk of failure and maximize impact.

5. Create a Flexible Work Environment to Accommodate Employees' Life Changes

Companies will be better positioned to attract and retain untapped sources of talent – such as career changers – if they adapt working conditions to the increasingly diverse generations and needs of employees. Across the board, traditional views of compensation and benefits are being challenged. Employers that recruit and manage across generations are finding that it is imperative to understand that the different life-stage needs of employees require flexibility across the enterprise. For example, younger workers may be motivated by income potential; middle-aged workers may be seeking income accumulation and retirement planning; and older workers, in contrast, may be interested in income but motivated by a combination of meaningful work and flexible hours.

Many of the subjects we interviewed – Argyro, Tim and Mui Gek to name just a few – left jobs for personal reasons, often feeling that either resigning or negotiating their departure was the only way to take care of their family. Each was able subsequently to bounce back, finding a new role in another organization and resuming his or her career with success. However, in hindsight, if you think about it from their original employer's perspective, wasn't it a loss of talent that could have been prevented?

The more progressive companies understand the importance of organizational family-friendliness for recruitment and retention. By offering attractive benefits, flexible working practices and a supportive work-family culture, they are in an advantageous position to both recruit and retain talent with diverse situations and needs. Here are some recent examples:

- Nike announced in 2016 the extension of its paid family leave. Full-time U.S. employees of the sportswear maker who are new parents or who are needed to care for sick family members are now eligible to receive eight weeks of paid leave. Birth mothers are now eligible for a minimum of 14 paid weeks of leave (versus six previously).

- Since 2016, U.S. Deloitte professionals – from the parent celebrating the arrival of a new child, to the professional caring for a spouse or significant other to the professional supporting aging parents – now have an extra layer of support from Deloitte's new family leave program, and are eligible for up to 16 weeks of fully paid family leave to support a range of life events impacting them and their families. Also under this family leave program, mothers who give birth to a child are eligible for up to six months of paid time off when factoring in short-term disability for childbirth.

Deloitte has gone beyond offering flexible benefits or work arrangements, introducing a few years ago the notion of "Mass Career Customization".[103] When looking closely at how people's careers unfold over time, they saw that career paths for knowledge workers were increasingly not a straight climb up the corporate ladder but rather an undulating journey of climbs, lateral moves, and planned descents. A professional, at some point in her life and career, may want to reduce travel and work less than 10 to 12 hours a day. The manager of a large team might wish to step back for a while and go back to an individual contributor role for some time and then take up a leadership position again.

Mass Career Customization (MCC) is a way for an organization to allow employees to both "dial up" and "dial down". Deloitte's MCC framework articulates a set of options along four core dimensions of a career: Pace (options relating to the rate of career progression), Workload (choices relating to the quantity of work output), Location/Schedule (options for when and where work is performed) and Role (choices in position and responsibilities). In collaboration with their managers, employees periodically select options along each dimension based on their career objectives and life circumstances within the context of the needs of the business.

There are no limits to organizations in creating innovative work practices. To stimulate your imagination, consider the idea from Avivah Wittenberg-Cox, who has brainstormed ways to help companies manage longer lives and postponed retirements:[104]

> Yesterday, companies were reluctant to employ both halves of a couple, fearing issues of nepotism. Tomorrow, they may shift to managing "family" careers by strategically choosing to hire both people. It may prove a lot easier to manage dual career couples when they both work for you. For many of the larger multinationals with big graduate training programs, a lot of people end up marrying a colleague anyway. Embracing this fact, and working with it, rather than ignoring or discouraging it, could optimize and encourage the skills of two people, rather than enmeshing them in today's often painful tradeoffs and choices between whose career should "take the lead" and who should "follow."

6. Provide "Disruptive Experiences" to Your Own Talent, Build More Mobility

In this book, we have discussed nine types of career change, which we characterized as uncharted transitions. By and large, these career changes were handled by each of the forty-four individuals whose stories you have discovered. Now, let's pause and ponder this question: What if these career moves could instead be facilitated, managed and supported by companies? What if we could have individual development outcomes from these transitions – such as greater awareness, adaptability, resilience – without the pains and uncertainties that these people had to overcome by themselves, and with greater chances for organizations of retaining these talented people? In other words, can companies offer disruptive career experiences to their own employees?

There are different ways to respond to this question. First, we should recognize that a number of companies, especially the larger international ones, are already doing some of this. The most obvious example is with international mobility. Companies like Schlumberger, Shell, GE, Nestlé, Unilever and many others are reputed for using international assignments as a way to develop high potential talent and create strong pools of global leaders. Another, perhaps less common, example is providing experience as a consultant inside the company. Several large corporations, such as Deutsche Post DHL or GSK, operate in-house consulting departments which offer stints of various lengths to their most promising talent as a way to sharpen their strategic and analytical skills and accelerate their readiness to larger roles. No need to go to McKinsey or BCG!

What about the move from profit to purpose which we discussed in two of this book's chapters? Are there ways to enable this remarkable transformative experience "from within"? Consider the following company programs:

- The PULSE Volunteer Partnership is GSK's skills-based volunteering initiative. Through PULSE, employees are matched to a non-profit organization for three or six months full-time, contributing their skills to solving healthcare challenges at home and abroad. In addition to developing their leadership capability, employees bring fresh ideas and new energy back to GSK to activate change in step with global health needs.

- Through MySkills4Afrika, Microsoft employees from all over the world volunteer to share their experience to build world-class skills and increase innovation and affordable technology access across Africa. Participants support organizations, ranging from start-ups and SMEs to schools, universities and government agencies, and individuals such as students, graduates and job seekers.

- Becton Dickinson's Volunteer Service Trip Program celebrated ten years of operation in 2015. The program sends teams of skilled BD employee volunteers from all over the world on two- to three-week service trips working in hospitals and clinics. In addition to sending volunteers, BD works with the organizations over the longer term to ensure that the partnerships and projects are sustainable.

- The EY Vantage Program connects future EY leaders with market leaders of tomorrow to accelerate growth and create jobs. During a six week, pro bono assignment, top-performing managers and senior managers work alongside entrepreneurs in emerging markets to help them address their biggest obstacles to growth. In turn, Vantage advisors gain once-in-lifetime leadership development opportunities and the global mindset that comes with an overseas work experience.

The idea of providing "extra" experiences such as those mentioned above can be expanded to other disruptive or unfamiliar environments – start-ups or research labs, for example. Ideally, a large corporation can use its own ecosystem of external partners to offer secondment opportunities. The potential benefits are numerous; the employee learns from working in an innovative and agile work environment, may help strengthen the relationship between the two partners and can import some of the innovations and practices back to her organization of origin.

Overall, we encourage companies to build more opportunities of internal mobility for their talent. This means creating a culture of development in which job changes are encouraged and risk is accepted. Companies that excel at this are ready to offer stretch assignments to accelerate their employees' learning, while at the same time providing them with the right level of support to maximize their success in new roles. To make this happen, companies need to institute programs, processes, tools and rewards to help people move from job to job. This includes many things which may not be in place today, as suggested by Josh Bersin in his recent LinkedIn blog on careers:[105]

- Open posting of positions internally so people can find, register interest, and apply for internal positions

- Tools to help people assess themselves and ready themselves for the job they want next
- Reward systems that incentivize managers to hire internally, even though an external candidate may be more qualified
- Recognition and social rewards that motivate people to take lateral, but developmental jobs, that help the company and their own career
- Managers who think about their jobs as "developing talent" not "hoarding talent", and are rewarded for moving people out of their groups
- Story-telling, open communications, and executive dialogue about how important it is to move around and contribute across the company

In the future, companies will use more diverse talent sources. As they are rapidly expanding their definitions of workforce beyond full-time, "balance-sheet" workers, they will have to create career management strategies that account for a new variety of nontraditional workers: contractors, contingent workers, interns, specialized consultants and more – in addition to conventional talent sources. Watch this space!

7. Enable Frequent, Quality Career Discussions
Our final piece of advice, while seemingly simple, is meant to provide the input, direction, support and energy needed to make career management happen in every organization. It starts with the recognition that the basic "units" of career management, namely career discussions, are not happening in companies, or when they do, their impact is limited. A CRF study from 2011 paints a gloomy picture of the situation:[106]

- The main employee challenges include finding out about opportunities in other parts of the business, encouraging the organization to take a risk on them if they do not have the exact skill set for a role, and coping with inconsistency in managers' coaching capabilities.
- 37 percent of employees had never had a career conversation with their manager.

- There is a danger of missing important conversations with high potentials and making assumptions about their future aspirations.

- The line manager is one of a network of people whom employees talk to about their careers. However, managers can feel ill-equipped for such discussions, partly because of a lack of knowledge. Many employee respondents valued access to a coach or mentor from a different part of the business with whom they felt they could be more open.

- HR seems to be relatively removed from career conversations, except at senior levels or where there are local talent managers. Typically, HR contributions focus on process and tools rather than engaging with individuals.

Facilitating purposeful career conversations should be at the heart of an effective career management strategy. Great career conversations are inspiring and thought-provoking and help to bring clarity to career goals. But as we learned, employees have identified the quality of career conversations – when they happen – as the weakest area of career management practices. Line managers are notoriously poor at helping people develop their career, and HR seems to be busy with other things.

One way to remedy this is to provide separate "career coaches", independent of line leaders. The career coach role, which is an important one in some big companies, is to help people find the next best job with everyone's interests at heart. Most of the time, the career coach operates inside the company.

Additionally, organizations should provide access to external career coaches. In some situations, these are better equipped to introduce an unbiased perspective and to deal with sensitive issues. They are not concerned about how their advice and recommendations might impact their standing within the company.

A Glimmer of Hope

We have seen endless examples of how the individual has to struggle, typically, to create any kind of career management, whether he/she is coming at this from a career transition perspective or from an internal company career perspective. Our subjects' stories show this clearly, and the relevant peripheral articles we have found underline how it is becoming an obvious priority to focus on career development in the face of talent scarcity.

Companies are just beginning to perceive the value of taking a proactive stance in this challenging environment, but are lagging way behind, leaving the responsibility with our friends the individuals. Yet they know they need to change in the face of an enormous war for talent. Some current examples of initiatives give rise to hope, and thus to an expectation that there is more to come.

Given the glaring nature of this challenge, those organizations that wish to take advantage of this situation, and which see the benefits to creating a genuinely proactive career development strategy, will see the fruits of this approach quickly and consistently.

At the same time, we know that our current world situation is leading to increasingly frequent career change, and thus the whole career paradigm is changing. As we observe the discrepancies and the opportunities, we can see that the issue – for the individual, for the corporation – becomes one of building lifelong career agility.

Conclusion

Embrace Disruption,
Build Lifelong Career Agility

As we move towards a life in which it is quite reasonable to expect to be alive at 90 or 100, we must all be clear about the need to reinvent ourselves, possibly several times. Avivah Wittenberg-Cox wrote recently that "we will want to relearn and be open to repetitive re-training. Lifelong learning will become an essential part of adult development".[107]

In this environment, what are the influencers of our career? Are they external or internal? We have found an underlying tension via our research. On the one hand, we are implicitly arguing in favor of the individual obtaining and having a greater choice or control over their career. On the other hand, we have found that a number of influences – such as family, society, or culture – are external and not always controllable by the individual. This chicken-and-egg question leaves us asking many more questions, cognizant of the fact that the answers are neither simple nor obvious.

What does stand out is that multiple transitions are possible and even likely. Lily, having started her career on the other side of the world, may well decide to go "home", one day soon, or on to a third location. Thomas has made such multiple moves, both from consultancy to CEO of businesses, and now to "encore". Subhanu Saxena, an accomplished global executive whose experience has spanned markets in Europe, North America, Africa and Asia, has already made so many transitions they are nearly impossible to count. He has worked with Citigroup, BCG, PepsiCo and Novartis, and more recently as CEO of CIPLA, an India-based pharmaceutical company. He recently returned to the UK, where he is currently settling in as a director of the Bill and Melinda Gates Foundation, as well as running a small and specialized private equity firm, offering coaching and mentoring services, and planning to create a leadership academy in India. He is the consummate example of career agility. The chances of our younger subjects following this kind of path are ever-increasing. Evidently, even if we do not all aspire to such mobility or lofty heights, we do need to hone the skills of adaptation and flexibility.

Our view here is that experiencing more career transitions makes you more adaptable, more resilient, and in turn more likely to succeed at further transitions. It is like learning several languages: the more languages you know, the easier it becomes to learn a new one. We also believe that it is desirable to start these transitions as early as possible in your career. Going overseas early, for example, accepting some risk and discomfort rather than waiting for the "perfect" opportunity, then building on these initial experiences is an effective approach to grow your career.

Chicken or Egg?

Back to our question of chicken or egg; the "luck" that some perceive may well play a role. Family and socio-economic background certainly have a big influence − but not only. Kavitha and Eric, for example, had siblings who did not rise to the same great heights in competitive sports. We do see, however, that individual conditions are likely to support success; so from there, it is logical for each of us as individuals to heed advice:

- Know yourself well: your personality, preferences, values, motivations, talents, aspirations. This way you can imagine a range of career or role options for yourself.

- Be explicitly aware of how your environment (your family, organization, communities, society, etc.) creates opportunities and constraints that might support or limit your individual choices.

- When needed, deliberately extract yourself from any environment that stifles your career progression, and force yourself to enter into new environments that will support your development.

Stay Flexible While Keeping a Clear Purpose in Mind

Beyond the recognition of influencers, and our earlier advice to "manage" them, we need to recognize that the world is changing. "65 percent of children entering primary school today will ultimately end up working in completely new job types that don't yet exist", according to a 2016 World Economic Forum report.[108] This means we have to be adaptable, flexible and versatile in our career planning and implementation.

We feel strongly that you need to not only be flexible and open to job or industry changes, but also keep a framework in mind to build up your career capital. What this means in practice is that while at first sight someone's career might appear random, inconsistent or messy, if indeed this individual has moved from one role to another over time, there might actually be a common thread, and progression, in his or her career.

Ultimately, your career and career decisions should be based on your core purpose — the why and how of your work life — and your core competencies. The notion of "career capital" is used by Georgetown University Professor Cal Newport, who defines it as "the skills you have that are both rare and valuable and that can be used as leverage in defining your career".[109] He adds that if you want something that's both rare and valuable, you need something rare and valuable to offer in return — basic supply and demand. And thus it follows that if you want a great job, you need something of great value to offer in return. Newport's idea is based on the principle of craftsmanship: building skills over time. He talks about three traits that define great work: creativity, impact and control.

Our advice is that you build your career capital using deliberate and consistent practice as well as a variety of situations in which those skills can be built and strengthened over time. The trifecta referred to by several of our subjects in the non-profit chapter, whereby some individuals accumulate experience and skills in profit, non-profit and government, illustrates this well. Another great example is Subhanu Saxena, whose career has spanned investment banking, top strategy consulting firms, CEO roles and more recently NGOs. Creating strategies, making deals, leading global teams and driving cultural change are just some of the core competencies that Subhanu grew to superior levels throughout his career. It is no wonder that these distinctive skills, together with his mindset to always keep improving and growing himself, are in high demand.[110]

Edgar Schein, one of the founders of the field of modern organizational psychology, suggests that every one of us has a particular orientation towards work, and that we all approach our work with a certain set of priorities and values. He calls this concept our "Career Anchors".[111] Few people have an early career calling, while many others start university without a clear idea of what they want to do for a living. For the majority of us, therefore, career anchors evolve through the process of our career development, which involves testing ourselves in various kinds of work settings and in different kinds of jobs until we have a clearer picture of our talents, needs and values. With this in mind, uncharted career transitions will help you in this process, and we recommend them as a basis for your development.

So, our career anchors and career capital are what form the backbone of our career. Where we go – which profession, industry, organization, role, etc. – can be seen as random or inconsistent. But it will make sense both to us, and to the observer, if it is tied to our work values, orientations and core competencies.

Build Career Agility

Career agility is not an optional extra anymore. It has become essential. Research indicates that the less adaptable we are in our careers, the more likely we are to be stressed by our work, and conversely the more we adapt, the more likely we are to be happy. But what exactly does this mean, and how do we become "career agile"? In Chapter 11, we proposed a framework to navigate career transitions, starting by following these 4E steps:

- **Explore:** Reflect on who you are, Think about why and what you want to change and Consider your career options
- **Experiment:** Try out new things in small steps, Build new connections and Reframe and zero in your search
- **Engage:** Find and launch yourself into your new role, Unlearn old skill sets and relearn new ones
- **Expand:** Deliver and thrive in your new role, Consolidate and expand your capabilities and Continue to reflect on your career journey

This framework can be used as a roadmap to orient anyone through the sometimes tortuous, emotional and lengthy process of changing roles or careers. We also highlighted the need to build the capability and the capacity to navigate transitions – which we named The 6 C's:

- **Commitment:** the extent to which you are focused and engaged in the process of managing your career
- **Control:** the extent to which you feel some control over your career and a responsibility for building it
- **Curiosity:** the extent to which you are exploring the world of work and seeking information about roles, careers and their requirements
- **Change Agility:** the extent to which you like to experiment, explore new options and cope effectively with the discomfort of change
- **Connections:** the extent to which you are building your network, and the efforts you are making to meet people and create connections
- **Confidence:** the extent to which you have faith in your ability to make and carry out wise career decisions and realistic choices

Former Uber executive Frederique Dame, reflecting on her Silicon Valley career, provides an inspiring example of what the above mindset and capabilities mean in real life. Her testimonial starts with acknowledging that a career journey is no smooth sailing: "Make no mistake, the path you're on right now is not straight. (…) Things will go wrong. Plans will fall apart. The only thing in your control is how you'll respond."[112] She follows with a list of powerful lessons she has learned from her experience in Silicon Valley – all of which you can apply:

- **Confidence and control:** "What if you just decided that you were going to be fine no matter what? You'd probably do a lot of things differently. You'd test your boundaries. You'd trust yourself more. The trick is that feeling this way is just a choice you make. You decide to believe it or not. (…) Being daring is all about trusting yourself to handle the results. (…) Shifting your confidence from one area of your life to another gives you the safety net you need to take more chances."

- **Change agility and curiosity:** "If you were to weather a transition or a tough time elegantly, what would that look like? You'd be honest and allow yourself to mourn the lost opportunity, an unexpected hiccup, whatever it is. You'd let yourself feel it with the self-assurance that the pain is impermanent because life changes fast. You'd look for hidden opportunities to hasten your recovery. You'd get comfortable with the uncomfortable. Sometimes you'd even seek out the uncomfortable because that's how you grow and get better."

As we see with Frederique's story, building career agility starts with a particular mindset and also requires a great deal of courage. Intrinsically, building career agility and longevity means to excel at learning from experience and succeed in changing times. To achieve this, the Center for Creative Leadership suggests working on these four things:[113]

- **Be a Seeker.** Seek out new and diverse experiences. Immerse yourself in situations that broaden your skills and perspective. Explore new pathways. Embrace the challenge of the unfamiliar.

- **Hone Your Sense-Making.** Take an active approach to making sense of the new challenges you face. Ask: "Why?" "How?" and "Why not?" Find another way to understand a problem. Use multiple techniques, engage different senses and tap into your emotions to wrest understanding, insight and meaning from the experience.

- **Internalize Experiences and Lessons Learned.** You need this to solidify insight and lessons learned for recall and application later. Ask for feedback, be open to criticism and take time to think about what happened and what you are learning. Reflect on feedback so you can see patterns (and changes) over time.

- **Adapt and Apply.** Through your experiences, you have created principles and rules of thumb to guide you. Over time, you get better at applying them to navigate new and challenging situations. Use your intuition, be flexible, and do not shy away from experimentation as you venture into new territory.

If you pay attention to and make the most of your experience by seeking, sense-making, internalizing and applying, you will do more, learn more and build the track record you need for a long and successful career.

Future-Proofing Your Career

"There is no future in any job. The future lies in the person who holds the job", said the writer, journalist and world traveler John Crane. This is a simple way of stating, again, that we all need to be flexible, to navigate endless changes, embrace lifelong learning and occasionally reinvent ourselves. In the new world of work, with automation, robots and AI looming large, we must constantly update our skills, and we would all do well to ask ourselves if we have a "sell-by date". In their 2016 book "Stretch!", Karie Willyerd and Barbara Mistick recommend that we go beyond our capabilities of today in order to be ready for tomorrow.[114] To remain relevant in spite of change, they say, you need to know how to open your thinking to a world beyond where you are now, connect to the people who can help you make your future happen and seek experiences that will prepare you for tomorrow – reinforcing many of the points we have tried to make in this book.

Final Thoughts

What are the implications for the future? While nature may well play a role in creating adaptable and agile leaders, we strongly recommend that this approach can and should be taught. Beyond our inspiring stories, models and frameworks, we are convinced that teamwork, agility and leadership, demanding adaptability across a variety of activities, are key elements of education.

Most importantly, this all means that we should each look for and value experiences. Beyond the traditional work experience, we need to find and try out our creativity, our innovation and our comfort with ambiguity.

Assuming we can each build our career capital in this way, we then need to ensure that companies and recruiters are formally recognizing our changing portfolio of assets and valuing our travel adventures or uncomfortable stretches outside the traditional work environment, so that organizations can benefit from this new, previously unexplored goldmine.

Embrace disruption and build lifelong career agility! Look as early on as possible for breadth and depth of experience. Variety, intensity, diversity and adversity will accelerate your career, make you feel fulfilled and expand your potential.

About the Authors

Antoine Tirard is an international talent management advisor, leadership development facilitator and executive coach to large global organizations. In 2010, he founded Paris-based NexTalent, a consulting firm specializing in talent management, leadership development and human capital strategy.

He builds on 20 years of leadership experience in talent and human resources within international corporations, including LVMH, Novartis, L'Oréal and Clifford Chance in Europe and the United States.

Antoine received an MBA from INSEAD and a master's degree in human resources management from Paris Sorbonne University.

He is the co-author of a book on psychometric tools for development and a French-English dictionary of human resources management. He is a regular guest lecturer at INSEAD and Paris Sorbonne University and speaks frequently at international HR and talent management conferences.

Claire Harbour-Lyell is passionate about creating the global leaders of the future using the wisdom acquired through thirty years of career the world over, and as many years of focus on nurturing talent across borders.

A multilingual, multicultural background gave her the chance to learn and appreciate diverse styles and points of view, and allowed her to take full advantage of her education at Cambridge and her MBA from INSEAD. All along the way, she built bridges between individuals and connected people with ideas.

All of Claire's latter career has been focused on the question of how best to optimize talent. From headhunting, through cross-cultural training, right through to the executive and career coaching she practices today, she is dedicated to helping people capture the abundant gifts they have inside them so that they can use these to create their own luck and success.

Claire speaks in order to inspire people to seek out the best of themselves – to fire up a disruptive career without borders. She travels the world in the aim of convincing young people to be courageous and ambitious, and to give themselves the best gift possible: career agility.

Acknowledgments

This book is a collaborative effort, that has been built on the contributions of many. What follows is only a partial list of those deserving our thanks:

Our subjects – all the career changers featured in this book, who were so patient and generous while we interviewed, double checked and even filmed them. We learned so much from them, with surprises, revelations and confirmations along the way.

The numerous executives of companies we interviewed as references and thought leaders. They shared their insights and advice, gave us faith and credibility, not to mention inspiration, as we saw them doing such a good job of developing talent, each in their own way.

Our beta readers – those who plowed through the book, despite the early typos and editorial mess, and compelled us to sharpen our ideas and writing: Rhonda Bernard, Martin Castellan, Caryn Kaftal, Sabine Kennedy, David Lange, Angela Negro, Elliott Nelson, Katherine Philips-Kaiser, Drew Shagrin, Mafalda Tenente and Sarah Tirard.

All those who took the time to read and reflect on our initial articles on LinkedIn and INSEAD Knowledge. Their stories and comments really counted for us, and spurred us on our mission.

Those who contributed to this book's creation process: Josiah Wartak, who worked tirelessly to make our manuscript legible; Laurence McCormack, our designer and typesetter, who had to endure endless naïve suggestions from us, while subtly allowing her expertise to shine through; and finally, Ravi Shah and his fine team in India, who helped our ideas to come alive through some amazing graphics for publicity and presentations.

Chris Howells and the team at INSEAD Knowledge, for understanding intuitively from the outset what we were attempting to achieve, and for brilliantly cutting down whatever subject we threw at him into sharp, 1,200 word articles.

The INSEAD Alumni Association, who have offered space, coffee, and unconditional support for our enterprise, throughout.

Our mentors and teachers: in Antoine's case, Norman Walker, David Dotlich, Jim Noel, Kevin Cashman, Doug Ready, Charles O'Reilly and Alain Nutkowicz, who have been powerful sources of inspiration and growth throughout his career; in Claire's, Michael and Linda Brimm, who crystallized her interest in organizational behavior and developing talent; Jane Upton, Angela Negro and Liema Law, who encouraged her to write this book, no matter what.

All those who offered advice, support and general encouragement about the diverse range of questions, doubts and hesitations we had along the way: Kate Hardy, Brid T. Rodgers, Celia Berk, Terry Brake, David Lange, Ali Tisdall, Mike Stanford and Fabienne Tailleur.

Our colleagues and clients over the years, who have encouraged our thinking and development into impassioned advocates of career management and disruption: for Claire, Fred Chin at the Swire Group, François Poirel at LVMH, Chris Crosby, Terry Brake, Hans van der Linden and the team at TMA World, Alaric Mostyn at Stonecourt, Celia Berk at WPP Group and the original team at GlobalEnglish, including Deepak Desai, Mahesh Ram et al, whose spirit and beliefs spurred her on for many years. For Antoine, his many bosses and colleagues at Novartis, LVMH and Pivot Leadership, Rhonda Bernard at Estée Lauder, Kim Lafferty at GSK, Chantal Gaemperle at LVMH, Sonia d'Emilio at LafargeHolcim, Peter Gasteiger at Apsen, Laurent Zermati at Groupe La Poste, Karin Priarollo at PPG Industries, Nadège Besson at Imerys, Stephanie Parry, Julie Jessup, Nicolas Bontron, Ruud and Margaret Rikhof, Michel Buffet, Greg Burns, Ashley Clark, Alain Verstandig, Luciana Balduino, Stéphane Moriou and Kathryn Clutz; and for both of us, all the many coaching clients across the world, whose insight has been such an inspiration.

Our families and friends, who have had to put up with our erratic availability while struggling over research or a turn of phrase: Antoine's wife Nathalie and his children Alice, Maximilien and Adrien for their patience, constructive criticism and encouragements; Claire's children, Grace, Georgia, Billy and Kitty, who always egg her on, even if half the time they have been unable to grasp what she was doing: finally they will understand when they can actually see and touch a paper book. Tom Dickson and Angela Negro have offered endless cups of coffee and wine, while listening to ideas and struggles, while Lone Nielsen has been an unconditional supporter from a distance. Now the book is done, maybe we both will be able to visit more of those distant friends who have not seen much of us for the past two years!

And finally, we would like to thank you for reading our book. Our hope is that *Disrupt Your Career* will help you have a better life.

Notes

Chapter 1

1. Lynda Gratton, Andrew Scott, *"The 100-Year Life: Living and Working in an Age of Longevity"*, Featherstone Education (2016).

2. William Bridges, *"Managing Transitions: Making the Most of Change"*, Da Capo Lifelong Books (2009).

3. Nigel Nicholson, Michael West, *"Transitions, work histories and the myth of careers"*, Handbook of career theory, Editors: Michael B Arthur; Douglas T Hall; Barbara S Lawrence, Cambridge University Press (1989): 181-199.

4. Herminia Ibarra, *"Our Many Possible Selves: Re-Working our Identities to Re-invent our Careers"*, INSEAD Working Paper (2004).

5. Herminia Ibarra, *"Career Transition and Change"*, INSEAD Working Paper (2004).

6. Margaret A. Cole, *"They Gain, You Retain: Creating a Culture of Career Development"*, Right Management (2013).

7. Esther L. Cruz, Allison Schnidman, Akansha Agrawal, Bo De Koning, *"Why & How People Change Jobs"*, LinkedIn Talent Solutions (2015).

8. Boris Groysberg, Robin Abrahams, *"Five Ways to Bungle a Job Change"*, Harvard Business Review (2010).

9. Peter Capelli, *"Talent Management for a New Generation"*, Harvard Business Review (2008).

10. Edgar H. Schein, *"Career anchors revisited: Implications for career development in the 21st century"*, Academy of Management Executive (1996): 80-88.

11. Linda Croll Howell, *"An Emerging Paradigm in Career Development: Task vs. Space & Time"*, First Annual Career Development Week (2010).

12. Yehuda Baruch, *"The Transforming careers: from linear to multidirectional career paths"*, Career Development International, Vol. 9 No. 1 (2004): 58-73.

Chapter 2

13. Robin Pascoe, *"Young Global Professionals: The 'Hidden' Expats"*, The Expat Expert (2012).

14. Corina Cristal, *"Seeking International Careers: Expatriation in the View of Young Graduates"*, M.Sc. paper, Aarhus School of Business, University of Aarhus (2010).

15. Uwe Brandenburg, Sonja Berghoff, Obdulia Taboadela, *"The Erasmus Impact Study: Effects of Mobility on the skills and employability of students and the internationalisation of Higher Education Institutions"*, European Commission, Publications Office of the European Union (2014).

16. Margaret Malewski, *"GenXpat: The Young Professional's Guide to Making a Successful Life Abroad"*, Intercultural Press (2005).

17. Michael Dickmann, Hilary Harris, *"Developing career capital for global careers: The role of international assignments"*, Journal of World Business (2005): 399-408.

18. Jean-Marc Hachey, *"The Big Guide To Living And Working Overseas"*, 4th Edition, ISSI Inc./Intercultural Systems (2004).

19. John Molony, Quacquarelli Symonds, Ben Sowter, *"QS Global Employer Sur-vey Report 2011: How Employers Value an International Study Experience"*, QS Intelligence Unit (2011).

20. Dimitrios Georgakakis, Tobias Dauth, Winfried Ruigrok, *"Too much of a good thing: Does international experience variety accelerate or delay executives' career advancement?"*, Journal of World Business (2016).

Chapter 3

21. Pablo S. Torre, *"How (and Why) Athletes Go Broke"*, Sports Illustrated (2009).

22. Pascale Witz, *"3 Lessons Executives can Learn from Athletes"*, Fortune Insiders (2015).

23. S. Cecić Erpič, S., Wylleman, P. and Zupani, M., *"Characteristics of the sports career termination and adaptation to post career transitions in perspective"*, Psychology of Sport and Exercise (2004): 1, 45–60.

24. Bruce Ogilvie, Maynard Howe, *"The trauma of termination from athletics."*, In J.M. Williams (Ed.), Applied Sport psychology: Personal growth to peak performance, Mayfield Publishing Co. (1986): 365–382.

25. D. Anderson, T. Morris, *"Athlete lifestyle problems"*. In David Lavallee and Paul Wylleman, (Eds.) Career transitions in sport: international perspectives (pp. 59-80). Morgantown, WV.: Fitness Information Technology (2000).

26. *"Les sportifs de haut niveau à l'honneur chez Allianz – du sport à la reconversion"*, YouTube video (https://youtu.be/Zxm6wZt4l4A), Allianz France (September 2014).

27. EY Women Athletes Business Network, Athletes interviews: http://www.ey.com/br/pt/about-us/our-sponsorships-and-programs/women-athletes-global-leadership-network---in-the-locker-room-with

Chapter 4

28. "How soon could our Army lose a war", The Daily Telegraph, cited in HC Defence Committee, Duty of Care, Vol 1, 28 (April 1998).

29. David Gee, *"Informed choice? Armed forces recruitment practice in the United Kingdom"*, report by David Gee funded by the Joseph Rowntree Charitable Trust (November 2007).

30. Michael Abrams, Julia Taylor Kennedy, *"Mission Critical: Unlocking the Value of Veterans in the Workforce"*, Center for Talent Innovation, (2015).

31. J. Michael Haynie, Dean Shepherd, *"Toward a Theory of Discontinuous Career Transition: Investigating Career Transitions Necessitated by Traumatic Life Events"*, Journal of Applied Psychology Vol. 96, No. 3 (2011) : 501 524.

32. Christine Giordano, *"Turning Points"*, Wharton Magazine (Spring 2016).

33. Megan McCloskey, *"Vets' transition to civilian jobs often includes a perceived step down"*, Stars and Stripes (February 2012).

34. Abigail Stevenson, *"Johnson & Johnson CEO explains why America should hire more veterans in business"*, CNBC (2016).

35. Adam Lashinsky, *"How Amazon learned to love veterans"*, CNN Money, Fortune (May 2012).

36. Chris Hitch, *"Ready to Serve: How and Why You Should Recruit Veterans"*, UNC Executive Development (2012).

37. Tim Duffy, *"Military Experience & CEOs: Is There a Link?"*, Korn Ferry International report written in cooperation with the Economist Intelligence Unit (2006).

38. Efraim Benmelech, Carola Frydman, *"Military CEOs"*, Journal of Financial Economics, Volume 117, Issue 1, (July 2015): 43–59.

Chapter 5

39. *"Is Your Next Great CEO a Management Consultant?"* By Gretchen Gavett, Harvard Business Review Blog (November 2013).
40. Fabrice Desmarescaux, *"Is there life after consulting?"*, LinkedIn Post (September 2016).
41. Duff McDonald, *"The CEO Factory: Ex-McKinsey Consultants Get Hired to Run the Biggest Companies"*, Observer (September 2013).
42. Bruce R. Raines, *"From Management Consulting to CEO: The Fork in the Road"*, Consulting Track (April 2012).

Chapter 6

43. Alexander Friedman, *"How banks can help the world's poor"*, Financial Times, (March 2010).

Chapter 7

44. Roy Maurer, *"Attitude on Rehiring Boomerang Workers Changing"*, SHRM (2015).
45. *"Welcome Back ... Or Not?"*, by Accountemps, a Robert Half company (February 2016).
46. Bob Nardelli, *"Leaving Is Painful. Coming Back Is Amazing"*, LinkedIn Pulse article (September 2016).
47. John Sullivan, *"Boomerangs: The Strategic Process Of Rehiring Your Former Employees"*, ERE Media (May 2006).
48. Eilene Zimmerman, *"The Boom in Boomerangs, Workforce Management* (January 2006).
49. Christine Giordano, *"Turning Points"*, Wharton Magazine (Spring 2016).
50. Boris Groysberg, Sarah Abbott, *"A.P. Møller - Maersk Group: Evaluating Strategic Talent Management Initiatives"*, Harvard Business School Case (June 2012, revised May 2013).

Chapter 8

51. Eileen Daspin, *"The Sad and Inspiring Reason This Top Novartis*

Exec Stepped Down", Fortune (May 2016).

52. Sue Shellenbarger, *"Getting From At-Home to On-the-Job, Even Now"*, The Wall Street Journal (July 2009).

53. Eve Tahmincioglu, *"Return to work not easy for stay-at-home dads"*, NBCNews.com (August 2007).

54. Suzanne Bearne, *"Failure to re-engage with mums who have left the workforce costs firms £2m per year"*, Campaign Magazine (May 2015).

Chapter 9

55. Didem Tali, *"Returnees boost Nigerian economy"*, Deutsche Welle (DW) (November 2014).

56. Gwen Vogel, Justin Stiebel, Rachele Vogel, *"Reentry Trauma: The Shock of Returning Home"*, Psychology International (December 2011).

57. James Lamont, Neil Munshi, *"The rigours of India's 'repatriates'"*, The Financial Times (April 2012).

58. Su Zhou, *"Overseas returnees tell of difficulties in starting their own businesses"*, China Daily (September 2015).

59. Peter S. Adler, *"The transitional experience: An alternative view of culture shock"*, Journal of Humanistic Psychology (1975): pp. 13–23.

60. Ramana Nanda, Tarun Khanna, *"Diasporas and Domestic Entrepreneurs: Evidence from the Indian Software Industry"*, HBS Working Paper 08-003 (February 2009).

61. James Lamont, Neil Munshi, *"The rigours of India's 'repatriates'"*, Financial Times (April 2012).

62. Tinghua Duan, Wenxuan Hou, *"The Curse of Returnee CEOs"*, Working Paper, University of Edinburgh Business School (August 2015).

Chapter 10

63. Marci Alboher, *"The Encore Career Handbook: How to Make a Living and a Difference in the Second Half of Life"*, Workman Publishing Company (2012).

64. Kevin Cashman, *"The Pause Principle: Step Back to Lead Forward"*, Berrett-Koehler Publishers, Inc. (2012).

65. Mark Feffer, "3 Great Ideas For Encore Careers", The Huffington Post (December 2014).

66. Stratford Sherman, Alyssa Freas, "The Wild West of Executive Coaching", Harvard Business Review (November 2004).

67. Emma Jacobs, "Working Older", FT Magazine (July 2015).

68. Richard Eisenberg, "Encore Careers for the Rest of Us", Forbes (February 2013).

69. Emma Jacobs, "Working Older", FT Magazine (July 2015).

Chapter 11

70. Blake E. Ashforth, "Role Transitions in Organizational Life: An Identity-based Perspective", Routledge (2000).

71. Herminia Ibarra, "Career Transition and Change", INSEAD Working Paper (2004).

72. "The 2016 Deloitte Millennial Survey : Winning over the next generation of leaders", Deloitte (2016).

73. Jenny Blake, "Pivot: The Only Move That Matters is Your Next One", Portfolio Penguin (2016).

74. Marguerite Ward, "Ex-Google career coach reveals the biggest mistake she sees people make", CNBC (September 2016).

75. Jelena Zikic and Douglas T. Hall, "Toward a More Complex View of Career Exploration", The Career Development Quarterly, Volume 58, Issue 2 (December 2009) : 181–191.

76. Herminia Ibarra, "Working Identity: Unconventional Strategies for Reinventing Your Career", Harvard Business School Press (2004).

77. Ron Ashkenas, "Navigating the Emotional Side of a Career Transition", Harvard Business Review (April 2016).

78. Adam Grant, "Originals: How Non-Conformists Move the World", Penguin Books (2017).

79. Steve Blank, "The Key to Startup Success? 'Get Out of the Building'", Inc. Video (2014).

80. Michael Watkins, "The First 90 Days: Critical Success Strategies for New Leaders at All Levels", Harvard Business School Publishing (2003).

81. Adam Grant, "Originals: How Non-Conformists Move the World", Penguin Books (2017).

82. Helen Rose Fuchs Ebaugh, *"Becoming an Ex: The Process of Role Exit"*, University of Chicago Press (1988).

83. Ray Williams, *"CEO Failures: How On-Boarding Can Help"*, Psychology Today (2010).

84. Mark L. Savickas, *"Career adaptability: An integrative construct for life-span, life-space theory"*, The Career Development Quarterly, (1997): 45, 247-259.

Chapter 12

85. Yehuda Baruch, *"Transforming careers: from linear to multidirectional career paths: Organizational and individual perspectives"*, University of East Anglia (November 2003).

86. Mollie Lombardi, Madeline Laurano, *"Human Capital Management Trends 2013 : It's a Brave New World"*, Aberdeen Group (January 2013).

87. Margaret-Ann Cole, *"They Gain, You Retain: Creating a Culture of Career Development"*, Right Management webinar (December 2013).

88. *"Talk The Talk: How Ongoing Career Conversations Drive Business Success"*, Right Management Global Career Conversation Study (2016).

89. *"Talent Shortage Survey Results"*, Manpower Group (2011).

90. *"Competing for Critical Talent"*, White Paper, CEB Recruiting Leadership Council (2016).

91. *"Competing for Critical Talent"*, White Paper CEB Recruiting Leadership Council (2016).

92. *"LinkedIn Talent Trends Report 2016"*, LinkedIn (2016).

93. Yvonne Sonsino, Tanya Viscovich, *"Age-Friendly Employer Research"*, Mercer, (September 2015).

94. "Why & How People Change Jobs", LinkedIn Survey (March 2015).

95. Jacquelyn Smith, *"The Pros and Cons of Job Hopping"*, Forbes (March 2013).

96. Whitney Johnson, *"Disrupt Yourself"*, Harvard Business Review (July-August 2012).

97. *"Optimizing the Talent Pool: Best Practices for Driving a Successful Talent Acquisition Strategy in Any Economic Climate"*, Manpower (2012).

98. *"Attitude on Rehiring Boomerang Workers Changing"*, SHRM, Roy Maurer (September 2015).

99. Luisette Mullin, *"Trends in Corporate Recruitment 2015"*, DAV Strategic Staffing Solutions (September 2015).

100. *"Why & How People Change Jobs"*, LinkedIn Survey (March 2015).

101. *"Competing for Critical Talent"*, White Paper CEB Recruiting Leadership Council (2016).

102. Adam Grant, *"Originals: How Non-Conformists Move the World"*, Penguin Books (2017).

103. Cathy Benko, Anne Weisberg, *"Mass Career Customization: A New Model for How Careers are Built"*, Ivey Business Journal (May-June 2008).

104. Avivah Wittenberg-Cox, *"What Happens When Careers Last 20 Years Longer?"*, Harvard Business Review (October 2016).

105. Josh Bersin, *"Hacking The Career: What Should Organizations Do?"*, LinkedIn blog (April 2016).

106. *"Talent, Careers and Organizations: Where Next?"*, CRF Research (May 2011).

Conclusion

107. Avivah Wittenberg-Cox, *"What Happens When Careers Last 20 Years Longer?"*, Harvard Business Review (October 2016).

108. *"The Future of Jobs: Employment, Skills and Workforce Strategy for the Fourth Industrial Revolution"*, World Economic Forum (January 2016).

109. Laura Shin, *"7 Steps To Developing Career Capital – And Achieving Success"*, Forbes (May 2013).

110. *"More Than Money – Executive Interview of Subhanu Saxena"*, CEO Magazine (August 2016).

111. Edgar H. Schein, John Van Maanen, *"Career Anchors: The Changing Nature of Careers Self Assessment"*, Pfeiffer; 4th Edition (May 2013).

112. Frederique Dame, *"Harnessing Happiness to Build Your Career - Advice from an Uber Product Leader"*, originally published at firstround.com (May 2016).

113. *"Here's How to Enjoy a Long Career"*, website article, Center for Creative Leadership.

114. Karie Willyerd, Barbara Mistick, *"Stretch: How to Future-Proof Yourself for Tomorrow's Workplace"*, Wiley (June 2016).

Index